Leipziger Altorientalistische Studien

Herausgegeben von
Michael P. Streck

Band 7, 1

2018
Harrassowitz Verlag · Wiesbaden

Michael P. Streck

Supplement to the Akkadian Dictionaries

Vol. 1: B, P

with the collaboration of Nadezda Rudik

2018
Harrassowitz Verlag · Wiesbaden

Bibliografische Information der Deutschen Nationalbibliothek
Die Deutsche Nationalbibliothek verzeichnet diese Publikation in der Deutschen Nationalbibliografie; detaillierte bibliografische Daten sind im Internet über http://dnb.dnb.de abrufbar.

Bibliographic information published by the Deutsche Nationalbibliothek
The Deutsche Nationalbibliothek lists this publication in the Deutsche Nationalbibliografie; detailed bibliographic data are available in the Internet at http://dnb.dnb.de.

For further information about our publishing program consult our website http://www.harrassowitz-verlag.de

Printed on permanent/durable paper.
Printing and binding: Hubert & Co., Göttingen
Printed in Germany

ISSN 2193-4436
ISBN 978-3-447-10978-9

Table of Contents

Introduction vii
Bibliography xix
Bibliographical Abbreviations xxxiii
Other Abbreviations xliii
Supplement B 1
Supplement P 55

Introduction

1. A Short History of Akkadian Lexicography

1.1. Friedrich Delitzsch: Assyrisches Handwörterbuch

Friedrich Delitzsch was the actual founder of Akkadian lexicography,[1] the initial beginnings of which date to the second half of the 19th century. Delitzsch[2] was the first to habilitate within the new academic discipline of Assyriology in Germany, in 1874. In the following years, he published three fascicles of an "Assyrisches Wörterbuch" (Delitzsch 1887–1890) totaling 488 pages, which contained the first half of the letter aleph. Delitzsch then gave up this unrealistic project and wrote a concise "Assyrisches Handwörterbuch" on the basis of his unpublished manuscript (Delitzsch 1894–1896). This masterful dictionary was 730 pages long and contained approximately six thousand lemmata and between thirty and thirty-five thousand references.[3] Wolfram von Soden later referred to the title of Delitzsch's dictionary when he published his own "Akkadisches Handwörterbuch".

1.2. William Muss-Arnolt: A Concise Assyrian Dictionary of the Assyrian Language

Between 1894 and 1905 William Muss-Arnolt[4] published 19 fascicles, 1202 pages altogether, of "A Concise Assyrian Dictionary of the Assyrian Language." Whereas the first fascicles can be regarded as almost scientifically useless, the following fascicles relied on Delitzsch's "Handwörterbuch" but offered more material than Delitzsch's dictionary.[5] For decades, the "Muss-Arnolt" was used side-by-side with the "Handwörterbuch" in cuneiform studies.

1.3. Carl Bezold: Babylonisch-assyrisches Glossar

In 1912, Carl Bezold[6] (at Heidelberg since 1894) decided to write an Assyrian thesaurus, a project similar to the one which Delitzsch had abandoned. In the space of nine years Bezold produced 200,000 file cards. Upon realizing that he would not live to publish his extensive collections, he prepared a short glossary (343 pages without references), which appeared posthumously (Bezold 1926). It contained approximately 12,000 lemmata, twice as much as Delitzsch's "Handwörterbuch."[7] Bezold's file cards were removed to the "Semitistisches

---

1 For the first glossaries and dictionaries of Akk. s. CAD A/1, ix; Borger 1984, 79f.

2 On Delitzsch s. Streck 2009, 345–349.

3 Borger 1984, 82.

4 On Muss-Arnolt s. Borger 1993–1997a.

5 On Muss-Arnolt's dictionary s. CAD A/1, x; Borger 1984, 85–89.

6 On Bezold s. Weißbach 1938.

7 On Bezold's glossary s. CAD A/1, x; Borger 1984, 90–93. A copy of Bezold's glossary, which had belonged to Bruno Meissner and later to Wolfram von Soden, is kept in the Altorientalisches Institut of the University of Leipzig. It shows some annotations by the latter.

Institut" of the University of Leipzig, which was the center of Ancient Near Eastern studies in 1930s Germany. The file cards were destroyed by bombings in 1943.[8]

1.4. Bruno Meissner

In the nineteen-twenties, Bruno Meissner[9] (Berlin) began to prepare a new Akkadian dictionary. At the time of his death in 1947, the manuscript contained only the letters b, g, d, w, z, ḫ, ṭ, j, and k, as well as half of the letter l; in other words, the first letters of the Hebrew alphabet omitting the difficult aleph. This manuscript was transferred to Wolfram von Soden in 1949, who mentions it as one of the reference materials he used on the title page of his "Akkadisches Handwörterbuch".[10] Meissner's plentiful file cards had also been in von Soden's keeping, but were mostly disposed of after the latter's death in Münster in 1996. Two hundred of Meissner's original file cards were saved in a Mon Chéri box, which was kept by Walter Sommerfeld, who transferred them to the present author in 2016. These materials now repose in the Altorientalisches Institut of the University of Leipzig (s. fig. 1).

1.5. Wolfram von Soden: Akkadisches Handwörterbuch

Wolfram von Soden[11] showed a marked lexicographical interest long before he began to publish his "Akkadisches Handwörterbuch" (AHw, von Soden 1958–1981).[12] His dissertation on the hymnic-epic register of Akk. literature, written in Leipzig under the guidance of Benno Landsberger (von Soden 1931/1933), contained a chapter on the vocabulary of literary texts.[13] In 1933, he published an edition of the synonym lists of the Vorderasiatisches Museum in Berlin (von Soden 1933). During World War II he wrote an Arabic-German dictionary of military language, which is today almost totally forgotten or overlooked (von Soden 1942). In 1946 von Soden initiated a series of articles in the periodical Orientalia, entitled "Zum akkadischen Wörterbuch." These were continued until 1958, one year before the first fascicle of the "Akkadisches Handwörterbuch" appeared, and the treated Akkadian words were labelled with consecutive numbering from 1–104 (von Soden 1946–1958).

In 1959 the first fascicle of the AHw appeared, which included the letters A, B and the first section of D. The final fascicle, out of a total sixteen, was published in 1981. The three volumes of the AHw contain more than 1,600 pages and 14,611 lemmata,[14] which is twice as many lemmata as in Delitzsch's dictionary and 2,500 more lemmata than in Bezold's glossary. Table 1 presents the publication dates for each letter of the AHw, and table 3 the number of lemmata for each letter.

---

8 The reasons behind the reprinting of Bezold's glossary in 2008 by the publishing house Wipf and Stock, after the publication of AHw, CAD and CDA, remains a mystery.

9 On Meissner s. Borger 1993–1997.

10 On Meissner's manuscript s. CAD A/1, xf.; Borger 1984, 100f.

11 On von Soden s. Borger 2009–2011.

12 This should be noted, even if Borger 1984, 102 n. 65 may be right in recording that von Soden had not intended to write an Akk. dictionary.

13 Von Soden 1933, 160–173.

14 Borger's (1984, 107) estimate of 19,000 lemmata is wrong.

A B D	D **E** **G**	**G** **Ḫ** **I**	**I** **J** K	K L	M	M N	N P	P Q R	R S	**Ṣ** Ṣ̌	Š	Š T	T Ṭ U	U W **Z** Ntr.
59	60	62	63	65	66	67	69	71	72	74	76	77	79	81

Table 1: Publication dates of the AHw (in bold the volumes which appeared after the same letters as treated by the CAD).

In the pre-digital era the references were collected on thousands of file cards by von Soden and his assistants.[15] Von Soden marked the words chosen for his dictionary in the text editions of his private library, now in the Altorientalisches Institut of the University of Leipzig (fig. 2).

It seems that von Soden rather neglected the Assyriological secondary literature, with one important exception: the Assyrian Dictionary of the Oriental Institute of the University of Chicago (CAD). His private copy of the CAD is full of annotations (fig. 3).

The typewritten manuscripts of the AHw, as sent to the publisher, look quite different from the "clean" manuscripts written with the help of computers today (fig. 4).[16]

More than half of the volumes of the CAD appeared at the same time as von Soden's AHw (table 2).[17]

G Ḫ	E	I J	D	Z	Ṣ	**A** **/1**	**B**	**A** **/2**	**K**	**L**	**M**	**N**	**Q**	**S**	**Š/** **1**	**Š/** **2-** **3**	**R**	**P**	**T** **Ṭ**	**U** **W**
56	58	59	59	61	62	64	65	68	71	73	77	80	82	84	89	92	99	05	06	10

Table 2: Publication dates of the CAD (in bold the letters which appeared after the AHw).

1.6. The Assyrian Dictionary of the Oriental Institute of the University of Chicago

The CAD[18] was initiated in 1921; by the 1950s it had produced between 1,500,000 and 1,750,000[19] file cards. After Ignace Gelb had withdrawn from the project, the CAD was overseen by three editors-in-charge over the course of the years: A. Leo Oppenheim, Erica Reiner and Martha Roth. The first volume of the CAD was published in 1956, the last in 2010, covering a time-span of fifty-four years. The CAD consists of 21 volumes with 9,164 pages in total. It contains 16,526 lemmata – nearly 2000 more than the AHw (table 3).[20]

---

15 Cf. Borger 1984, 106 and 108.

16 I thank W. Sommerfeld who handed over to me in 2016 the typewritten manuscripts of the AHw (starting with the letter T) saved from destruction after von Soden's death. They are kept in the Altorientalisches Institut of the University of Leipzig.

17 On the relationship between the AHw and the CAD s. Reiner 2002, 77f.

18 On the history of the CAD s. CAD A/1, xix–xiii; Borger 1984, 94–100; Reiner 2002.

19 This was estimated by Ignace Gelb (Borger 1984, 97).

20 Cf. also Streck 2014b, 105 for a survey of lemmata and loanwords in the CAD.

Whereas the AHw presented the references in an abbreviated form – frequently only the reference itself – the CAD was designed to provide the word within a larger context.[21]

	A	B	D	E	G	Ḫ	I/J	K	L	M
AHw	1,169	513	361	622	412	976	525	1,143	410	1,271
CAD	1,315	570	380	630	480	1,250	600	1,170	431	1,662

	N	P	Q	R	S	Ṣ	Š	T	Ṭ	U	W	Z
AHw	968	637	335	417	708	387	1,589	860	133	621	161	383
CAD	1,170	850	424	480	860	285	1,560	1,116	143	753	72	325

Table 3: A comparison of the total lemmata by letter in AHw and CAD.

1.7. Concise Dictionary of Akkadian

The last Akkadian dictionary to be mentioned here is the CDA, which is for the most part an English translation of the AHw, however, with all references omitted and updated by the information contained in the CAD and in a limited amount of other secondary literature.

2. The Supplement to the Akkadian Dictionaries

2.1. The Development of the Project

The Supplement to the Akkadian Dictionaries (SAD) was planned as a by-product of the Etymological Dictionary of Akkadian (EDA), directed by Manfred Krebernik, with the collaboration of Leonid Kogan. It was meant to provide the EDA with the most important new lexical material (primary sources and secondary literature) which appeared after the completion of the two standard Akkadian dictionaries, the AHw and the CAD. The original concept envisaged a three-year project, the results of which would be published on the internet, and subsequently continued on a small scale for another seven years, in order to process new text editions and lexicographical studies. The Deutsche Forschungsgemeinschaft approved this plan.

However, SAD has since shared the same fate as many dictionaries: "Ein Leitmotiv (oder Leidmotiv) jeglicher lexikographischer Arbeit ist zeitliche Planung, die sich nicht entfernt einhalten läßt".[22] We too underestimated the amount of new lexicographical material available. Moreover, the original idea to scan all reviews of AHw and CAD and the numerous word indices in text editions in order to make them available online under the proper entries proved to be time-consuming and ineffective from a lexicographical standpoint. This idea was thus given up, and other aspects of the concept have also changed during the first three years of funding:

---

21 Reiner 2002, 1 stressed that the contexts provided by the CAD are not so much necessary "in syntactic terms but in cultural and semantic terms" and thus became a "tool for recapturing an ancient civilization".

22 Borger 1984, 76. In this regard, Borger speaks of "typischen Lexikographen-Optimismus", a quality which shows up in Borger's essay more than once (p. 76, p. 81 n. 17, p. 98).

First it was decided not to include every Akkadian text, nor all the secondary literature published after the completion of the dictionaries AHw and CAD, but to evaluate only a strictly defined text corpus and a limited amount of secondary literature. The reason for covering only a selection of texts and secondary literature is one of efficiency: the project is, of course, limited in time and resources and therefore forced to concentrate on sources that produce the most fruitful results within a given time. A further limitation of the SAD should be mentioned here: SAD does not cover the Ebla texts because a separate Ebla glossary is part of the EDA program.

Secondly, the supplement will appear in separate volumes in print, as well as being published on the internet. As in the EDA, the order of the volumes does not follow strict alphabetic order but is organized according by phonetically related letters:

Fascicle 1: Letters B and P.
Fascicle 2: Letters D, T and Ṭ.
Fascicle 3: Letters G, K and Q.
Fascicle 4: Letters S, Ṣ, Š and Z.
Fascicle 5: Letters L, M, N and R.
Fascicle 6: Letters A, E, Ḫ, I, U, W and Y.

Thirdly, the entire project will continue for seven years on the same scale as during the first three years of funding. The Deutsche Forschungsgemeinschaft has approved these changes.

The daily work was organized as follows: the present author is responsible for including material from new text editions, with Nadezda Rudik fulfilling the duty of sifting through the secondary literature. The results were discussed in weekly sessions by both of the above authors. Every week, the new material was uploaded to the internet (http://www.altorient.gko.uni-leipzig.de/etymd.html). Last minute additions to and corrections for Old Assyrian material were kindly sent to us by Bert Kouwenberg. Finally, the entire manuscript was revised by the present author. English corrections were made by Emily Zeran. The print version was formatted by Ellen Rehm in collaboration with Rudik.

2.2. The Corpus

The corpus covered by the SAD is a selection of texts and text groups which seem to be especially important for the Akkadian lexicon. Three criteria define the selection of texts:

1) We prefer texts from periods and/or places hitherto not well-documented in the dictionaries. Particular examples are the Middle Babylonian texts from Qatna and the Neo-Babylonian texts from Nippur.

2) We prefer texts and text genres which produce rich lexicographical materials due to their content. Examples are the letters from the palace archives from Mari which touch on so many subjects not attested elsewhere in the cuneiform corpus, or the Old Babylonian literary texts from the Schøyen collection.

3) We prefer texts edited in full, preferably with complete indices, as this facilitates the work of the lexicographer. Good examples are the Old Babylonian texts from Tuttul or the Middle Assyrian texts from Dūr-katlimmu.

For the fascicle B/P of the SAD the following texts were used:[23]

2.2.1. Old Akkadian

- Tall Baydar: Subartu 2 and 12.
- Sargonic letters: FAOS 19.
- Garšana, Ur III documents: CUSAS 4.
- For royal inscriptions see Kienast / Sommerfeld 1994 under secondary literature, below.

2.2.2. Old Babylonian

- Early OB letters from Ešnunna: AS 22.
- Late OB texts from the sealand dynasty: CUSAS 9.
- Letters from Babylonia: AbB.
- Mari, texts from the palace archive: ARM (esp. the latter volumes), FM, MARI.
- Tuttul: KTT.
- Shemshara, letters: Shemshara 1.
- Šubat-Enlil, Royal Archives: RATL (Eidem).

2.2.3. Middle Babylonian

- Ekalte: WVDOG 102.
- Emar: Emar 6/1–4.
- Qatna: QS 3.
- Ur: Gurney 1983.

2.2.4. Neo-Babylonian

- Nippur, Early Neo-Babylonian Governor's archive: OIP 114.
- Letters: SAA 17, 18 (esp. new texts from CT 54).

2.2.5. Late Babylonian

- Letters: AOAT 414/1.
- Bēl-rēmanni archive: Bēl-rēmanni (index).

2.2.6. Old Assyrian

- Letters and documents (all texts new): AKT 1–7 (AKT 3 = FAOS Bh. 3). Prag 1 (Hecker et al.); TPAK 1 (Michel; Garelli).

2.2.7. Middle Assyrian

- Dūr-Katlimmu: BATSH 4/1, BATSH 9.
- Giricano: Subartu 14.
- Tall Chuera: Jakob 2009.

---

23 With series like AbB and ARM only the volumes not already covered by AHw and CAD were used.

2.2.8. Neo-Assyrian

- Aššur: documents, STAT 1–3.
- Dūr-Katlimmu: BATSH 6.
- Kalḫu, Ninive etc.: SAA (esp. new texts such as those in CT 53 and CTN 5).

2.2.9. Literary Texts

- Aššur literary texts: KAL 1–4.
- Babylonian divinatory texts in the Schøyen Collection: CUSAS 18.
- Emar literary texts: Emar 6/4.
- Epic of Gilgameš: George 2003 and recent publications.
- Mesopotamian Incantations and Related Texts in the Schøyen Collection: CUSAS 32.
- Old Babylonian literary texts in the Schøyen Collection: CUSAS 10.
- Old Babylonian Flood Account: Finkel 2014.
- Ugarit literary texts: Arnaud 2007.
- Uruk literary texts: SpTU 1–4 (indices).
- For further literary texts from the OAkk, OB, MB, OA and MA periods see www.seal.uni-leipzig.de.

2.2.10. Lexical Texts

- Edubba 7, 100: list of birds.
- Lexical texts in the Schøyen Collection: CUSAS 12.
- Malku-šarru, synonym list: AOAT 50.
- UET 7, 93.

2.2.11. Secondary Literature

The following is a selection of the secondary literature which was used. We prefer lexicographic studies:

- Reviews of AHw and CAD.
- Abraham / Sokoloff, AfO 52 (2011) 22–76: Aramaic Loanwords.
- Beaulieu 2003, Pantheon of Uruk: philological notes.
- Bulletin on Sumerian Agriculture: terminology of plants and agriculture.
- Jursa 2009: Late Babylonian list of aromatic plants and substances.
- Kienast / Sommerfeld 1994: glossary of Old Akkadian inscriptions.
- Mayer 2016 and 2017: additions to the Akk. dictionaries.
- Michel / Nosch (ed.) 2010: textile terminology (esp. the articles by Michel / Veenhof on Old Assyrian and by Zawadzki on Late Babylonian textiles).
- McEwan 1988 (Babylonia in the Hellenistic Period, Klio 70, 412–421): Greek loanwords.
- Moran 1992: The Amarna Letters.
- Pentiuc 2001: West Semitic Loan Words in Middle Babylonian texts from Emar.
- Sallaberger 1996: Terminology of pottery.
- Sivan 1987: Northwest Semitic loanwords in Akk. texts of the Middle Babylonian period.

- Streck 2000, 82–123: Amorite Loanwords.
- Streck 2003a: Verbal stems with ta-infix.
- Moreover, we went through the Archiv für Orientforschung, after W. Sommerfeld (ed.), https://www.uni-marburg.de/cnms/forschung/dnms/apps/agi.

The above corpus is preliminary and will be modified and supplemented during the course of this project.

2.3. Selection of References

None of the standard dictionaries, the AHw and CAD nor the SAD, aim to serve as a thesaurus. Therefore, even within the narrow corpus defined above (2.2), not all references for words starting with B and P have been here collected. Rather, we paid particular attention to references according to the following criteria:

1) New words not listed in AHw or CAD. They are marked by a preceding +. Examples are *baq(a)ru* "cow", *barkarrû* "a coarse textile", *pādu* "fetter, handle" or *pāḫu* "breathing".

2) New verbal stems not attested in AHw or CAD, marked by a preceding +. Examples include *bâru* I N "to be caught", *batāqu* Š "to take away", *paḫāru* DRt "to gather" or *parāqu* D "to separate".

3) New references for hapax legomena and other rare words, which may help to define the meaning, form, or etymology of a word. An example is the word *papātu*, previously attested in Alalaḫ (in the dictionaries as *papatu*, etymology unknown) and translated in AHw 824 as "ein Holzgegenstand", in CAD P 106 as "a wooden implement or furnishing". New attestations from MB Qaṭna make clear that the word designates a container, that the second syllable contains a long /ā/ and that the word is probably of Hurrian origin (note the Hurrian plural-suffix *-na*). Another example is the word *burṭiš* "yak(?)"; the new reference shows that the reading *burḫiš* in AHw and CAD is incorrect.

4) References which testify to new variants of words, marked by a preceding +. Examples are the by-forms *b/pi/enzurru* and *pezzurru* of *bunzerru* "web", or the by-form *perʾazu* of *piʾāzu* "mouse".

5) References which expand the distribution of a word. The word *pargallu*, for example, is listed in the dictionaries as Late Babylonian. The new references expand its distribution into Old and Middle Babylonian. The word *buṣinnu* "lamp wick" is now also attested in Old Assyrian. New periods/dialects are marked by a preceding +.

6) References which testify to a new use of a well-attested word. The word *baʾālu* "to be exceptionally big", for example, is now also attested with the abstract subject *ibissû* "loss", and the word *pasāsu* "to erase" is attested with the object *dīnī* "my verdict".

2.4. Statistics

The following table provides the numerical breakdown for the fascicle B/P of the SAD.

	B	P	Total
Number of entries in AHw	513	637	1,150
Number of entries in CAD	570	850	1,420
Number of entries in SAD	295	296	591
New words in SAD in total	70	57	127
New nouns	60	50	110
New verbs	9	4	13
New adverbs	1	3	4
New verbal stems in total	9	11	20
New Gt-stems		1	1
New Gtn-stems	1	2	3
New D-stems	2	2	4
New Dtn-stems		2	2
New DRt-stems		1	1
New Š-stems	1		1
New Štn-stems	2		2
New N-stems	2	2	4
New Ntn-stems	1	1	2

Table 4: Numerical breakdown for the fascicle B/P of SAD

Thus the number of lemmata commented upon in the SAD is ca. 50 % of the lemmata in AHw and 40 % of the lemmata in CAD. The B/P volume of the SAD increases the number of lemmata in the Akkadian the B/P section of the lexicon by ca. 10 %. The overwhelming majority of new lemmata are nouns, whereas verbs and adverbs are much less represented.

2.5. Layout of the Supplement to the Akkadian Dictionaries

- In general, the reader is referred to the website of the project where one can find the material collected for all letters of the alphabet and additional material for the letters B/P: <http://altorient.gko.uni-leipzig.de/etymd.html>
- See also the two abbreviation lists and the bibliography in this fascicle for bibliographical abbreviations, other abbreviations and the secondary literature quoted.
- Homonymous lemmata are numbered according to the AHw.
- Lemmata of verbs are structured by the verbal stems in the order of the AHw.
- In general, the order of references within a lemma or verbal stem follows from the oldest period to the youngest (OA before OB, SB after OB, NB and LB are distinguished). However, sometimes the order of references follows semantic reasoning. In most cases, each reference gets a separate number; sometimes, several references are assembled under a single number, further subdivided by small letters (a, b, c etc.). In some cases, a discussion follows the references.

- The drafts of the articles were written by different authors. At the end of each lemma, the responsibilities are indicated by the following abbreviations: NR = Nadezda Rudik, NJCK = Bert Kouwenberg, MPS = Michael P. Streck. The drafts of all lemmata not claimed by any author remain the responsibility of MPS, as does the final manuscript.

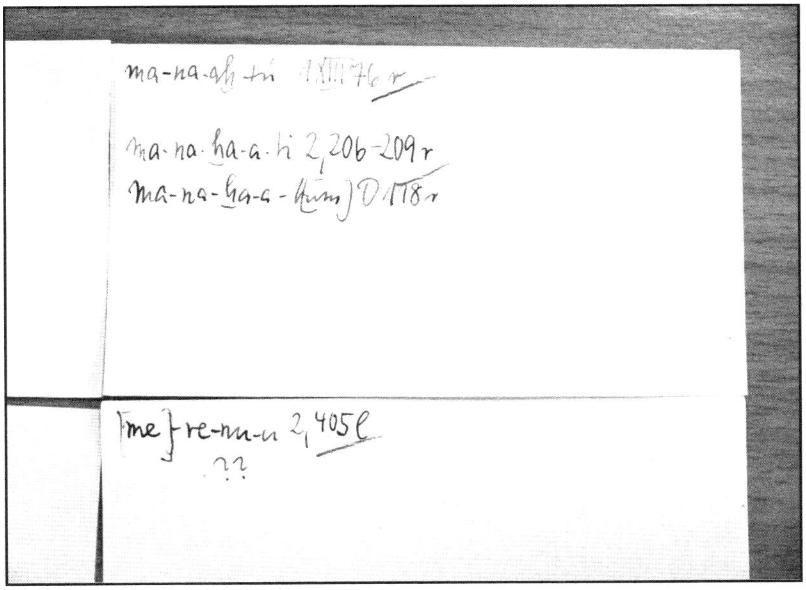

Fig. 1: Some of Meissner's file cards kept in the Altorientalisches Institut of the University of Leipzig (photo: M. P. Streck)

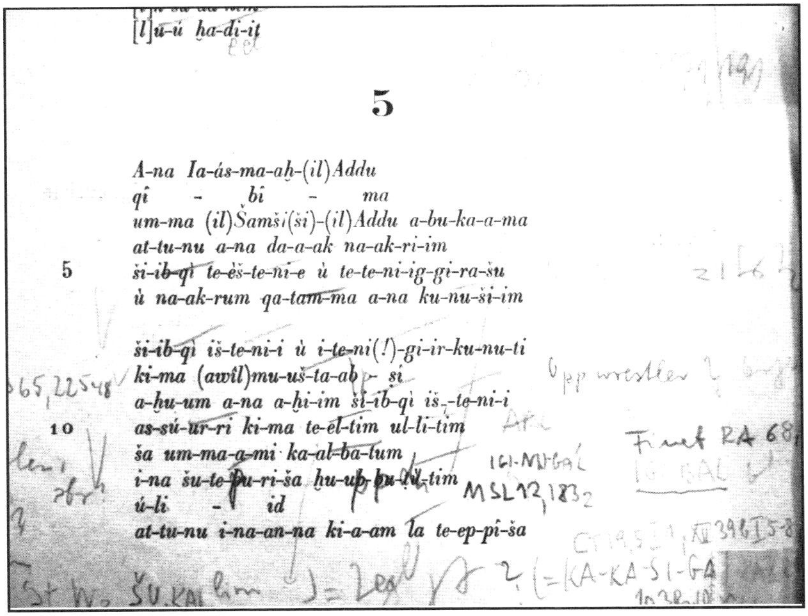

Fig. 2: Page of ARM 1 with annotations by W. von Soden (photo: M. P. Streck)

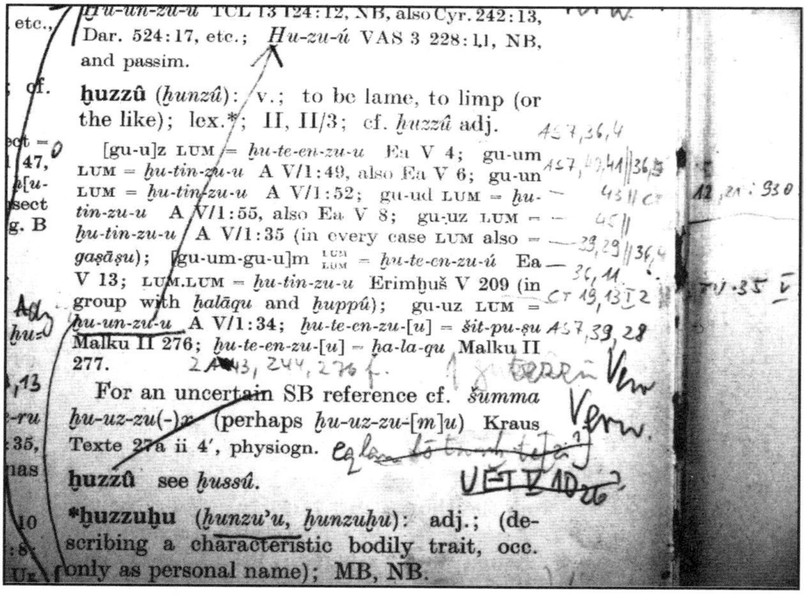
Hu-un-zu-u TCL 13 124:12, NB, also Cyr. 242:13, Dar. 524:17, etc.; Hu-zu-ú VAS 3 228:11, NB, and passim.

ḫuzzû (*ḫunzû*): v.; to be lame, to limp (or the like); lex.*; II, II/3; cf. *ḫuzzû* adj.

[gu-u]z LUM = *ḫu-te-en-zu-u* Ea V 4; gu-um LUM = *ḫu-tin-zu-u* A V/1:49, also Ea V 6; gu-un LUM = *ḫu-tin-zu-u* A V/1:52; gu-ud LUM = *ḫu-tin-zu-u* A V/1:55, also Ea V 8; gu-uz LUM = *ḫu-tin-zu-u* A V/1:35 (in every case LUM also = *gaṣāṣu*); [gu-um-gu-u]m LUM LUM = *ḫu-te-en-zu-ú* Ea V 13; LUM.LUM = *ḫu-tin-zu-u* Erimḫuš V 209 (in group with *ḫalāqu* and *ḫuppû*); gu-uz LUM = *ḫu-un-zu-u* A V/1:34; *ḫu-te-en-zu-[u]* = *šit-pu-ṣu* Malku II 276; *ḫu-te-en-zu-[u]* = *ḫa-la-qu* Malku II 277.

For an uncertain SB reference cf. *šumma ḫu-uz-zu(-)x* (perhaps *ḫu-uz-zu-[m]u*) Kraus Texte 27a ii 4′, physiogn.

ḫuzzû see *ḫussû*.

***ḫuzzuḫu** (*ḫunzu'u*, *ḫunzuḫu*): adj.; (describing a characteristic bodily trait, occ. only as personal name); MB, NB.

Fig. 3: Page of CAD vol. Ḫ with annotations by W. von Soden (photo: M. P. Streck)

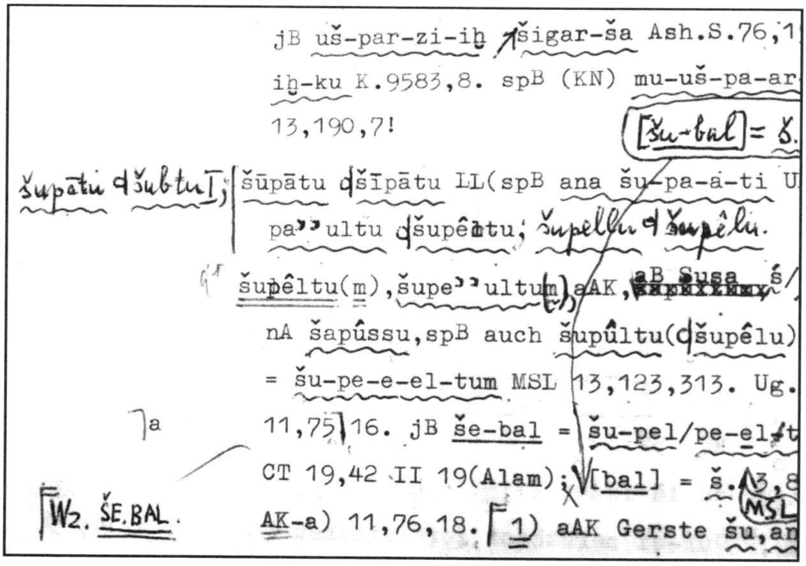
jB uš-par-zi-iḫ šigar-ša Ash.S.76,1
iḫ-ku K.9583,8. spB (KN) mu-uš-pa-ar
13,190,7!
šūpātu šīpātu LL(spB ana šu-pa-a-ti U
pa''ultu šupêltu;
šupêltu(m), šupe''ultu(m), aAK, aB Susa š/
nA šapûssu, spB auch šupûltu(šupêlu)
= šu-pe-e-el-tum MSL 13,123,313. Ug.
11,75,16. jB še-bal = šu-pel/pe-el-t
CT 19,42 II 19(Alam); [bal] = š. 13,8
AK-a) 11,76,18. 1) aAK Gerste šu,ar

Fig. 4: Typewritten manuscript of AHw (photo: M. P. Streck)

Bibliographie

Abraham K. / Sokoloff M. 2011: Aramaic Loanwords in Akkadian. A Reassessment of the Proposals, AfO 52, 22–76.

Adamthwaite M. R. 2001: Late Hittite Emar: the chronology, synchronisms, and socio-political aspects of a Late Bronze Age fortress town (= ANES Suppl. 8). Louvain.

Adler H.-P. 1976: Das Akkadische des Königs Tušratta von Mitanni (= AOAT 201). Kevelaer.

Arkhipov I. 2012: Le vocabulaire de la métallurgie et la nomenclature des objets en métal dans les textes de Mari (= ARM 32) Paris.

Arnaud D. 1985–1987: Recherches au pays d'Astata: Emar VI.1–4: Les textes sumériens et accadiens. Paris.

Arnaud D. 1987: La Syrie du moyen-Euphrate sous le protectorat Hittite: contrats de droit privé, AulaOr. 5, 211–241.

Arnaud D. 2007: Corpus des textes de bibliothèque de Ras Shamra-Ougarit (1936–2000) en sumérien, babylonien et assyrien (= AulaOr. Suppl. 23).

Balkan K. 1986: Betrothal of Girls During Childhood in Ancient Assyria and Anatolia, in: H. A. Hoffner, Jr. / G. M. Beckman (eds.), Kaniššuwar. A tribute to Hans G. Güterbock on his seventy-fifth birthday, May 27, 1983 (= AS 23, Chicago) 1–11.

Beaulieu P.-A. 1989: Textes administratifs inédits d'époque hellénistique provenant des archives du Bīt Rēš, RA 83, 53–87.

Beaulieu P.-A. 2003: The Pantheon of Uruk during the Neo-Babylonian Period (= CunMon. 23). Leiden / Boston.

Beckman G. 1996: Texts from the Vicinity of Emar in the Collection of Jonathan Rosen (= HANEM 2). Padua.

Bezold C. 1926: Babylonisch-assyrisches Glossar. Heidelberg.

Black J. A. / Al-Rawi F. N. H. 1987: A Contribution to the Study of Akkadian Bird Names, ZA 77, 117–126.

Böck B. 2000: Die babylonisch-assyrische Morphoskopie (= AfO Bh. 27). Wien.

Borger R. 1971: Review of CAD A Part II and B, BiOr 28, 65–67.

Borger R. 1984: Altorientalische Lexikographie. Geschichte und Probleme (= Nachrichten der Akademie der Wissenschaften in Göttingen. I. Philologisch-Historische Klasse, 1984/2). Göttingen.

Borger R. 1987: *puṣuddu*, Or. 56, 145–146.

Borger R. 1993–1997: Meissner, RlA 8, 33.

Borger R. 1993–1997a: Muss-Arnolt, RlA 8, 497–498.

Borger R. 2008: Review of CAD P, BiOr 65, 437–447.

Borger R. 2009–2011: Von Soden, RlA 12, 584–585.

Borger R. 2010b: Mesopotamisches Zeichenlexikon (= AOAT 305). Münster.

Bottéro J. 1995: Textes culinaires mésopotamiens. Winona Lake.

Charpin D. / Durand J.-M. 1988: Nouveaux exemples de "R-Stems", NABU 1988/17.

Charpin D. / Ziegler N. 2003: Mari et le Proche-Orient à l'époque amorrite. Essai d'histoire politique (= FM 5). Antony.

Charpin D. 1991: Le "temple aux peintures" d'Aššur, NABU 1991/78.

Charpin D. 1993: Review of AbB 12, RA 87, 87–89.

Charpin D. 2005: Les dieux prêteurs dans le Proche-Orient Amorrite (c. 2000–1600 av. J.-C.), Topoi 12–13, 13–34.

Civil M. 1987b: Feeding Dumuzi's Sheep: The Lexicon as a Source of Literary Inspiration, Fs. Reiner (= AOS 67, New Haven) 37–55.

Civil M. 2006: BE$_5$/PE-EN-ZÉ-ER = *BIṢṢŪRU*, in: A. K. Guinan et al. (eds.), If a Man Builds a Joyful House. Assyriological Studies in Honor of Erle Verdun Leichty (= CunMon. 31, Groningen / Leiden) 55–61.

Collon D. 1986: Catalogue of the Western Asiatic Seals in the British Museum, Cylinder Seals III. London.

Da Riva R. 2002: Der Ebabbar-Tempel von Sippar in frühneubabylonischer Zeit (640–580 v. Chr.) (= AOAT 291). Münster.

Delitzsch F. 1887–1890: Assyrisches Wörterbuch zur gesamten bisher veröffentlichten Keilschriftliteratur, unter Berücksichtigung zahlreicher unveröffentlichter Texte. Leipzig.

Delitzsch F. 1894–1896: Assyrisches Handwörterbuch. Leipzig.

Deller K. 1966: Review of CAD B, Or 35, 304–318.

Deller K. 1985: *kurru* "Mehlbrei", Or 54, 327–330.

Deller K. 1987: Review of VS 21, AfO 34, 58–66.

Dercksen J. G. 1996: The Old Assyrian Copper Trade in Anatolia (= PIHANS 75). Leiden.

Dercksen J. G. 2005: Metals according to documents from Kültepe-Kanish, in: Ü. Yalçin (ed.), Anatolian Metal III (= Der Anschnitt Beiheft 18, Bochum) 17–34.

Dietrich M. / Loretz O. 2008: Die sozialen Gruppen der *bidalūma* and *mhrm* in Ugarit, in: M. Dietrich (ed.), Orbis Ugariticus. Ausgewählte Beiträge von Manfried Dietrich und Oswald Loretz zu Fest- und Gedenkschriften anlässlich des 80. Geburtstages von Oswald Loretz (= AOAT 343, Münster) 287–295.

Dietrich M. 2003: The Babylonian Correspondence of Sargon and Sennacherib (= SAA 17). Helsinki.

Dombradi E. 1996: Die Darstellung des Rechtsaustrags in den altbabylonischen Prozeßurkunden (= FAOS 20/1). Stuttgart.

Donbaz V. 1993: Some Remarkable Contracts of 1-B Period Kültepe Tablets II, in: Fs. N. Özgüç, 131–157.

Donbaz V. 1999: Cuneiform Texts in the Sadberk Hanim Museum. Istanbul.

Driver G. R. 1967: Review of CAD B, JSS 12, 105–109.

Durand J.-M. / Marti L. 2003: Chroniques du Moyen-Euphrate. 2. Relecture de documents d'Ekalte, Emar et Tuttul, RA 97, 141–179.

Durand J.-M. 1983: Textes administratifs des salles 134 et 160 du Palais de Mari: transcrits, traduits et commentés (= ARM 21). Paris.

Durand J.-M. 1984: Sur un Emploi du Verb *bulluṭum*, MARI 3, 260–263.

Durand J.-M. 1987: Villes Fantômes de Syrie et Autres Lieux, MARI 5, 199–234.

Durand J.-M. 1988: Archives Epistolaires de Mari I/1 (= ARM 26/1). Paris.

Durand J.-M. 1989a: Compte Rendu: Daniel Arnaud, Recherches au Pays d'Aštata, Emar VI, RA 83, 163–191.

Durand J.-M. 1989b: L'Assemblée en Syrie à L'Époque Pré-Amorite, QuadSem 16, 27–44.

Durand J.-M. 1990a: Documents pour l'histoire du royaume de haute-mesopotamie II, MARI 6, 271–301.

Durand J.-M. 1991a: *pârum* et *parrum*, NABU 1991/30.

Durand J.-M. 1991b: *Baddum* = Devin fantôme, NABU 1991/53.

Durand J.-M. 1992: Unité et Diversités au Proche-Orient à L'Époque Amorrite, CRRAI 38, 97–128.

Durand J.-M. 1997: Documents épistolaires du palais de Mari I (= LAPO 16). Paris.

Durand J.-M. 1998: Documents épistolaires du palais de Mari II (= LAPO 17). Paris.

Durand J.-M. 2000: Documents épistolaires du palais de Mari III (= LAPO 18). Paris.

Durand J.-M. 2002: Le Culte d'Addu d'Alep et l'Affaire d'Alahtum (= FM 7). Paris.

Durand J.-M. 2004a: A. Les textes antérieurs à la babylonisation, RA 98, 122–130.

Durand J.-M. 2004b: Peuplement et sociétés à l'époque amorrite: (1) les clans bensim'alites, in: C. Nicolle (ed.), Nomades et sédentaires dansle Proche-Orient ancien. Compte-Rendu de la XLVIe Rencontre Assyriologique Internationale (= Amurru 3, Paris) 111–197.

Durand J.-M. 2005: Le culte des pierres et les monuments commémoratifs en Syrie Amorrite (= FM 8). Paris.

Durand J.-M. 2009: La nomenclature des habits et des textiles dans les textes de Mari (= ARM 30). Paris.

Edzard D. O. 1964: Mari und Aramäer? ZA 56, 142–149.

Edzard D. O. 1970a: Review of CAD A Part I, A Part II and B, ZA 60, 157–160.

Edzard D. O. 1970b: Die *bukānum*-Formel der altbabylonischen Kaufverträge und ihre sumerische Entsprechung, ZA 60, 8–53.

Farber W. 1977: Beschwörungsrituale an Ištar und Dumuzi. *attī Ištar ša ḫarmaša Dumuzi* (= Veröffentlichungen der Orientalischen Kommission, Akademie der Wissenschaften und der Literatur 30). Wiesbaden.

Farber W. 1989b: Schlaf, Kindchen, Schlaf! Mesopotamische Baby-Beschwörungen und -Rituale (= MesCiv. 2). Winona Lake.

Farber W. 2014: Lamaštu: An Edition of the Canonical Series of Lamaštu Incantations and Rituals and Related Texts from the Second and First Millennia B. C. (= MesCiv. 17). Winona Lake.

Feliu L. 2003: The God Dagan in Bronze Age Syria (= CHANE 19). Leiden.

Finkel I. 2014: The Ark before Noah. London.

Frahm E. 1997: Einleitung in die Sanherib-Inschriften (= AfO Bh. 26). Wien.

Frayne D. 1990: Old Babylonian Period (2003–1595 BC) (= RIME 4). Toronto.

Freydank H. 1991: Beiträge zur mittelassyrischen Chronologie und Geschichte. Berlin.

Fuchs A. 1994: Die Inschriften Sargons II. aus Khorsabad. Göttingen.

Gelb I. J. / Kienast B. 1990: Die altakkadischen Königsinschriften des dritten Jahrtausends v. Chr. (= FAOS 7). Stuttgart.

George A. R. 1986: Sennacherib and the Tablet of Destinies, Iraq 48, 133–146.

George A. R. 2003: The Babylonian Gilgamesh-Epic. Oxford.

George A. R. 2013: Babylonian Divinatory Texts Chiefly in the Schøyen Collection (= CUSAS 18). Bethesda.

Gesche P. D. 2000: Schulunterricht in Babylonien im ersten Jahrtausend v. Chr. (= AOAT 275). Münster.

Gong Y. 2000: Die Namen der Keilschriftzeichen (= AOAT 268). Münster.

Görg M. 1989: Beiträge zur Zeitgeschichte der Anfänge Israels (= ÄAT 2). Wiesbaden.

Hecker K. 1966: Die Keilschrifttexte der Universitätsbibliothek Giessen. Giessen.

Heimpel W. 1997a: A case of BA = *pá*, NABU 1997/5.

Heimpel W. 1997b: Cases of belated and premature initiative, NABU 1997/113.

Heimpel W. 2003: Letters to the King of Mari (= MesCiv. 12). Winona Lake.

Heimpel W. 2009: Workers and Construction Work at Garšana (= CUSAS 5). Bethesda.

Hertel T. 2013: Old Assyrian Legal Practices (= PIHANS 123). Leiden.

Hirsch H. / Hunger H. 1980: Assyriologie, Register: 1. Realien, 2. Wörter, 3. Textstellen, AfO 27, 335–461.

Hirsch H. 1961: Zu einer neuen Edition altassyrischer Texte, WZKM 57, 43–58.

Huehnergard J. 1983: Five Tablets from the Vicinity of Emar, RA 77, 11–43.

Huehnergard J. 1987: Ugaritic Vocabulary in Syllabic Transcription (= HSS 32). Winona Lake.

Hunger H. / Sachs A. 1988: Astronomical Diaries and Related Texts from Babylon, I, Diaries from 625 BC. to 262 B.C. Wien.

Hurowitz V. 1989: Isaiah's Impure Lips and Their Purification in Light of Akkadian Sources, HUCA 60, 39–89.

Ikeda J. 2003: A New Contribution to Northwest Semitic Lexicography (Review of Pentiuc 2001), BiOr 60, 263–279.

Jacquet A. 2011: Documents relatifs aux dépenses pour le culte (= FM 12 = Mémoires de NABU 13). Paris.

Jahn B. 2005: Altbabylonische Wohnhäuser. Eine Gegenüberstellung philologischer und archäologischer Quellen (= Orient-Archäologie 16). Rahden.

Jakob S. 2009: Die mittelassyrischen Texte aus Tell Chuēra in Nordost-Syrien. Wiesbaden.

Jiménez E. 2017: The Babylonian Disputation Poems (= CHANE 87). Leiden.

Joannès F. 1989: Archives de Borsippa. La famille Ea-ilûta-bâni. Geneve.

Jursa M. 1995: Die Landwirtschaft in Sippar in neubabylonischer Zeit (= AfO Beih. 25). Wien.

Jursa M. 1999: Das Archiv des Bēl-rēmanni (= PIHANS 86). Leiden.

Jursa M. 2009: Die Kralle des Meers und andere Aromata, in: W. Arnold et al. (eds.), Philologisches und Historisches zwischen Anatolien und Sokotra: Analecta Semitica In Memoriam Alexander Sima, Wiesbaden, 147–180.

Kienast B. / Sommerfeld W. 1994: Glossar zu den altakkadischen Königsinschriften (= FAOS 8). Stuttgart.

Kouwenberg N. J. C. 2010: The Akkadian Verb and Its Semitic Background (= LANE 2). Winona Lake.

Kouwenberg N. J. C. 2017: A Grammar of Old Assyrian (= HdO 118). Brill.

Kraus F. R. 1984a: Nominalsätze in altbabylonischen Briefen und der Stativ. Amsterdam.

Kraus F. R. 1984b: Königliche Verfügungen in altbabylonischer Zeit (= SD 11). Leiden.

Kühne C. 1973: Ammistamru und die Tochter der „Großen Dame“, UF 5, 175–184.

Kupper J.-R. 1992: Le bois à Mari, BSA 6, 163–170.

Kwasman T. 1999: *bunbullu*, NABU 1999/60.

Labat R. 1960: Review of AHw Lieferung 1–2, BiOr 17, 166–168.

Labat R. 1973: Review of AHw Lieferung 9–10, BiOr 30, 57–58.

Larsen M. T. 2002: The Aššur-nādā Archive (= OAA 1). Leiden.

Lauinger J. 2015: Following the Man of Yamhad: Settlement and Territory at Old Babylonian Alalah (= CHANE 75). Leiden.

Limet H. 1985: Bijouterie et Orfèvrerie a Mari, MARI 4, 509–221.

Luukko M. / van Buylaere G. 1987: The Political Correspondence of Esarhaddon (= SAA 16). Helsinki.

Malul M. 1985: The *bukannum*-Clause – Relinquishment of Rights by Previous Right Holder, ZA 75, 66–77.

Matouš L. 1964: Einige Bemerkungen zur akkadischen Lexikographie (Review of CAD E, D, I/J, Z, Ṣ; AHw Lief. 2–4), ArOr 32, 127–138.

Mayer W. 2001: Tall Munbāqa – Ekalte II: Die Texte (= WVDOG 102). Saarbrücken.

Mayer W. R. 1976: Untersuchungen zur Formensprache der babylonischen „Gebetsbeschwörungen“ (= StPohl series minor 5). Rom.

Mayer W. R. 1989: Die Verwendung der Negation im Akkadischen zur Bildung von Indefinit- bzw. Totalitätsausdrücken, Or. 58, 145–170.

Mayer W. R. 1990: Sechs Šu-ila-Gebete, Or. 59, 449–490.

Mayer W. R. 2008: Akkadische Lexikographie: CAD P, Or. 77, 94–105.

Mayer W. R. 2016: Zum akkadischen Wörterbuch A–L, Or. 85, 181–235.

Mayer W. R. 2017: Zum akkadischen Wörterbuch M–S, Or. 86, 1–40.

McEwan G. J. P. 1988: Babylonia in the Hellenistic Period, Klio 70, 412–421.

Michel C. / Veenhof K. R. 2010: The Textiles Traded by the Assyrians in Anatolia (19th–18th centuries BC), in: C. Michel / M.-L. Nosch (eds.), Textile Terminologies in the Ancient Near East and Mediterranean from the Third to the First Millennia BC (= Ancient Textiles 8, Oxford) 210–271.

Michel C. 1997: Une incantation paléo-assyrienne contre Lamaštum, Or. 66, 58–64.

Michel C. 2004: The *perdum*-mule, a mount for distinguished persons in Mesopotamia, in: B. S. Frizell (ed.), PECUS. Man and Animal in Antiquity, Proceedings of the conference at the Swedish Institute in Rome, September 9–12, 2002 (Rom) 190–200.

Milano L. 1993–1997: Mehl, RlA 8, 22–31.

Militarev A. / Kogan L. 2000: Semitic Etymological Dictionary, Vol. 1: Anatomy of Man and Animals (= AOAT 278/1). Münster.

Militarev A. / Kogan L. 2005: Semitic Etymological Dictionary, Vol. 2: Animal Names (= AOAT 278/2). Münster.

Moran W. L. 1987: Review of AbB 10, JAOS 107, 134–135.

Moran W. L. 1992: The Amarna Letters. Baltimore / London.

Muss-Arnolt W. 1894–1905: A Concise Dictionary of the Assyrian Language. Berlin / New York.

Olmo Lete G. del / Sanmartín J. 2004: A Dictionary of the Ugaritic Language in the Alphabetic Tradition (= HdO 112). Leiden.

Oshima T. 2011: Babylonian Prayers to Marduk (= ORA 7). Tübingen.

Oshima T. 2014: Babylonian Poems of Pious Sufferers (= ORA 14). Tübingen.

Parpola S. 1979: Review of AHw Lieferung 7–12, OLZ 74, 23–35.

Parpola S. 1993: Letters from Assyrian and Babylonian scholars (= SAA 10). Helsinki.

Pentiuc E. J. 2001: West Semitic Vocabulary in the Akkadian Texts from Emar (= HSS 49). Winona Lake.

Postgate, J. N. / Streck, M. P. 2011–2013: Terebinthe, RlA 13, 594–596.

Postgate, J. N. 1976: Fifty Neo-Assyrian Legal Documents. Warminster.

Powell M. A. 1984: Sumerian cereal crop, BSA 1, 48–72.

Powell M. A. 1987–1990: Masse und Gewichte, RlA 7, 457–517.

Radner K. 1997: Die neuassyrischen Privatrechtsurkunden als Quelle für Mensch und Umwelt (= SAAS 6). Helsinki.

Radner K. 2006–2008: Šabirēšu, RlA 11, 474f.

Reiner E. 2002: An Adventure of Great Dimension. The Launching of the Chicago Assyrian Dictionary (= Transactions of the American Philosophical Society Vol. 92/3). Philadelphia.

Reschid F. / Wilcke C. 1975: Ein ‚Grenzstein' aus dem ersten(?) Regierungsjahr des Königs Marduk-šāpik-zēri, ZA 65, 34–62.

Richter T. 2012: Bibliographisches Glossar des Hurritischen. Wiesbaden.

Sack R. H. 1994: Cuneiform Documents from the Chaldean and Persian Periods. Selingsgrove.

Saggs H. W. F. 2001: The Nimrud Letters, 1952 (= CTN 5). Baghdad / London.

Sallaberger W. 1996: Der babylonische Töpfer und seine Gefäße nach Urkunden altsumerischer bis altbabylonischer Zeit sowie lexikalischen und literarischen Zeugnissen (= MHEM 3). Ghent.

Sallaberger W. 2004: A Note on the Sheep and Goat Flocks. Introduction to Texts 151–167, in: L. Milano, W. Sallaberger / P. Talon / K. Van Lerberghe (eds.), Third Millennium Cuneiform Texts from Tell Beydar (seasons 1996–2002) (= Subartu 12, Turnhout) 13–21.

Sallaberger W. 2011: Sumerian Language Use at Garšana. On Orthography, Grammar, and Akkado-Sumerian Bilingualism, in: D. I. Owen (ed.), Garšana Studies (= CUSAS 6, Bethesda) 335–372.

San Nicolò M. 1954: Materialien zur Viehwirtschaft in den neubabylonischen Tempeln IV, Or. 23, 351–382.

Sassmannshausen L. 2001: Beiträge zur Verwaltung und Gesellschaft Babyloniens in der Kassitenzeit (= BagF 21). Mainz am Rhein.

Sasson J. M. 2001: Ancestors Divine? Fs. Veenhof, 413–428.

Schramm W. 1989/1990: Review of RIMA 1, AfO 36/37, 120–124.

Schuster-Brandis, A. 2008: Steine als Schutz- und Heilmittel. Untersuchung zu ihrer Verwendung in der Beschwörungskunst Mesopotamiens im 1. Jt. v. Chr. (= AOAT 46). Münster.

Scurlock, J. A. / Andersen, B. R. 2005: Diagnoses in Assyrian an Babylonian Medicine. Urbana.

Scurlock, J. A. 1989–1990: Was there a "Love Hungry" *Ēntu*-priestess Named Eṭirtum?, AfO 36–37, 107–112.

Sivan D. 1984: Grammatical analysis and glossary of the northwest Semitic vocables in Akkadian texts of the 15th–13th c.b.C. from Canaan and Syria (= AOAT 214). Kevelaer.

Sjöberg Å. W. 1996: UET 7 no. 93. A Lexical Text or a Commentary?, ZA 86, 220–237.

Sokoloff M. 2009: A Syriac Lexicon. Winona Lake.

Sommerfeld W. 1990: Review of AbB 10, ZA 80, 141–143.

Sommerfeld W.: Akkadische Glossare und Indizes. https://www.uni-marburg.de/cnms/forschung/dnms/apps/agi

Sövegjarto S. 2014: CBS 1596. A Sumerian Composition with Akkadian Translation, NABU 2014/66.

Starr I. 1983: The Rituals of the Diviner (= BiMes. 12). Malibu.

Stol M. 1982: State and Private Buisness in the Land of Larsa, JCS 34, 127–230.

Stol M. 1983: Review of CT 55–57, ZA 73, 296–300.

Stol M. 1987–1990: Malz, RlA 7, 322–329.

Stol M. 1987a: The Cucurbitaceae in the Cuneiform Texts, BSA 3, 81–92.

Stol M. 1987b: Garlic, Onion, Leek, BSA 3, 57–80.

Stol M. 1988: Old Babylonian Fields, BSA 4, 173–188.

Stol M. 1993a: Mohrhirse, RlA 8, 348–349.

Stol M. 1993b: Epilepsy in Babylonia (= CunMon. 2). Leiden.

Stol M. 1995: Old Babylonian Cattle, BSA 8, 173–213.

Stol M. 2000: Birth in Babylonia and the Bible. Its Mediterranean Setting (= CunMon. 14). Leiden.

Stol M. 2004a: Review of VS 29, BiOr 61, 133–134.

Stol M. 2004b: Wirtschaft und Gesellschaft in Altbabylonischer Zeit, OBO 160/4, 641– 975.

Stol M. 2008: Review of CAD P, OLZ 103, 348–355.

Streck M. P. / Wasserman N. 2011: Dialogues and Riddles. Three Old Babylonian Wisdom Texts, Iraq 73, 117–125.

Streck M. P. / Wasserman N. 2012: More Light on Nanāya, ZA 102, 183–201.

Streck M. P. 1994: Funktionsanalyse des akkadischen Št_2-Stamms, ZA 84, 161–197.

Streck M. P. 1995: *ittasab ibakki* „weinend setzte er sich“: *iparras* für die Vergangenheit in der akkadischen Epik. Or. 64, 33–91.

Streck M. P. 1999: Review of OIP 114, ZA 89, 286–295.

Streck M. P. 2000: Das amurritische Onomastikon der altbabylonischen Zeit (= AOAT 273/1). Münster.

Streck M. P. 2003a: Die akkadischen Verbalstämme mit *ta*-Infix (= AOAT 303). Münster.

Streck M. P. 2006: Sibilants in the Old Babylonian texts of Hammurapi and of the Governors in Qaṭṭunān, in: G. Deutscher / N. J. C. Kouwenberg (eds.), The Akkadian Language in its Semitic Context (= PIHANS 106, Leiden) 218–254.

Streck M. P. 2007: Review of CAD P, ZA 97, 149–152.

Streck M. P. 2009: Altorientalistik, in: U. von Hehl / U. John / M. Rudersdorf (eds.), Geschichte der Universität Leipzig 1409–2009, Band 4: Fakultäten, Institute, Zentrale Einrichtungen (Leipzig) 345–366.

Streck M. P. 2013: Remarks on Two Recent Studies on Amorite, UF 44, 309–328.

Streck M. P. 2014a: Altbabylonisches Lehrbuch, Wiesbaden (2nd rev. Edition).

Streck M. P. 2014b: Review of CAD U/W, ZA 104, 104–107.

Streck M. P. 2014–2016: Türhütergottheiten, RlA 14, 163–164.

Streck M. P. 2017: The Terminology for Times of the Day in Akkadian, in: Y. Heffron / A. Stone / M. Worthington (eds.), At the Dawn of History. Ancient Near Eastern Studies in Honour of J. N. Postgate (Winona Lake) 583–609.

Tropper J. 2012: Ugaritische Grammatik (= AOAT 273). Münster.

Tsukimoto A. 1991: Akkadian Tablets in the Hirayama Collection (II), ASJ 13, 275–333.

Tsukimoto A. 1998: Review of G. Beckman, Texts from the Vicinity of Emar in the Collection of Jonathan Rosen, WO 29, 184–190.

Tsukimoto A. 1999: "By the Hand of Madi-Dagan, the Scribe and *Apkallu*-Priest". A Medical Text from the Middle Euphrates Region, in: K. Watanabe (ed.), Priests and Officials in the Ancient Near East (Heidelberg) 187–200.

Van Driel G.1995: Cattle in the Neo-Babylonian period, BSA 8, 215–240.

van Koppen F. 2002a: Redeeming a Father's Seal, in: Fs. Walker, 147–176.

van Koppen F. 2002b: Equids in Mari and Chagar Bazar, AoF 29, 191–30.

van Soldt W. H. 1980: MA and ḪUR in Kassite Texts, RA 74, 77–80 (and p. 170).

van Soldt W. H. 1990: Fabrics and Dyes at Ugarit, UF 22, 321–357.

Veenhof K. 2006: Sisterly Advice on an Endangered Marriage in an Old Assyrian Letter, AS 27, 284–303.

Veenhof K. 2015b: *Baʾārum*, "to start a fight", in Old Assyrian, NABU 2015/11.

Veenhof K. R. 1972: Aspects of Old Assyrian Trade and Its Terminology. Leiden.

Veenhof K. R. 1981–1982: Babylonian Expressions for "over/at a Distance of ...", JEOL 27, 65–75.

Veenhof K. R. 1987: 'Dying tablets' and 'hungry silver'. Elements of figurative language in Akkadian commercial terminology, in: M. J. Geller et al. (eds.), Figurative Language in the Ancient Near East (London) 41–75.

Veenhof K. R. 2015a: Some Contributions to the Old Assyrian Lexicon, Or. 84, 217–275.

Villard P. 2001: Les administrateurs de l'époque de Yasmah-Addu, Amurru 2, 9–141.

Vincente C. A. 1992: The 1987 Tell Leilan tablets dated by the Limmu of Habil-kinu. Ann Arbor.

Volk K. 1989: Die Balaĝ-Komposition úru àm-ma-ir-ra-bi (= FAOS 18). Stuttgart.

Von Soden W. 1931: Der hymnisch-epische Dialekt des Akkadischen, Teil I, ZA 40, 163–227.

Von Soden W. 1933: Der hymnisch-epische Dialekt des Akkadischen, Teil II, ZA 41, 90–183, 236.

Von Soden W. 1933a: Die lexikalischen Tafelserien der Babylonier und Assyrer in den Berliner Museen. II: Die akkadischen Synonymenlisten. Berlin.

Von Soden W. 1942: Arabische wehrsprachliche Ausdrücke. Leipzig.

Von Soden W. 1946–1958: Zum akkadischen Wörterbuch. Or. 15 (1946) 423–431; Or. 16 (1947) 66–84; Or. 16 (1947) 437–458; Or. 18 (1949) 385–403; Or. 20 (1951) 151–165; Or. 22 (1953) 251–261; Or. 24 (1955) 136–145; Or. 24 (1955) 377–394; Or. 25 (1956) 241–250; Or. 26 (1957) 127–138; Or. 27 (1958) 252–261.

Von Soden W. 1958–1981: Akkadisches Handwörterbuch. Unter Benutzung des lexikalischen Nachlasses von Bruno Meissner (1868–1947). Wiesbaden.

Von Soden W. 1966: Review of CAD A/1, OLZ 61, 356–360.

Von Soden W. 1967: Review of AbB 2, BiOr 24, 334–335.

Von Soden W. 1968: Review of CAD B, OLZ 63, 458–459.

Von Soden W. 1977: Aramäische Wörter in neuassyrischen und neu- und spätbabylonischen Texten. Ein Vorbericht. III, Or. 46, 183–197.

Von Soden W. 1978: Review of AbB 7, BiOr 35, 206–208.

Von Soden W. 1980: Review of M. De J. Ellis, Agriculture and the State in Ancient Mesopotamia. An Introduction to Problems of Land Tenure, ZA 69, 270–271.

Von Soden W. 1982: Review of AbB 9, BiOr 39, 590–592.

Von Soden W. 1987: Review of ARM 21, ARM 22/1, ARM 23 and ARM 24, Or. 56, 97–105.

Von Soden W. 1988: Weitere mittelassyrische Briefbruchstücke aus Hattusa, in: E. Neu / C. Rüster (eds.), Documentum Asiae minoris antiquae. Festschrift für Heinrich Otten zum 75. Geburtstag (Wiesbaden) 333–346.

Waetzoldt H. 1972: Untersuchungen zur neusumerischen Textilindustrie. Rom.

Waetzoldt H. 1980–1983b: Leinen, RlA 6, 583–594.

Walker C. B. F. 1973: Cuneiform Tablets in the County Museum and Art Gallery, Truro, Cornwall, AfO 24, 122–127.

Walker Ch. / Dick M. 2001: The Induction of the Cult Image in Ancient Mesopotamia. The Mesopotamian Mis Pi Ritual (= SAALT 1). Winona Lake.

Wasserman N. / Ziegler N. 1994: *Qātum baʾʾīṭum* – A Check-list, NABU 1994/30.

Wasserman N. 2012: Most Probably. Epistemic Modality in Old Babylonian (= LANE 39). Winona Lake.

Wasserman N. 2013: Treating Garments in the Old Babylonian Period: "At the Cleaners" in a Comparative View, Iraq 75, 255–277.

Watanabe K. 1987: Die *adê*-Vereidigung anlässlich der Thronfolgeregelung Asarhaddons (= BagM Beih. 3). Berlin.

Watson W. G. E. 2002: Emar and Ugaritic, NABU 2002/9.

Weißbach F. H. 1938: Bezold, RlA 2, 23–24.

Westenholz J. G. 1997: Legends of the Kings of Akkade (= MesCiv. 7). Winona Lake.

Weszeli M. 2011–2013: Stachelschwein, RlA 13, 49–50.

Wilcke C. 1985: Familiengründung im Alten Babylonien, in: E. W. Müller (ed.), Geschlechtssreife und Legitimation zur Zeugung, Historische Anthropologie 3 (Freiburg) 213–317.

Wilcke C. 2010: Die Inschrift „Tukultī-Ninurta I 1". Tukultī-Ninurtas I. von Assyrien Feldzug gegen Gutäer und andere, nordöstliche und nordwestliche Feinde und der erste Bericht über den Bau seines neuen Palastes, in: J. C. Fincke (ed.), Festschrift für Gernot Wilhelm anlässlich seines 65. Geburtstages am 28. Januar 2010 (Dresden) 411–446.

Wilhelm G. 1985: Das Archiv des Šilwa-Teššup, 3: Rationenlisten II. Wiesbaden.

Wilhelm G. 1998: Hurr. *šinussi* "Scheuklappe"?, in: D. I. Owen / G. Wilhelm (eds.), General Studies and Excavations at Nuzi 10/2 (= SCCNH 9, Winona Lake) 173–176.

Worthington M. 2006: Edition of BAM 3, Le Journal des Médecines Cunéiformes 7, 18–48.

Wunsch C. 1995/96: Die Frauen der Familie Egibi, AfO 42/43, 33–63.

Zaccagnini C. 1994: Joint Responsibility in Barley Loans in the Neo-Assyrian Period, SAAB 8, 28–42.

Zadok R. 1991: Notes on the West Semitic Material from Emar, AION 51, 113–137.

Zadok R. 1993: On the Amorite Material from Mesopotamia, in: M. E. Cohen / D. C. Snell / D. B. Weisberg (eds.), The tablet and the scroll: Near Eastern studies in honor of William W. Hallo (Bethesda) 315–333.

Zawadzki S. 2010: Garments in non-cultic context, in: Michel, C. / Nosch, M.-L. (eds.), Textile Terminologies in the Ancient Near East and Mediterranean from the Third to the First Millennia BC (= Ancient Textiles 8, Oxford) 409–429.

Zgoll A. 2003: Die Kunst des Betens. Form und Funktion, Theologie und Psychagogik in babylonisch-assyrischen Handerhebungsgebeten zu Ištar (= AOAT 308). Münster.

Zsolnay I. 2010: Ištar, "Goddess of War, Pacifier of Kings": An Analysis of Ištar's Martial Role in the Maledictory Sections of the Assyrian Royal Inscriptions, in: L. Cogan (ed.), Language and City Administration in the Ancient Near East, Vol. 1 (Winona Lake) 389–402.

Bibliographical Abbreviations

ÄAT	Ägypten und Altes Testament. Studien zu Geschichte, Kultur und Religion Ägyptens und des Alten Testaments.
aATU	K. Hecker, Altassyrische Texte in Umschrift. https://www.hethport.uni-wuerzburg.de/HPM/index.php
AbB	Altbabylonische Briefe in Umschrift und Übersetzung.
ABL	R. F. Harper, Assyrian and Babylonian letters belonging to the Kouyounjik collection of the British Museum.
AfO (Beih.)	Archiv für Orientforschung (Beihefte).
AHw.	W. von Soden, Akkadisches Handwörterbuch.
AION	Annali dell'Istituto (Universitario) Orientale di Napoli.
AJBI	Annual of the Japanese Biblical Institute.
Akkadica	Akkadica. Revue semestrielle de la Fondation Assyriologique Georges Dossin.
AKT	Ankara Kültepe Tabletleri (Ankaraner Kültepe-Tafeln).
ALL	N. Wasserman, Akkadian Love Literature of the Third and Second Millennium BCE (= Leipziger Altorientalische Studien 4).
AMD	(Studies in) Ancient Magic and Divination.
Amurru	Amurru (Paris 1996ff.).
ANES	Ancient Near Eastern Studies. An annual (publ.) by the School of Fine Arts, Classical Studies and Archaeology University of Melbourne.
AnSt.	Anatolian Studies. Journal of the British Institute of Archaeology at Ankara.
AO	Tablets in the collections of the Musée du Louvre.
AOAT	Alter Orient und Altes Testament.
AoF	Altorientalische Forschungen.
AOS	American Oriental Series.
ARM	Archives Royales de Mari.
ArOr.	Archív Orientální.

ARRIM	Annual Review of the Royal Inscriptions of Mesopotamia Project.
AS	Assyriological Studies (Chicago).
ASJ	Acta Sumerologica.
Ass.	Field number of tablets excavated at Assur.
Astronomical Diaries	A. J. Sachs / H. Hunger, Astronomical Diaries and Related Texts from Babylonia.
ATHE	B. Kienast, Die altassyrischen Texte des Orientalischen Seminars der Universität Heidelberg und der Sammlung Erlenmeyer-Basel.
Atra-ḫasīs	W. G. Lambert / A. R. Millard, Atra-ḫasīs. The Babylonian story of the flood.
AulaOr.	Aula Orientalis. Revista de estudios del Próximo Oriente Antiguo.
AWTL	F. Ismail, Altbabylonische Wirtschaftsurkunden aus Tall Leilān Syrien (PhD thesis Tübingen 1991).
BabA	Babylonische Archive (Dresden 2002ff.).
BagF	Baghdader Forschungen.
BagM	Baghdader Mitteilungen.
Ballad of Early Rulers	Line numbering after Y. Cohen, Wisdom from the Late Bronze Age (Atlanta 2013) 132–139.
BAM	F. Köcher et al., Die babylonisch-assyrische Medizin in Texten und Untersuchungen.
BATSH	Berichte der Ausgrabung Tall Šēḫ Ḥamad / Dūr-Katlimmu.
BBR	H. Zimmern, Beiträge zur Kenntnis der babylonischen Religion.
Bēl rēmanni	M. Jursa, Das Archiv des Bēl-rēmanni (= PIHANS 86).
BiMes.	Bibliotheca Mesopotamica.
BiOr.	Bibliotheca Orientalis.
BIWA	R. Borger, Beiträge zum Inschriftenwerk Assurbanipals.
BM	Tablets in the collections of the British Museum.
BMS	L. W. King, Babylonian magic and sorcery.

Bo.	Field number of tablets excavated at Boghazköy.
BSA	Bulletin on Sumerian Agriculture.
BWL	W. G. Lambert, Babylonian wisdom literature.
CAD	The Assyrian Dictionary of the University of Chicago.
Cagni Erra	L. Cagni, L'epopea di Erra (= Studi Semitici 34).
CBS	Tablets in the collections of the University Museum of the University of Pennsylvania, Philadelphia).
CDA	J. A. Black / A. George / N. Postgate, A concise dictionary of Akkadian.
CH	Codex Hammurapi.
CHANE	Culture and History of the Ancient Near East.
Chuera	S. Jakob, Die mittelassyrischen Texte aus Tell Chuēra in Nordost-Syrien.
CRRAI	Compte rendu, Rencontre Assyriologique Internationale.
CT	Cuneiform Texts from Babylonian Tablets in the British Museum.
CTMMA	Cuneiform Texts in the Metropolitan Museum of Art.
CTN	Cuneiform Texts from Nimrud.
CunMon.	Cuneiform Monographs.
CUSAS	Cornell University Studies in Assyriology and Sumerology.
DCCLT	N. Veldhuis (ed.), Digital Corpus of Cuneiform Lexical Texts. http://oracc.museum.upenn.edu/dcclt/.
EA	J. A. Knudtzon, Die El-Amarna-Tafeln. Cf. W. L. Moran, The Amarna letters.
Edubba 7	F. N. H. Al-Rawi / S. Dalley, Old Babylonian Texts from Private Houses at Abu Habbah, Ancient Sippir.
Ee	Enūma elîš (W. G. Lambert, Babylonian Creation Myths [2013]; T. R. Kämmerer / K. A. Metzler, Das babylonische Weltschöpfungsepos Enūma elîš [= AOAT 375, 2012]).
Emar	D. Arnaud, Recherches au Pays d'Aštata. Emar 6/1–4. Textes sumériens et accadiens.
FAOS (Beih.)	Freiburger Altorientalische Studien (Beihefte).

FLP	Tablets in the collections of the Free Library of Philadelphia.
FM	Florilegium Marianum (= Mémoires de NABU).
Fs. De Meyer	H. Gasche / M. Tanret / C. Janssen / A. Degraeve (eds.), Cinquante-deux réflexions sur le Proche-Orient ancien: offertes en hommage à Léon De Meyer (= MHEO 2, 1994).
Fs. Garelli	D. Charpin / F. Joannès (eds.), Marchands, diplomates et empereurs. Études sur la civilisation mésopotamienne offertes à Paul Garelli (Paris 1991).
Fs. Hoffner	G. M. Beckman / R. H. Beal / G. McMahon (eds.), Hittite studies in honor of Harry A. Hoffner Jr. on the occasion of his 65th birthday (Winona Lake 2003).
Fs. Lambert	A. R. George / I. L. Finkel (eds.), Wisdom, gods and literature: Studies in Assyriology in Honour of W. G. Lambert (Winona Lake 2000).
Fs. Matouš	B. Hruška / G. Komoróczy (eds.), Festschrift Lubor Matouš, 1–2 (Assyriologia 5/1–2 = Az Eötvös Loránd tudományegyetem Ókori történeti tanszékeinek kiadványai 24–25, Budapest 1978).
Fs. N. Özgüç	M. J. Mellink / E. Porada / T. Özgüç (eds.), Aspects of Art and Iconography. Anatolia and its Neighbors. Nimet Özgüç'e armağan. Studies in Honor of Nimet Özgüç (Ankara 1993).
Fs. Reiner	F. Rochberg-Halton (ed.), Language, Literature and History. Philological and Historical Studies Presented to Erica Reiner (= AOS 67, 1987).
Fs. Sjöberg	H. Behrens / D. Loding / M. T. Roth (eds.), DUMU-E_2-DUB-BA-A. Studies in honor of Åke W. Sjöberg (= OccPubl. S. N. Kramer Fund 11, 1989).
Fs. Veenhof	J. G. Dercksen et al. (eds.), Veenhof Anniversary Volume. Studies presented to Klaas R. Veenhof on the occasion of his sixty-fifth birthday (= PIHANS 52, 2001).
Fs. Walker	C. Wunsch (ed.), Mining the archives. Festschrift for Christopher Walker on the occasion of his 60th birthday 4 October 2002, (= BabA 1, 2002).
Fs. Wilcke	W. Sallaberger / K. Volk / A. Zgoll (eds.), Literatur, Politik und Recht in Mesopotamien. Festschrift für Claus Wilcke (= Orientalia Biblica et Christiana 14, 2003).
GAG	W. von Soden, Grundriß der akkadischen Grammatik.

Gilg.	A. R. George, The Babylonian Gilgamesh-Epic (Oxford 2003), and recent publications.
Gs. Sachs	E. Leichty / M. deJong Ellis / P. Gerardi (eds.), A scientific humanist. Studies in memory of Abraham Sachs (= OccPubl.S. N. Kramer Fund 9, 1988).
HAL	L. Koehler / W. Baumgartner / J. J. Stamm, Hebräisches und Aramäisches Lexikon zum Alten Testament.
HANEM 2	G. Beckman, Texts from the Vicinity of Emar in the Collection of Jonathan Rosen (History of the Ancient Near East 2).
Hermitage	Tablets in the collections of the Hermitage St. Petersburg.
Ḫg	Lexical series ḪAR-gud, published MSL 5–11.
Ḫḫ	Lexical series ḪAR-ra = *ḫubullu*, published MSL 5–11.
HSAO	Heidelberger Studien zum Alten Orient.
HSS	Harvard Semitic Series.
HUCA	Hebrew Union College Annual.
IM	Tablets in the collections of the Iraq-Museum.
Imdilum	M. Ichisar, Les archives cappadociennes du marchand Imdilum.
Iraq	Iraq. Journal of the British Archaeological Institute.
Ištar Bagdad	M. P. Streck, Die Klage „Ištar Bagdad“, in: Fs. Wilcke, 304–309.
IV R	H. C. Rawlinson et al., The Cuneiform Inscriptions of Western Asia.
Izi	Lexical series izi = *išātu*, published MSL 13, 154ff.
JAOS	Journal of the American Oriental Society.
JCS	Journal of Cuneiform Studies.
JEOL	Jaarbericht van het Vooraziatisch-Egyptisch Genootschap “Ex Oriente Lux”.
JRAS	Journal of the Royal Asiatic Society.
JSS	Journal of Semitic Studies.
KAL	Keilschrifttexte aus Assur literarischen Inhalts.
KAR	E. Ebeling, Keilschrifttexte aus Assur religiösen Inhalts.

KKS	L. Matouš / M. Matoušov-Rajmová, Kappadokische Keilschrifttafeln mit Siegeln aus den Sammlungen der Karlsuniversität in Prag.
KTT	M. Krebernik, Keilschrifttexte aus Tuttul.
KUB	Keilschrifturkunden aus Boghazköi 1–60 (Berlin 1921–1990).
Lamaštu	W. Farber, Lamaštu. An Edition of the Canonical Series of Lamaštu Incantations and Rituals and Related Texts from the Second and First Millennia B.C.
LANE	Languages of the Ancient Near East (Winona Lake 2008ff.).
Langdon Tammuz	S. H. Langdon, Tammuz and Ishtar.
LAPO	Littératures Anciennes du Proche-Orient (Paris 1967ff.).
LBAT	Th. G. Pinches et alii, Late Babylonian astronomical and related texts.
LE	Laws of Eshnunna. Editions: A. Goetze, The Laws of Eshnunna. R. Yaron, The Laws of Eshnunna.
Lie Sg.	A. G. Lie, The inscriptions of Sargon II, king of Assyria.
LKA	E. Ebeling, Literarische Keilschrifttexte aus Assur.
M.	Field number of tablets excavated at Mari.
MAD	I. J. Gelb, Materials for the Assyrian Dictionary.
Malku	Lexical series *malku* = *šarru*, published AOAT 50.
MARI	MARI. Annales de recherches interdisciplinaires.
MARV	H. Freydank et al., Mittelassyrische Rechtsurkunden und Verwaltungstexte.
MBLET	O. R. Gurney, The Middle Babylonian legal and economic texts from Ur.
MCS	Manchester Cuneiform Studies.
MDP	Mémoires de la Délégation en Perse.
MesCiv.	Mesopotamian Civilizations (Winona Lake 1989ff.).
MesZL	R. Borger, Mesopotamisches Zeichenlexikon (= AOAT 305).
MHEM / MHET / MHEO	Mesopotamian History and Environment. Memoirs /Texts / Occasional Publications.
MRS	Mission de Ras Shamra (Paris 1936–1978).

MSL	Materialien zum sumerischen Lexikon / Materials for the Sumerian lexicon.
NABU	Nouvelles Assyriologiques Brèves et Utilitaires (Paris / Rouen 1987ff.).
NBC	Tablets in the collections of the Nies Babylonian Collection (Yale University, New Haven).
NCBT	Tablets in the collections of the Newell Collection of Babylonian Tablets (Yale University, New Haven).
ND	Field number of tablets excavated at Nimrud (Kalḫu).
OAA	Old Assyrian Archives (Leiden 2002ff.; in PIHANS).
OBO	Orbis Biblicus et Orientalis.
OBTR	S. Dalley / C. B. F. Walker / J. D. Hawkins, Old Babylonian Tablets from Tell al Rimah.
OccPubl. Bab. Fund	Occasional Publications of the Babylonian Fund.
OECT	Oxford Editions of Cuneiform Texts.
OIP	Oriental Institute Publications (Chicago 1924ff.).
OLA	Orientalia Lovaniensia Analecta.
Or.	Orientalia.
ORA	Orientalische Religionen in der Antike (Tübingen 2009ff.).
Parfümrezepte	E. Ebeling, Parfümrezepte und kultische Texte aus Assur.
PBS	The Museum Publications of the Babylonian Section, University of Pennsylvania.
Persika	Persika (Paris 2001ff.).
PIHANS	Publications de l'Institut Historique-Archéologique Néerlandais de Stamboul.
PNA	K. Radner et al. (eds.), The Prosopography of the Neo-Assyrian Empire.
Prag	K. Hecker / G. Kryszat / L. Matouš, Kappadokische Keilschrifttafeln aus den Sammlungen der Karlsuniversität Prag.
PRU	C. F.-A. Schaeffer (ed.), Le Palais Royal d'Ugarit.
PSBA	Proceedings of the Society of Biblical Archaeology.

PSD	Å.W. Sjöberg et al. (eds.), The Sumerian dictionary of the University Museum of the University of Pennsylvania.
QS 3	T. Richter / S. Lange, Das Archiv des Idadda (Qaṭna Studien 3).
QuadSem.	Quaderni di Semitistica.
RA	Revue d'Assyriologie et d'Archéologie Orientale.
RATL	J. Eidem, The Royal Archives from Tell Leilan (= PIHANS 117).
RGTC	W. Röllig et al. (eds.), Répertoire géographique des textes cunéiformes.
RIME	The Royal Inscriptions of Mesopotamia. Early Periods.
Rm.	Rassam. Tablets in the collections of the British Museum.
SAA	State Archives of Assyria.
SAAB	State Archives of Assyria. Bulletin.
SAALT	State Archives of Assyria. Literary Texts.
SAAS	State Archives of Assyria Suppl.
SCCNH	Studies on the Civilization and Culture of Nuzi and the Hurrians.
SD	Studia et Documenta ad Iura Orientis Antiqui Pertinentia.
SEAL	M. P. Streck / N. Wasserman, Sources of Early Akkadian Literature. http://www.seal.uni-leipzig.de.
Sefarad	Sefarad. Revista de la Escuelade Estudios Hebráicos.
Shemshara 1	J. Eidem / J. Læssøe, The Shemshara Archives. Vol. 1: The Letters (Copenhagen 2001).
SpTU	Spätbabylonische Texte aus Uruk.
ŠRT	C. D. Gray, The Šamaš Religious Texts.
StAT	Studien zu den Assur-Texten.
StBoT	Studien zu den Boğazköy-Texten.
StPohl SM	Studia Pohl. Dissertationes scientificae de rebus Orientis antiqui, Series Maior.
Streck Asb.	M. Streck, Assurbanipal (= Vorderasiatische Bibliothek 7).

STT	O. R. Gurney / J. J. Finkelstein / P. Hulin, The Sultantepe tablets.
Subartu	Subartu, edited by the European Centre for Upper Mesopotamian Studies (Turnhout 1995ff.).
Sumer	Sumer. A Journal of Archaeology and History in Arab World.
Šūpê-amēli	Line numbering after Y. Cohen, Wisdom from the Late Bronze Age (Atlanta 2013) 84–101.
TCL	Textes Cunéiformes. Musée du Louvre.
TDP	R. Labat, Traité akkadien de diagnostics et pronostics médicaux.
TIM	Texts in the Iraq Museum.
TMH	Texte und Materialien der Frau Professor Hilprecht Collection of Babylonian Antiquities im Eigentum der Universität Jena.
TPAK	C. Michel / P. Garelli, Tablettes paléo-assyriennes de Kültepe.
UET	Ur Excavations. Texts.
UF	Ugarit-Forschungen. Internationales Jahrbuch für die Altertumskunde Syrien-Palästinas.
UFBG	W. R. Mayer, Untersuchungen zur Formensprache der babylonischen „Gebetsbeschwörungen".
VAT	Tablets in the collections of the Vorderasiatische Abteilung (Staatliche Museen zu Berlin).
VOM	A. Finet (ed.), La Voix de l'opposition en Mésopotamie.
VS	Vorderasiatische Schriftdenkmäler.
WAG	Tablets in the collections of the Walters Art Gallery.
Weidner Tn.	E. F. Weidner, Die Inschriften Tukulti-Ninurtas.
WHM	Tablets in the collections of The Welcome Institute of the History of Medicine, London.
Wiseman Treaties	Wiseman, D. J., The Vassal-Treaties of Esarhaddon, Iraq 20 (1958) 1–99.
WVDOG	Wissenschaftliche Veröffentlichungen der Deutschen Orientgesellschaft.
WZKM	Wiener Zeitschrift für die Kunde des Morgenlandes.

YBC	Tablets in the Babylonian Collection, Yale University.
YOS	Yale Oriental Series.
ZA	Zeitschrift für Assyriologie.
ZABR	Zeitschrift für Altorientalische und Biblische Rechtsgeschichte.

Other Abbreviations

acc.	accusative
adj.	adjective
Amor.	Amorite
Arab.	Arabic
Aram.	Aramaic
Assyr.	Assyrian
astron.	astronomical
Bab.	Babylonian
cf.	confer
coll.	collation, collated
comm.	commentary
corr.	correction
det.	determinative
dict.	dictionary
diff.	different
disc. sect.	discussion section
disc.	discussion
DN	divine name
ed.	edition / edited
etym.	etymology
f.	following
fem.	feminine
ff.	following pages
Gilg.	Gilgameš
GN	geographical name
gramm.	grammtical
Hebr.	Hebrew
Hitt.	Hittite
Hurr.	Hurrian
i. e.	id est
ib.	ibidem
incant.	incantation
inf. constr.	infinitive construction
inscr.	inscription
interpret.	interpretation
LB	Late-Babylonian
lex.	lexical
lex. sect.	lexical section
lit.	literature / literary / literally
logogr.	logogram / logographical(ly)
lw.	loanword
MA	Middle-Assyrian
masc.	masculine
MB	Middle-Babylonian
med.	medical
mng.	meaning
n	unknown number of items
n.	note
NA	Neo-Assyrian
NB	Neo-Babylonian
NN	nomen nominandum
no.	number
NWSem.	Northwest-Semitic
OA	Old-Assyrian
OAkk.	Old-Akkadian
OB	Old-Babylonian
p.	page
pl.	plural / plate
PN	personal name
PNf	personal name feminine

pret.	preterite
prob.	probably
r.	reverse
ref.	reference
s. v.	sub verbo / sub voce
s.	see
SB	Standard Babylonian
sg.	singular
stat.cstr.	status constructus
Sum.	Sumerian
Ugar.	Ugaritic
unkn.	unknown
unpubl.	unpublished
WSem	West-Semitic

B

baʾālu "to be exceptionally big, bright; to be in force, forceful"

G OB *mādiš ib-il* AbB 13, 15: 11 "he was very forceful(?)". *ibissû ... mādiš ib-ta-il* AbB 10, 32: 36 "the loss has become very great".
D OB "to make important, exaggerate, enlarge" (s. AHw 1546 for other D- and Dtn-stem forms): *apītam ub-ta-aḫ-i-il* AbB 13, 85: 18 "I have enlarged the fallow land".

baʾāšu "to smell bad, be of bad quality"; + OB

G 1. OB *karānu bé-iš ana lêmim ul naṭū* FM 7, 48 no. 19: 16. "the wine smells bad. It is not fit for consumption".
2. *li-ib-ši* Wiseman Treaties 605 (CAD B 4b, *baʾāšu* 1a and CAD B 151b, *bašû* n1') is with Deller 1966, 306 and SAA 2, 6: 605 a form of *baʾāšu* "to stink": s. the duplicates *lib-ʾ-iš*, *lib-ʾ-ši*, *lib-iš* etc. Cf. also D, below.

Gtn *ib-ta-na-šu* (AfO 11, 224: 75, s. CAD under *baʾāšu* A 1a) is interpreted by von Soden 1968, 458 (s. also AHw 846; CDA 270) as *ip-ta-na-šu* (from *pašû*). Cf. also the disc. CAD P 267a ***pašû*.

D Deller 1966, 306: The duplicate X 21 (Iraq 20 pl. 46) of Wiseman Treaties 605 has *nipiškunu [l]u-ba-i-šu* "may they (the gods) make your breath stinking". Cf. also G 2, above.

MPS (G), NR (G, Gtn, D)

babbanû, + *banbanû* "good"

The postulated original form *banbanû* is attested for the first time: NA lit. *ana kirî ba-an-ba-nat* SAA 3, 14: 18, 24 "beautiful garden". SB *ba-⌜an!⌝-ba-nu-u* ib. 7 r. 1 in broken context.

+ bab(b)iltu "tribute"; OB

mê GN *ša ba-bi-il₅-ta-šu-nu ušātiqa ḫursāni Idiqlat u Puraāāttum* CUSAS 18, 2: 5 "water of GN, whose tribute the Tigris and Euphrates caused to pass the mountains".

babbilu "bearer"

1. Unparalleled plene spelling OB *ba-ab-bi-i-li* AbB 8, 78: 26 "bearers". Mistake for *-li-i*? Probably not noun pattern *PaRRĪS*.

2. Kraus 1984b, 236f.:
a) *aššum* ^lú^*ba-ab-bi-li*^meš^ PN *ana šar-ri iqbīma* AbB 10, 81: 16' "because of the bearers PN has spoken with the king".
b) *ba-bi-lam* AbB 1, 42: 7.

3. *ba-ab-bi-li* YOS 13, 77: 2; CT 47, 80: 37 (as ration recipients, s. von Soden 1980, 271).

MPS (1), NR (2–3)

babbilūtu "transportation"

OB *ba-ab-bi-lu-tim ša šamaššammī* AbB 13, 156: 10 "transportation of sesame".

bābtu I "city quarter, district"

"Residential unit" (Dombradi 1996, 245 with further lit.): *awīltum ša ina bīt abīka ušbu aššūssa ba-ab-ta-ka! īdû kīʾamma ittallak* CT 45, 86: 32 "the woman who has been living in your father's house and of whose married status your *b*. knew – shall she go out thus?" (s. RA 70, 153ff.; AfO Beih. 23, 120). NR

bābtu II "commercial goods; remainder(?)"

"Remainder(?)" in NB astron. diaries in river level statements (Hunger/Sachs 1988, 35): *itu-bi illu ta* 10 *en* 13 5 *si gin* 32 *na* <*ta*> 23 *en* 25 8 *si ba-ab-tú* 5/6*kùš gin* Astronomical Diaries 2, no. -203: 7 (= LBAT 304) "that month, the river level from the 10th to the 13th rose 5 fingers, 32 was the na (gauge); <from> the 23 until the 25th, – remainder(?) 5/6 cubit – it rose 8 fingers". NR

bābu "gate, door; city quarter"

1. OA *apputtum iʾidma ba-bi4-iš* TÚG[há] *u* AN.NA *re-e-šu-nu na-áš-ú-ni* CTMMA 1, 79: 26 "please take care at the gate of the textiles and tin, which are being checked!"

2. OB lit. *ba-ba-am ša wālittim ... pārikat* YOS 11, 19: 6 "(Lamaštu) is blocking the gate of the woman giving birth".

3. OB lit. *ba-ab laʾî ibāma ... ba-ab wāli[d]ātim ibāma* ZA 71, 61–63: 4, 6 "she passed the gate of the babies ... she passed the gate of the women in labor".

4. OB *i[n]a šībūt* GN *u* IGI *ba-bi-im* CT 2, 9: 5 "in (the council of) the elders of GN and in front of the gate".

5. SB *akī iṣi damqi elâku ina* KÁ *mālakāni* STT 360 r. 16 "I stand up like a healthy tree at the gate of the processions" (Deller 1966, 307; CAD M/1, 159a s. v. *mālaku* A).

6. "city quarter":

a) OA KÙ.BABBAR *iqqaqqad šalmišunu u kēnišunu ibbītīšunu u ba-a-bi4-šu-nu rakis* FAOS Beih. 3, 25 no. 10: 21 "(the obligation to pay back) the silver is guaranteed by whoever among them is (financially) sound and (legally) responsible, by their houses and by their city quarter".

b) OB *kīma ba-ab dūrija lā ibarrīʾū* AbB 12, 166: 36 "that (oxen and sheep) do not starve at the 'gate of my wall'". Van Soldt, ib. p. 133 "in my *city* quarter" with comm. "probably refers to (a sector) of the city wall".

c) NA *ana lappanī šēʾī* KÁ-*ia-a* [*t*]*arruṣā qātāya* STT 65: 16 "my hands are stretched out to (even) my poor neighbors" (Deller 1966, 307; s. also CAD Š/2, 363b and CAD T 213a).

7. *ina* KÁ *buqūmi* 5 *immerī luterrakkum* AbB 12, 163: 15' "at the beginning of the plucking I will bring you 5 rams in return", s. van Soldt, ib. p. 129.

8. OB said of seals (unclear): *kunukkātim ša taknuku ba-ab qātīšina šuṭramma* AbB 13, 56: 6'–9' "the sealed documents which you sealed, write for me 'the gate of their hands'". Van Soldt, ib. p. 51: "in the gate of their ..." or "the beginning of their list". Stol apud van Soldt, ib.: perhaps "a part of the seal".

MPS (2–3), NR (1, 4–8)

badādu s. *buddudu*

+ **badāqu** "to repair"; NA, Aram. lw.

1. NA *a-a-i dullu ša šarru bēlī e-pu-su-su-nu u ba-di-qu-nu mar dul-lu!-nu ša šarru bēlī ep-pa-su-nu gabbišu dammuq* SAA 16, 126 r. 22' "which work (exists), that the king my lord has performed and (later) was repaired?"

2. For the Aram. etymon cf., e. g., Sokoloff 2009, 120, who distinguishes two roots BDQ, the one mng. "to disperse" (corresponding to Akk. *batāqu*), the other mng. "to repair"; other scholars assume only a single root BDQ. The form BDQ instead of BTQ (but there exists an OB by-form *bi-du-uq-tum* of *butuqtu* "sluice channel", CAD B 223 = AHw 144 *butuqtu* 1a) and the mng. "to repair", only attested in NA and LB (cf. *badqu*), suggest a loan from Aram.

baddu?, *baṭṭu*? "reconnoiterer(?)"; Amor. lw.?

Durand 1991b rejects (as already previously Edzard 1964, 144) the mng. "diviner", proposed by Driver 1967, 108 (s. also WO 2, 19f.), connects the word with hebr. BDD "alone" and translates "homme isolé" for ARM 2, 30. Heimpel 2003, 479: "reconnoiterer". Cf. also Akk. *buddudu* "to waste, dissipate" (SB, NA). For FM 9, 100 no. 13 s. *baddû*.

+ **baddû** "a musical instrument(?)"; OB

PN *nârum* [*ša*] *ba-ad-de-e ileʾʾû ana nargallūtim ina* GN *taškunšuma* FM 9, 100 no. 13: 6 "you appointed the musician PN, [who] is not able to hold *b.*s, to the office of chief musician in GN". Durand 1991b sees here the word *baddu* and translates "gens islólés"; Ziegler FM 9, 100 "solistes". The context rather speaks for a musical instrument. Moreover, the spelling *-de-e* points to a word *baddû* instead of *baddu*.

+ **badqu** "repair work"; NA and LB, Aram. lw.

1. Cf. the ref. collected in CAD B 167f. *batqu* 2d and disc. sect., supported by the new lemma *badāqu* (s. above). AHw B 115 *batqu* 6: "ellipsis" is unlikely to be correct.
2. Deller 1966, 311: NA *bēt rab tupšarrē qalal ... bad-qu maʾda ina libbi* SAA 16, 89: 14 "the house of the chief scribe is tiny ... much repair (must be done) there".
3. Deller 1966, 311: NA ^{lú}GAL *bad-qi* Iraq 23, pl. 12 ND 2374: 11 "supervisor of repairs".
4. Deller 1966, 311: ^{lú}A.BA *ša* GAL *bad-qí* VAT 10430: 11' "scribe of the supervisor of repairs". MPS (1), NR (2–4)

bāʾertu "huntress, fisherman"; + OB

Women in the harem of Mari, summarized as ^{f}ŠU.ḪA FM 4, 183 no. 13 viii 12.

bāʾeru "hunter, fisherman"

1. MB *u* ^{lú}ŠU.ḪA^{meš} *tâmti ša ana* GN$_1$ *u* GN$_2$ *ginâ izabbilū* DUMU PN *kī itbalušunūti ginû* KU$_6^{\text{meš}}$ *batiq* JCS 19, 97: 22 "and (concerning) the fishermen of the sea, who have been delivering a regular offering to GN$_1$ and GN$_2$, – when the son of PN has taken them away, the regular offering of fish was cut off". S. Sassmannshausen 2001, 115f.
2. SB *ba-i-ri-ma* Šūpê-amēli 29, cf. *pariktu*.
3. LB *adī* 2 MU.AN.NA^{meš} PN$_1$ ... *ina* IGI PN$_2$ ^{lú}*ba-ʾi-i-ri šummē ša šarri* ^{lú}*ba-ʾi-ru-*⌜*tu*⌝ *ša šummē ulammassu* WZKM 83, 31: 3 "for two years PN$_1$ is at the disposal of PN$_2$, the dormouse hunter of the king. He will teach him dormouse hunting".
4. S. also *bayyāru*. MPS (2), NR (1, 3)

bāʾerūtu "craft of hunter"

LB ^{lú}*ba-ʾ-ru-*⌜*tu*⌝ *ša šummē ulammassu* WZKM 83, 31: 4 "he will teach him dormouse hunting". NR

bagani "call"

S. the new ed. AOAT 414/1, 176 no. 61: 25; ib. 268 no. 152 r. 4 with comm.

+ baḫiltu, pl. *baḫ(i)lātu* "a vessel"; OB

1. 1 GAL *ba-ḫi-il₅-tum* ARM 31, 187: 17'.

2. 1 GAL *ba-ḫi-il-tum* KÙ.BABBAR ARM 31, 78: 1 (of silver).

3. 1 *ba-ḫi-il-tum ša* GÚ-*sà ṣipirtim* KÙ.SIG₁₇ ARM 31, 85: 17 "1 *b.*-vessel whose neck (is decorated) with a gold ornament".

4. [1] *libbu ša ba-ḫi-il-tim* KÙ.SIG₁₇ SÙ.A 2 1/3 GÍN KI.LÁ.BI 1 GAL *ba-ḫi-il-tum* GAL KÙ.SIG₁₇ 1/3 *mana* 5 GÍN KI.LÁ.BI 1 GAL *ba-ḫi-il-tum* TUR KÙ.SIG₁₇ *qadum libbiša* 4 GÍN KI.LÁ.BI ARM 31, 186: 5' "[1] *libbu* for a *b.*-vessel of fine gold, its weight (is) 2 1/3 shekels; 1 big golden *b.*-vessel, its weight (is) 1/3 mina 5 shekels; 1 small golden *b.*-vessel together with its *libbu*, its weight (is) 4 shekels".

5. 1 ⸢GAL⸣ *ba-ḫi-*[*il-tum* KÙ.SIG₁₇] *tamlī* ^na4^ZA.GÌ[N] *u* ^na4^*ṣí-*[*ir-pí-im*] *kawārum u ta*[*rbāṣum*] *ṣibbit* ARM 31, 203: 7 "1 [golden] *b.*-vessel, inlay of lapis lazuli and fired (clay), 'wall' and 'enclosure' (decorative elements) (are) golden *ṣ*".

6. Fem. pl.:
a) 2 GAL *ba-aḫ-la-tum* ZABAR ARM 31, 109: 6 (of bronze).
b) 2 GAL *ba-aḫ-la-tim* ARM 25, 2: 3 "(1 mina of gold, the weight of) 2 *b.*-vessels".
c) 2 *ba-ḫi-la-tim* ARM 31, 149: 3.
d) 12 *ba-ḫi-la-tum* ARM 31, 225: 9.
e) 2 GAL *ba-ḫi-la-tim* ARM 31, 287: 7.

7. Cf. *biʾiltu* "an alabastron": the same word? (after CAD B 223 and AHw 125, however, from *baʾāšu* "to smell bad"). For disc. and further ref. s. Guichard, ARM 31, 183ff. NR

baḫrû "a stone"

OB 60 *ba-aḫ-ru-ú*^urudu^ KI.LÁ.BI 1 GÚN 10 MA.NA YOS 5, 227: 3 (Edzard 1970a, 160) "60 copper *b.* with a total weight of 1 talent and 10 minas". NR

baḫû II "to be(come) thin, scarce"; + OB

ul i-ba-aḫ-ḫi AbB 10, 177: 34 "does not become scarce"(?, context uncl.).

bāʾiru "hunter" s. *bāʾeru*

****bakīram** s. *šurrâ, makkāru*

Instead of *bakīram* (AHw 97 and 1548, CAD B 34) read *šurrâm* ARM 1, 70: 5 and *makkāram* VOM 181: 18. Cf. lit. Streck 2000, 85. NR

bākītu s. *bakkītu*

****bakta** s. *maqta*

bakkītu, *bākītu* "wailing woman"; + Bo.

bá-⸢*ki*⸣*-ti-ia* KBo. 36, 27: 18f. The many spellings with a single *k* point to a by-form *bākītu*.

bakkû "squalling, crying"; + NA

1. NA lit. *bak-ka-ni-i ṣar-piš ana* ^lú^NU.^giš^KIRI₆-*ni ni-ib-ki* SAA 3, 16: 20 "we are crying bitterly. We have cried for our gardener". Cf. Deller 1966, 307.
2. ZA 30, 220 (AHw 97a; CAD B 35a): Read with Farber 1989b, 52: 137 and comm. ib. p. 55 [*b*]*a-ʾ-ki-i* // *ba-ki-i*. Participle *bākî*? MPS, NR

bakû "to weep"

Gtn OB *anāku annīkī ūmiša ina bi-ta-ki īnāya ittaḫmaṭā* AbB 13, 175: 13 "as for me here, my eyes were burning feverishly every day because of (my) constant crying".

+ **D**(?) (they place five tables) *ina bīt bu-uk-ki ša ēntu* "in the house of weeping(?) of the *ēntu*-priestess". Disc. Pentiuc 2001, 42f. MPS (D), NR (Gtn)

+ **bakûtu** "weeping, mourning ceremony"; OB

1. OB (oil) *ana* 4 *ba-ku-ut šarrim* FM 3, 229 no. 60: 2 "for the 4 weeping ceremonies for the king".
2. S. also FM 3, 233: *inūma ba-ku-tim ša šarrim* "at the occasion of the weeping ceremony for the king". Cf. Jacquet 2011, 37.

balālu "to mix (up), alloy"

G 1. Beer:
a) OB *inūma lahtanam ib-lu*!?(ed.: *li*)-*lu* ARM 21, 130: 7f. "when they mixed (beer in) the l. vat".
b) MA *ú-ra-ṭu-bu i-ba-lu-lu* Chuera 12: 33f. "they will soak and brew". S. [*lu*]-*ub-lu-ul* in destroyed context ib. 30: 7'.
2. Blood: OB lit. *ba-al-la-at qerbetum ina damīšunu* FM 14, 19 iii 6 "The meadowland was smeared with their blood".
3. Alloy:
a) OB 3 MA.NA *annakum ana ba-la-al* 24 MA.NA URUDU *billi* 8-ÀM ARM 22, 205 ii 9' (cf. also ib. 17', iii 8') "3 minas of tin for making an alloy of 24 minas of copper, alloy of 8 (to one)".
b) OB 2 1/3 MA.NA URUDU LUH.HA <…> 1 MA.NA AN.NA *ina* 8-*su* TA.ÀM *ba-li-il* RA 64, 21 no. 1: 4 "2 1/3 minas of copper … 1 mina of tin at the rate of 8 shekels (of tin) pro (mina) are mixed". S. also Arkhipov 2012, 23f.
c) OB (metals) *ša* PN *ina kiškattī*[*m*] *ša* PN$_2$ *ib-lu-lu* ARM 21, 285: 12 "which made PN to an alloy in the kiln of PN2".
4. People (cf. CAD *b.* 1f, 2 and 7):
a) OB *mārī Si-im-a-al it-ti-šu-nu ab-lu-ul-ma a-*[*la*]*m i-n*[*a*]*-aṣ-ṣa-ru* ARM 26/1 p. 308 no. 144: 20' "I mixed sons of Simʾal with them and they guard the city (together)".
b) OB *u mārī* GN$_1$ *ša ištū* GN$_1$ *tassuham ana adaššim ša* GN$_2$ *šūribšunūti* [*i*]*tt*[*ī mārī*] *ālim bu-lu-ul-šu-nu-ti* CRRAI 38, 105 n. 63 "and the citizens of GN$_1$, which you have removed from GN$_1$, let them enter the enclosure wall of GN$_2$ and mix them with the citizens of the city".
5. Extispicy:
a) OB *têrtam ē*[*pušma*] *ba-a*[*l*]*-la-a* ARM 26/1 p. 300 no. 136: 4'f. "I m[ade] an extispicy [and] the (signs) were confused".
b) OB *ṭēmam ina nadānim ba-la-lum i-ba-al-la-lu* ARM 27, 162: 34f. "when they deliver the report, they cause much confusion".

Gtn OB *ana bi-ta-al-lu-*[*li-im*] *ana bīt sābītim ana mēlulim* "for constantly mixing, for alehouse, for play" ARM 1, 28: 16. Reading after Durand 1984, 135 n. 42 (s. copy on p. 147). He understands *b.* here sexually (s. also id. 1997, 66). Or mixing beer?

Št$_2$ OB *kakkī uš-ta-ba*[*-al-la-lu*] ARM 26/2 p. 268 no. 405: 18 "they constantly mix[ed] the weapons (in the battle)".

N 1. OB *ina šittīn lā ab-ba-al-la-al* ARM 26/2 p. 224 no. 392: 37 "I will not be mixed up in two-thirds" (Heimpel 2003, 338f. with n. 3).
2. OB lit. *ilū mātim* … ⸢*ib*⸣*-ba-lu in-epri* UET 6/2, 395: 11 "the gods of the land were spread with dust".

+ **Ntn** OB lit. *i-ta-ab-la-al elī inbī u dādī* YOS 11, 24 i 23 "constantly mingle on top of (my) fruits and desires!"
MPS (G, N, Ntn), NR (G, Gtn, Št$_2$)

balangu, + *bulukku*, + *bulungu*, + *pilaggu* "lyre"

1. MB Emar *bu-lu-uk-ki* Emar 6/4, 545: 103 and ^{giš}*balag* = *bu-lu-un-g*[*u*$_5$(KU)] ib. 380.
2. NA *arim pi-*⌜*lag*⌝*-gi* SAA 3, 8 r. 13' "the lyre is tuned(?) (lit. covered)". Diff. CAD P 372b *pilakku* a "spindle", but s. CAD P 359b *pigû* A. MPS (1), NR (2)

balāṣu I "to stare"

G OB lit. *ina pīka u šīnātika ib-ta-li-iṣ-ka* TIM 9, 53: 6 "it stared at you in your mouth and your urine". S. Streck/Wasserman 2011, 123.
D For CH § 159 UB-*ta-al-li*-IS-*ma* s. AHw 814a and CAD P 54a s. v. *palāsu*. Diff. Borger 1971, 66; id. 2008, 439.
MPS (G), NR (D)

balāt "without"

1. OA *ba-lá-at* (in broken context) AKT 5, 18: 49. OA occurences show that the word cannot, pace AHw 101, be a fem. pl. of *balûtu*, because a contraction **balū-at* is impossible.
2. NA *ba-lat* DN SAA 12, 96: 21 "without the permission of DN".
3. With prep. *ana* + loc. + suffix: NA *a-bal-la-tuk-ka memēni lā eppušū šumma mār šipri ettiq a-ba-la-duk-ka lā ettiqū* SAA 15, 241: 6, 9 "without you they should do nothing! If a messenger passes by, they must not pass by without you!"
4. Instead of *ba-lat* Gilg. SB VII 40, read *ba-šat*, s. *bašû*.
MPS (1, 3, 4), NR (2)

balāṭu I "life"

1. Note the spelling *bala-ṭí* in OB *šu-lum bala-ṭí ù da-ri-i lu-uš-me* CUSAS 9, 6: 22 "may I hear greetings of long life and being eternal".
2. EA [*i-n*]*a* TI-*ma* EA 17: 30 = *ina balāṭ* "next year". S. Moran 1992, 42 n. 5.
3. SB *ba-la-ṭa/ṭu/ṭù ša lā namāri ina muḫḫi mūti minâ utter* Ballad of Early Rulers 19 "a life without light, what has it more than death?" MPS (1, 3), NR (2)

balāṭu II "to live"

G 1. OB lit. [*u*]*l ib-lu-ṭú šunu imtūtū* FM 14, 23 iv 5 "they did not stay alive but died".
2. OB *še'am … šūbilamma bītī lū ba-li-iṭ-ṭì* AbB 10, 4: 36 "send me grain … may my household stay alive" (pace CAD B 301b *b.* 1a: *lu-ba-li-iṭ-ṭì* "so that I may keep alive"). For comm. s. Kraus, ib. p. 6 n. 4g.
3. SB *alka Adapa ammīni lā tākul lā taltīma lā ba-al-ṭa-ta* MesCiv. 10, 20: 68' "come, Adapa, why did you not eat nor drink? Hence you shall not live!".
4. Deller 1966, 305: MA *bal-ṭa-ku ma-ṭi-ma ša balāṭiya mētāku ma-ṭi-*[*ma ša mu-a-ti-ja*] "ich bin am Leben, aber ich habe zu wenig, um am Leben zu bleiben; ich bin tot, aber ich habe zu wenig, [um tot zu sein]" Bo. 845: 10'. Wrong von Soden 1988, 345: *bal-ṭa-ku-ma ṭé-ma ša balāṭiya mētāku ma-*?[...].
5. NA *libbinni ib-ta-a*[*l-ṭa*] SAA 10, 185: 15 "our hearts were delighted"; cf. ŠÀ-*bi lib-l*[*a-ṭa*] ib. e. 2 "may my heart be delighted!" (Deller 1966, 308).
6. NA *adi* UD^{meš} *ša* PN *bal-ṭu-u-ni ipalluḫū-šú* SAA 14, 208: 4' "as long as PN lives they shall serve him" (Deller 1966, 308).

7. PN *šarru māt Aššur i-bal-la-ṭá* SAA 4, 322 r. 1 "will Assurbanipal, king of Assyria, survive and escape this insurrection?" Incorrect in CAD B 73a *balû* 1b (ABL 1368, s. Deller 1966, 308).

D 1. OA/OB "to assess the value of, consider an asset or credit, render the account" (Prag p. 20 with lit.; cf. CAD B 62 *b.* 9):
a) OA *luqūtam ... ba-lí-ṭá-am* Prag 431: 6 "estimate the goods!" Stative *ba-lu-uṭ-ma* ib. 16 "is estimated".
b) OB "now take your tablets (records)and come here and *bu-ul-li-iṭ* the accounts/accounting of your barley" OBTR 311: 11.
c) *bu-ul-lu-uṭ kaspim* AWTL 103: 49.
d) *bu-ul-lu-uṭ* ZI.GA ŠE.Ì.GIŠ ARM 22, 276 iv 40 "drawing the balance of expenditures of sesame".
e) *bu-lu-uṭ* ZI.GA UD.KA.BAR ARM 22, 203 r. iv 8 "drawing the balance of the expenditures of bronze".
f) *ana bu-ul-lu-uṭ našpakim šakin* MARI 3, 262 M.11500: 9 "(this document) is established to render the account of the accumulation (of grain)".
g) For further ref. in Mari s. Durand 1984, 260ff. S. also Veenhof 1987, 49f.
2. MB Emar *ḫubbulāku u ana bubūti nuppuḫ* u PN *ub-tal-li-ṭá-ni-mi* AulaOr. Suppl. 1, 25: 7 "I am in debt and bloated(?) with hunger from famine and PN maintains me". For *bulluṭu* "maintaining alive (during time of distress)" s. disc. in Adamthwaite 2001, 148ff.

Dt 1. OB *mu-úš-ke-num* DUMU^{meš} GN *aš-šum bu-ta-al-lu-ṭì-im a-na-na-ba-al-ka-at-ti ša-di-im it-ta-al-ku* ARM 28, 51: 11 "The poor people from GN went to cross the mountain in order to provide themselves". S. also Kupper 1988 and Borger 2008, 439.
2. OB UD 5^{kam} *li-ib-ta-li-iṭ* AbB 12, 37: 8 "may he be kept alive for 5 days".
MPS (G, Dt), NR (G, D)

balittu s. *balītu*

balītu, *balittu* "backwater"
1. OB *eqel ba-li-tim* FM 2, 38 no. 11: 19, 25 "field at the backwater".
2. OB *ba-li-tum šī* (in broken context) FM 2, 71 no. 36: 5.
3. OB *ḫarrānum ša ba-li-tim* ARM 22, 328 ii 20, 31 (*-tum*! correct?) "road (leading to) the pond" (in description of field).
4. There is prob. only one word *balītu* instead of two, *balittu* (CAD B 63 "reservoir, pond", and *balītu* (ib. "desert land"); AHw 99 only has *balittu* "Reservoir; Fischteich". *t* is never doubled, hence the form appears to be *balītu*, derived from the prep. *balū*. After Durand 2000, 545, the word has, at least in Mari, the mng. "backwater".

baliu "a synonym for lord, master"
For *ba-li-u*[*m*] CAD B 63b s. now AOAT 50, 430: 14. Prob. /baʿlīyu/ "lordly".

ballu "mixed"
Said of evil in NA EDIN ḪUL! *bal-li*! SAA 9, 2 ii 24 "steppe of mixed evil" (i. e., evil of all kind?), s. comm. of Parpola, ib. p. 16.

ballukku, *balluggu* "a tree; an aromatic substance"
1. OB 4 GÍN KÙ.BABBAR *šīm* 2 GÚ *ba-al-lu-gi* ARM 22, 261: 10 "2 shekels of silver, the price of 2 talents of *b.*" (in list of aromatic trees).
2. OB *ba-lu-gu-um* (besides *kikkirēnu*) FM 2, 25 no. 4: 14.

3. OB [n] MA.NA *ba-lu-ku* ... *[a-n]a diziptuḫḫim* ARM 21, 106: 1 "3 minas of *b.* (and sweet cane) for making sweet beer".
4. OB 5 MA.NA *šurmēnum* 5 MA.NA *asum* 5 MA.NA *ba-lu-ku ana kisamim* ARM 21, 106: 12 "5 minas of cypress, 5 minas of myrtle, 5 minas of *b.* for *kisamu*-drink(?)".
5. OB 20 MA.NA *ba-l[u-ku]* ARM 21, 119: 3 (besides other aromatics).
6. For OB Mari s. ref. in MARI 7, 266 (also *pa-lu-gu* ARM 9, 277).
7. Moran 1992, 59 n. 35 ad CAD B 64*b*. 1a: EA 22 iii 33 read ŠIM.BÚLUG, EA 25 iv 51 read ŠIM.GIG = *kanaktu*.
8. SB *erēnu* $^{\text{giš.šim}}$MUG-*ma nērebi ul īši* JCS 66, 76: 11 (Gilg.) "(entangled) were cedar and *b.* tree so that (the forest) had no ways in". MPS (1–6, 8), NR (7)

ballūṣītu "a bird; a lizard"

SB (if a falcon hunts for prey and) *bal-⸢lu⸣-ṣi-ti*^{mušen} *iššī* CUSAS 18, 36 ii 18 "picks up a *b.*-bird".

+ **baltām(mu)** "balsam"; LB, WSem. lw.

1. Jursa 2009, 156f. with etym.: ^{šim}⸢*ba-al-ta*⸣*-am* BM 77429: 22. ^{šim}*ba-al-tam-[(mu)]* BM 73126. ^{šim}*ba-al-tam-mu* BM 75774.
2. As PNf: ^{f}*Bal-ta-am-mu* Wunsch 1995/96, 57 no. 7: 7, 11. ib. 63 no. 12:4.
3. These LB ref. of *baltām(mu)* are the earliest found in non-biblical texts.

NR

baltu, *baštu* "thornbush"; + OB

1. OB 1 *majjālu ba-áš-tum*! ARM 22, 322: 46 "1 bed of *b.* wood". Whereas Kupper, ib. p. 499 translates "lit d'apparat", Kupper 1992, 164, correctly recognizes the tree *baltu* here; for further ref. from Mari texts s. ib.
2. OB lit. *assuḫ ba-aš-ta-am* ALL no. 23: 8 "I have torn the thorn".
3. OB lit. *aruḫ ša ba-aš-tim* CUSAS 32, 49: 4 "it is hurrying among the thornbush". Cf. George, ib. p. 113f. for further instances of OB *baštu*.
4. OB lit. *waruq ina ba-aš-tim* RA 66, 141ff. AO 7682: 7 "(the scorpion) is green in the thornbush".

balṭu "living, alive"

1. OA in PN: *Ba-al-ṭù-šar* AKT 7a, 249: 27 "The alive one is king/is just".
2. OB *ana ba-al-ṭì-im* DN *mimma ul ikallā* AbB 7, 80: 14 "DN withholds nothing from the (person) in good health".
3. OB 6 $^{\text{lú.meš}}$*pagrī iddû u kalûšu ba-al-ṭà-am iṣbat* ARM 26/2 p. 132 no. 357: 26' (Heimpel 2003, 315) "they abandoned 6 corpses; and all of them seized one (prisoner) alive".
4. SB In the sense of "magnetic" in *šadânu balṭu* (Ḫḫ XVI), s. DCCLT MB Ura 10.
5. "solvent", cf. Zaccagnini 1994, 32ff.: *kaspam ba-al-ṭum-ma umallā* AT 18: 16 "he who is solvent shall pay the silver in full". 60 GÍN("SU")$^{\text{ḫi-a}}$ *bal-ṭù-ma ippalšina* AT 47: 15 "he who is solvent shall pay 60 shekels".
6. For *ina balṭū u šalmū* as state of financial well-being s. Charpin 2005, 26f.; Veenhof 1987, 58ff.

MPS (1, 4), NR (2–3, 5-6)

balṭūtu "state of being alive"

1. OB *ba-al-ṭú-us-sú ul īdē kīma mītim kispam aktassipšum* AbB 13, 21: 7 "I did not know whether he (my son) was still alive and I kept making funerary offerings for him as if he were dead".
2. OB *u ṣābum b[a-a]l-ṭù-us-sú tūr* ARM 26/2 p. 132 no. 357: 27' "and the

troop (of Mari) has returned safe and sound".
3. For Wiseman Treaties 570 (CAD B 69b *b.* a1') s. SAA 2, 6: 570: *kī ša šá-aṣ-*⌜*bu?-tu?*⌝ *tul-tu takkuluni.* NR

ba᾿lu "(exceptionally) big"

SB *šumma erû ina ūri bīt amēli iṣṣūra lū* 1 *lū* 2 *ikkal bēl bīti šu᾿āti zitta ba-il-tam* [GU₇] Gs. Sachs p. 282 YBC 16934 i 8 "if an eagle eats a bird, either one or two, on the roof of a person's house, the owner of that house [will consume] an (exeptionally) large share". NR

balū "without"

1. With suffix (es. CAD B 71 *b.* c end):OB *kaspam ana mamman ba-lu-ia lā tušeṣṣē* AbB 12, 53: 17f. "do not issue the silver to anyone without my permission!"
2. Deller 1966, 305: MA *ana namāše ba-lu bēliya palḫāku* JCS 7, 167 no. 63: 21 "I am afraid to move on without my lord". MPS (1), NR (2)

balû I s. *belû* II

+ **balû II** "spare donkey"; SB, Sum. lw.

[MIN (= *anše*)*-á-*]⌜*bal*⌝*-lá* = *ba-lu-u* Emar 6/4, 550: 233 (Ḫḫ XIII). Parallel to *anše-á-bal* = *tēnû* MSL 8/1, 51: 365 (AHw 1347 *tēnû* 3, CAD T 344 *tēnû* lex. sect.).

baluḫḫu, *paluḫḫu*, *buluḫḫu* "an aromatic plant"

1. OB *aššum ḫīl ba-lu-ḫi u kukrim* AbB 3, 32: 4, 6 "as to the resin of *b.* and *kukrum*". *kukru ba-lu-ḫu* ib. 8.
2. OB 5 MA.NA *ᵍⁱˢba-lu-ḫu-um* FM 7, 94 M.12595: 9'. For OB Mari s. ref. in MARI 7, 265 (also *pa-lu-ḫu-um*).

balultu? "mixture"

von Soden 1968, 458 ad CAD B 75 denies the existence of *balultu* and refers to *balûtu* (AHw 101a) "in state of being empty". NR

balūt "without"

SB Ugar. *ba-lut šaḫḫi* AulaOr. Suppl. 23, 51: 23 "without *š.*-cloth".

balûtu s. *balāt*

bāmtu "half; chest; open country, plain"

1. OB *šê šibši u šê ba-ma-*[*tim*] Joannes 2006, 54 n. 11 fragm B: 5' (Haradum) "the barley of the *š.*-tax and the barley of the metayage agreements". S. also ib. 55 n. c.
2. OB *ba-ma-sú-nu lū wašbū ba-ma-sú-nu* [*l*]*illikū* AbB 13, 104: 5'f. "let half of them stay, half of them go".
3. OB *ba-ma-at riksim u ša ibaššû ma-ḫa-aṣ* AbB 12, 54: 16 "divide (lit. hit) half of the package and what (else) is there" (i. e., divide into two halves, s. van Soldt, ib. p. 45).
4. 4 *pelî ša lurmim ina ba-ma-tim ilqûnimma* ARM 27, 9: 32 "they gathered 4 ostrich eggs in the plains".
5. OB GIŠ.NI*-e-ĝu*$_{10}$ = *ba-am-ti ṣe-ḫ*[*e-er-*]*tum*, ⌜x⌝*-sa-ad-ĝu*$_{10}$ = *ba-am-ti ra-b*[*i-tu*]*m* CUSAS 12 p. 150: 12f. (Ugumu) "my small/big paunch".
6. In the dual: OB *ba-am-ti-šu ikūṣ* ARM 26/2 p. 337 no. 434: 39 "he skinned his chest (on both sides)". The dual is also attested in STT 87: 11, wrongly analysed as pl. in CAD B *bamtu* B a 3'.
7. For the question of a single *bāmtu* (as in AHw) against two (in CAD, + pl. *bamâtu*) s. Militarev/Kogan 2000, 190. MPS (2–7), NR (1)

bandillu, + *baddillu* "belly"; + NA

In lists of temple offerings: 10 *ban-dil*! SAA 7, 202 r. 3 "10 stomachs(?)" (after 3 ^{uzu}*lipšāt* "3 scrotums"). 10 *ba-dil*^{meš} ib. 189 r. 7. [*ba*]*n*!-*dil*! ib. 208: 15.

banduddû, + *banduttû* "bucket"; + NA

1. OB 1 GAL *ba-an-du-du-ú* KÙ.BABBAR ARM 31, 235: 3; 1 *ba-an-du-ud-ú* KÙ.BABBAR *ša* GN ib. 241: 1 "1 silver *b*.-bucket from GN". For further ref. and disc. s. Guichard ib. 187f.
2. MB Emar: New by-form *banduttû*: [*gú*]*r-ba-an-du*$_8$*-du*$_8$ = MIN (= *kippat*) *ba-an-du-ut-te-e* Emar 6/4, 545: 102 (Ḫ̮ḫ̮ VI).
3. Rare syllabic spelling: NA lit. [*m*]*ullâ mullâ ban-*(*du*)*-de-šu-un* SAA 3, 10: 11 "fill, fill their buckets!"

MPS (2–3), NR (1)

bannu, *bānu* "ewer"

SB lex. *ba-*⸢*an*⸣ *šipr-rum* = *nemsû* AOAT 50, 405: 204 (Malku) "ewer for a ritual = washing basin". With AHw 102 and CDA 37, against CAD B 95 *bānû* A 2, Sum. lw. < *bán* (cf. also *pānu* II), not deriving from Akk. *banû* "to create".

+ **bantû** "bucket"; MB Emar

Lex. *gúr-ba-an-du*$_8$ = MIN (= *kippat*) *ba-an-te-e* Emar 6/4, 545: 101 (Ḫ̮ḫ̮ VI) "handle of the *b*.-bucket".

banû I "well-formed, well-made, fine"

1. OB, said of musicians destined to be blinded:
a) ^{lú}TUR^{meš} *la ba-nu-tim* ARM 26/2 p. 25 no. 297: 15 "boys not good". Heimpel 2003, 287 translates "untrained", but perhaps their physical state of still having their eyes is meant.
b) OB ^{lú}TUR^{meš} *lā ba-nu-tim* FM 9, 220 no. 53: 9 "boys not beautiful".

2. Referring to an abstract in OB *ana ilūtika ba-ni-tim* AbB 12, 99: 21 "to your splendid divine power".

3. OB *aššum ana lā ba-ni-a-t*[*im pānīk*]*a taškunu* AbB 13, 103: 2' "because you have set [your mind] on improper matters".

4. MB 32 NA$_4$^{meš} *ba-nu-tu*$_4$ MBLET 20: 4 "32 fine stones".

MPS (1–4), NR (5)

banû II "to be(come) good, beautiful"

G Mayer 2016, 193: ref. in CAD B 91 *banû* B 1 "to grow" belong to *banû* IV "to create, build", except *bini arkāniš* Ee V 20 "become beautiful backwards!" (with D. O. Edzard apud Streck 1994, 168 n. 37). Pace Mayer, also *banī bu*ʾ*āru* RA 22, 170: 15 belongs to *banû* IV: "at her glance, prosperity is created".

D 1. "to make good": OB *tuppaka ana awīlim bu-un-ni-a-am-ma šūbilam* AbB 12, 113: 19 "Send a well-done letter of yours to the lord!".
2. Matouš 1964, 137: KAR 4 r. 20 (CAD B 91a *banû* B "to be beautiful") with DÍM = *ana bu-ni-*[*i*] belongs to *banû* A "to build".
3. Mayer 2016, 193f.: ref. CAD B 93 *banû* 6 "to grow" translate in fact "was decorated with", "was formed well".

MPS, NR

banûtu s. *rab-banûtu*

bappiru, *pappiru* "beer bread"

1. OA *še*ʾ*am lū taš*ʾ*amma bu-uq-lam ù ba-pi-ra-am-ma tēpuš* AKT 2, 26: 18 "may she buy grain and make malt and beer bread".

2. Stol 2008, 350: Syllabic spellings for *pappiru*:
a) OB *pa-pí-ri* TIM 9, 51: 9.
b) *buqlum u pa-ap-pí-ru-um* Iraq 42, 69 no. 10 i 12.
c) MA UDUN *pa-pi-ri* Deller 1987, 65.
MPS (1), NR (2)

baqāmu, *baqānu* "to pluck"

G 1. OB *ṣēnū kīma šaddaqdim tabqumu šalmā* AbB 5, 230: 10 "the livestock, that(?) (lit. as) you plucked last year, are well".
2. MB Ekalte 18 *immerū* MU 2 *ša šinīšu ba-aq-nu* WVDOG 102, 32: 2 "18 sheep, two years old, which were plucked twice".
3. MA (small cattle) *ba-aq-na* BATSH9/3, 21: 19; 28: 13 "has been plucked".
4. Deller 1966, 305f.: KAJ 88: 15–18 (CAD B 98 *b.* 1a5') read *ú-⸢la*!*-da*!⸣ instead of *ú-⸢la*⸣.

N 1. Lex. [*z*]*é-ba* = *na-ab-qí-im* CUSAS 12 p. 248: 25 (gramm. text) "be plucked!".
2. OB *li-ib-ba-qí-im-ma* MARI 8, 387 A.2459 r. 4, cf. *buqūmu*.
3. MA *ina muḫḫišu errīʾā ulladā i-ba-qa-an-na irabbīʾā* BATSH 9/3, 48: 26 "incumbent on him, (small cattle) will become pregnant, give birth, be plucked (and) grow". MPS (G, N), NR (G)

bāqilu "maltster"

1. MB É [lú]MUNU4[meš] BagF 21, 48: 32'; 50: 16; PBS 2/2, 77; 106: 7' "house of maltster" (always in connection with city gates).
2. MB 200 *qa* MUNU4.SAR *ina qāt* PN [lú]MUNU4.SAR CT 51, 29: 5 "200 litre of malt from PN, maltster (for brewer)". S. Sassmannshausen 2001, 80 for further ref. NR

+ **baq(a)ru** "cow"; OB; MB Emar; NWSem. lw.

1. OB 1! AMAR! GA! *ša*! *ba-aq-ri-im* ARM 24, 42: 2' "1 milk calf of a cow". Cf. Durand 1987, 210 n. 36, followed by Streck 2000, 85.
2. OB *ba-iq-ru-um ša ina ša-la-ta-im ša* GN KTT 55a: 6 "cows from the booty of GN". Cf. disc. of Krebernik, ib. p. 57 (*baqru* "to be claimed" or "cow") and Durand/Marti 2003, 170.
3. MB Emar (sheep) *ša ina ba-qa-ra* Emar 6/3, 327: 9 "which are in the flock". Cf. Pentiuc 2001, 36f.
4. Cf. *buqāru*. MPS (1, 3), NR (2–3)

bar *s. buru*

barakku "outbuilding"

Lex. *é-gal bar-ra* = *ba-rak-ku* CUSAS 12, 39: 5 (Kagal).

barāmu I "to be variegated, multicolored"

D OB lit. *libissunu bu-ur-ru-um* CunMon. 8, 22ff. ii 19 "their cloth is multicolored".

barāqu "to lighten, shine"

Š OB *tattakkipma kīma lîm tu-ša-ab-ra-aq-šu* Gilg. OB Nippur 5 "you will lock horns and strike him down like a bull". Cf. George 2003, 244; or *parāku* Š?
+ **N** SB *būlu ib-ba-riq* SpTU 4, 264: 15 "the animals are flashed down(?)".
Ntn KAH 2, 74: 5 (CAD B 105b *b.* 3) read *mut-tap-ri-š*[*u-ti*] (s. also CAD M/2, 308b, a1'). MPS (Š, N), NR (Ntn)

barārī "at dusk, evening"; + OB

1. OB *ba-ra-ri i-na* [giš]MÁ.TUR [*a-ra*]-*ak-ka-bu-ma* ARM 26/1 p. 197 no. 54: 42 "(so that) I can [em]bark at evening on a small boat".

2. OB *ba-ra-ri bitqam šâtu esekker*! FM 1, 94 A.250: 28 "at dusk I will block up that breach".
3. OB *ba-ra-ri* AbB 7, 2: 7.
4. MA *ina mūše ba-ra-ri-ma* BATSH 4/1, 2: 22 "in the night, at dusk".
5. Lit.: Streck 2017, 597.

barārītu, *barārtu*, + *barīrītu*, + *barīru*? "dusk, evening watch"

1. OB (sheep and tables for DN) *ni-iq ba-ra-⸢ar⸣-tim i-⸢na qa-ab⸣-li-tim* KTT 345: 4 "sacrifice of the evening watch, at midnight".
2. OB 4 *dipārī ana ba-ra-ar-tim qabśitim u nawā[rtim] anaššī* RATL 156: 30 "I will lift four torches at the 1., 2. and 3. watch of the night".
3. Fem. pl. *barārīʾātam* (for these frozen pl. forms s. Streck 2007, 597 § 11): OB *ba-ra-ri-a-t[a-am]* AbB 3, 66: 7 "at dusk". Diff. GAG § 113l*: adverb in *-attam*.
4. OB *šuttī annītum ša ba-ra-ar-tim* ARM 10, 50: 13 "this dream was (seen) during the evening watch".
5. New by-form *barīrītu* (cf. *barīrītu* "a female demon" CAD B 111): OB *šuttum šī ba-ri-ri-tum-ma* ARM 26/1 p. 306 no. 142: 22 "that dream was during the evening watch".
6. New by-form perhaps *barīru* (cf. *barīru* A "rays" CAD B 111f.): *mūšu mašil ... ba-ri-ri-im* ARM 26/2 p. 132 no. 357: 34f. "midnight ... evening watch(?)" (in broken context).
7. Lit.: Streck 2017, 597.

barāru I "to flicker" or "be dim"?

SB *ib-ru-ur* SpTU 4, 262 r. 6.

barāru II? "to speak blasphemously"

Cf. Durand 1997, 101: "proférer des injures". Pace Durand not related to Hebr. *brr* "purify, select". For *i*B-*ru-ur-ma* TDP 190: 26 s. *parāru*. NR

barbartu, + *barbaratu* "she-wolf"; + OB, + OA

1. OB *šī ba-ar-ba-ra-tum* YOS 11, 20: 3 "she (Lamaštu) is a she-wolf".
2. SB *bar-ba-rat* // OA *ba-ar-ba-ra-tum* Lamaštu i 37 (Farber 2014, 74).

MPS, NR

barbaru "wolf"

1. OB lit. *libbaka kīma* U[R.B]AR.RA *bāštum [kīma] nēšim ⸢šalummatum liklāka⸣* ZA 75, 202: 82 "may dignity, [like] a wolf, (restrain) your heart, may radiance, like a lion, restrain you".
2. OB lit. *kīma ba-ar-ba-ri-⸢im⸣ [b]āš⸢tam⸣ [kī] nē⸢šim⸣ šalummat[am lūṭ]erka* ZA 75, 180: 4 "vigor like (that of) a wolf, splendor like (that of) a lion, I will take away from you".
3. OB lit. *kīma ba-ar-ba-ri-im lakāta mādmi* UET 6/2, 399: 6 "like a wolf (the anger) is quick-running".
4. OB lit. *našāk ba-ar-ba-ri-im inaššak* YOS 11, 14 r. 3 "(the *maškadu* sickness) bites a wolf-bite".
5. OB lit. *ul iḫaddī ba-ar-ba-ru* YOS 11, 29 r. 25 // *bar-ba-ra* 15: 5 "the wolf shall not rejoice".
6. SB *ba-ra-ba-ra* OIP 114, 115: 2 (in list of Akk. words between *nēšu* "lion" and *imēru* "donkey").

+ **bardītu** "girl(?)"; OA

1. OA (silver) *ana* TÚG *ša ba-ar-dí-tí* Prag 429: 34 "for a garment of a girl(?)".
2. *bar-dí-tí* OIP 27, 55: 63. Cf. comm. Prag p. 14.
3. Perhaps a by-form of *wardatu*.

MPS (1–2), NJCK (3)

bardû "crosspiece"

SB *bar-da-a ana bar-di-i uštanār* // MB *ba-ar-da-a ana ba-ar-de-e* Lamaštu ii 166 (Farber 2014, 122) "crossbar after crossbar, she keeps leaning (into the window)".

+ **barḫu** "fugitive, rustic(?)"; Ugar. word

For ^{lú}*ba-ar-ḫu* and ^{munus}*ba-ri-iḫ-tu*$_4$ (AHw 1547a *barḫu* "shining") s. Huehnergard 1987, 114f. and 323f.; del Olmo Lete/Sanmartín 2004, 236f. NR

barī- "between, among"

ana barī-: *išarū a-na ba-ri-šu-nu-ma* AKT 1, 21: 10 "they are even".

barīrītu "the glittering one, (name of a female demon)"

Lex. [*b*]*a-ri-ri-tum* = [*kabittu*] AOAT 50, 431: 53 (exp. Malku) "the glittering one = [the important one]".

+ **barīru III** (mng. unkn.); OB

ba-ri-ri-ka nakru ile[*qqē*] CUSAS 18, 26: 15' "the enemy will ta[ke] your *b.*" *ba-ri-ri* ib. 17'. In spite of the divergent orthography, George, ib. p. 182, connects the word with *parīru*.

+ **barkarrû**, pl. f. *barkarrêtum* "a coarse textile"; OB

1. ŠU.NIGIN 16 ^{túg}*ba-ar-ka-ru-ú* ŠÀ.BA 1 TÚG SI.SÁ ÚS 3 ^{túg}GÚ.È. A^{ḫá} *iškar* É GN$_1$ 6 ^{túg}*ba-ar-ka-ru iškar bīt* GN$_2$ ŠU.NIGIN 25 ^{túg}*ba-ar-ka-ru-ú* 11 ^{túg}GÚ.È.A^{ḫá} *ba-ar-ka-re-tum iškar* 3 *bītātim* ⌜*ḫalaṣ*⌝ GN$_2$ *maḫrum* ARM 30 p. 552 M.5888 "total: 16 *b.*, among them 1 fabric of second quality, 3 *naḫlaptu* garments, the work assignment of the house of GN$_1$. 6 *b.*, the work assignment of the house of GN$_2$. Total: 25 *b.*, 11 *naḫlaptu* garments (made) of *b.*, the work assignments of 3 houses from the district of GN$_2$ received(?)".
2. 4 ^{túg}*bar-ka-ru-ú pirsu* ARM 30 p. 428 M.8599: 1 "4 *b.*, a piece (for repairing them?).
3. 4 ^{túg}BAR.KAR.RA ÚS *ana* TÚG.BA *kullizi* ARM 7, 147: 1 "4 *b.* of second quality, clothing allocation of the ox-driver".
4. 1 ^{túg}BAR.KAR *ana riksi ša* ANŠE ^{giš}GIGIR ARM 24, 181: 7 "1 *b.* for the harness of the donkey chariot".
5. 2 *gizzu* BAR.KAR.RA ARM 22, 119: 1 "2 *g.* cloths (made) of *b.*".
6. DAL.ÚŠ BAR.KAR.RA AWTL 88: 1; ib. 98: 2 "catapult of *b.*"
7. Lit. with further ref.: Durand 2009, 97–99. NR

barku s. *birku*

barmu "multicolored"

1. OB lit., said of cloths: *aprū ba-ar-mu-ti-im-ma* CunMon. 8, 22ff. ii 20 "their (head) is covered with multicolored (cloths)".
2. NA, said of animals: *erbiʾu* NUMUN! *bar*!*-mu kal-mu-tú* SAA 2, 6: 599 "locusts, the multicolored seed(?), bugs". Cf. SAA 2 p. 85: *barmu* "a pest".

barru III s. *bāru* II

barsillu "a garment"

Edzard 1970a, 160: hybrid from **bardullu* (< BAR.DUL$_5$) and *kusītu*? Veenhof 1972, 162 n. 276: *b.* based on a misunderstanding? NR

+ **baršu II** "a cereal"; OB

OB (^{še})*bar-šum* ARM 19 p. 164 (index). Limet, ib. p. 24 suggests a loan from

Sum. *bar-si*, for which s. Milano 1993–1997, 27 (emmer flour).

bārtu "revolt, rebellion"

1. OB *ina ba-ar-tim ilattakūka* ARM 10, 7: 9 "they will put you to a test by a rebellion".
2. Amarna Ḫ̮I.G[A.R]I K[I]-*ia* EA 138: 20 "revolt against me(?)" (Moran 1992, 223 n. 4). Note Ḫ̮I.GA.RI instead of normal Ḫ̮I.GAR. MPS (1), NR (2)

barû I "to see, look at"

Gt 1. OB *awātam ana bi-it-r*[*i*]-*i*-[*im*] AbB 13, 110: 19 "in order to consider thoroughly(?) the matter".
2. SB *urḫ̮ī bi-it-ri* AulaOr. Suppl. 23, 33: 29 "watch my path!"

D 1. "to announce, to disclose, to reveal" (CAD B 331 has a separate lemma *burrû*): NA *kētu anāku lā ú-bar-ri lā a-qa-ba-áš-šú-nu bēt šarru bēlī išapparšanuni* SAA 15, 4: 14 "truly, I have not disclosed nor told them where the king, my lord, is sending them".
2. *ú-bar-r*[*a*…] in broken context in ib. 61 r. 3'.

Dt "to be announced": OB *šumma šāpirī iqabbī li-ib-te-er-ri-šu-nu-ši-im-ma ṣibit ṭēmim liršû* AbB 13, 37: 32 "if my superior gives the order, it should be announced to them, so that they will take action". MPS (Dt), NR (Gt, D)

\+ **barû III** "to spend time, be stuck, be forced to stay"

G Disc. and OA ref. in Veenhof 2015a, 253–259, e. g.: *lā ta-ba-ri tibʾamma atalkam* AKT 3, 66: 15 "don't spend time in GN! Get ready and come!" Delete CAD *barû* C "to be available, to be on the market".

Gtn?: *ikrib ili u šarri lib-tar-ru-ú ina šaptīya dameqti Marduk bēliya lū kayyān ina pīya* Or. 59, 450: 9' "may a blessing for the god and the king constantly(?) endure on my lips, may a good (word) for my lord Marduk be always in my mouth". Mayer 1990, 454 ad 9': Gt *libtarû*.

Gt 1. Veenhof 2015a, 258: ref. in CAD *bitrû* (= AHw *barû* Gt) belong here. Also OA attested.
2. SB *ina īnēja bi-it-ra-at dili*[*ptu*] AulaOr. Suppl. 23, 33: 26 "anxiety lasts in my eyes".

Š "to let wait". Veenhof 2015a, 258f. for OA ref., e. g.: *aṣṣēr ša* GN *ú-ša-áb-ra-ki-im* Kt h/k 73: 18 "I will let you wait longer than in GN".

Št Ref. in AHw under *berû* "to be hungry", in CAD under *bitrû* belong here. But s. *berû* II. MPS (G, Gt, Š, Št), NR (Gtn)

bāru II, *barru*, pl. *ba*/*errātu* "open country; undeveloped land"; + OB, + LB

1. OB (field) *ša ba-a-ri* ARM 23, 590: 5 "situated in the open country". Pace Villard, ib. p. 557 unlikely to be *būru* "cistern" or *bārû* "diviner".

2. LB pl.(?) *ba*/*errātu*, s. von Soden 1977, 185:
a) ŠE.NUMUN *zaqpi u ber-ra-t*[*um*] Iraq 54, 132 BM 50021: 1 "arable land, planted and undeveloped land".
b) ŠE.NUMUN^{meš} *ā zaqpi u bar-rat-tum*^{meš} *makkūr šarri* BM 116622: 7 (Iraq 54, 132 ad. 1) "those fields, planted and undeveloped land, royal property".
c) *zaqpi adi bé-rat* CunMon. 20B, 19 no. 11 r. 1, 5 "(land) planted, including undeveloped land".
d) *ina libbi* n *zēru ša ina libbi* n2 *zēru bé*?!-*rat zittu ša* PN CunMon. 20B, 164 no. 130: 10', s. also ib. 16'.

e) *[zēr]a imaššaḫū ber-ra-tu4 isann[iqū]* CunMon. 20B, 214 no. 181: 28 "they will measure the arable land and check the undeveloped land".

MPS (1), NR (2)

bārû, MA *bāʾeru* "diviner; supervisor"

1. "supervisor" in OAkk. texts from Beydar: *ba-rí* UDU (NITA) "(male) supervisor of sheep", UGULA *ba-rí* UDU "overseer of supervisor(s) of sheep" Subartu 2 p. 176. Cf. disc. Sallaberger 2004, 18.
2. Said of Šamaš: *ilum namrum ba!-ru-ú* (// *a-zu*) *ebbu* CT 58, 28 r. 8 "bright god, the shining diviner".

bâru I "to catch, trap (with a net etc.)"

G 1. OB TU.TÚL[mušen.ḫi.a] *li-ba-ru* ARM 14, 41: 8 "let them catch *sukannīnu*-doves".
2. Said of persons:
a) OB *lā ta-ba-ra-né-ti lā tadukkanêti u ana mātim šanîm lā tanassaḫnêti* ARM 26/2 p. 277 no. 409: 28 "do not catch us, do not kill us, and do not move us toanother land!" (Heimpel 2003, 350).
b) *šaknī ša aškunakkunūšim lā ta-ba-ra-šu lā tadukkaššuma* ib. 32 "my governor whom I have installed over you, do not catch him, do not kill him!".
3. OB lit. *bāʾirum i-ba-ar nūnam* Fs. De Meyer 82ff. IM 95317: 19 "the fisherman is catching a fish".
4. OB lit. *ḫāwirī lu-ub-qú-ma-am* (// *ga-an-zé-e-še*) UET 6/2, 386: 10 "let me pluck my darling".

D 1. OB *tu-ba-aḫ-ḫi-ir*! (text: RI)*-ma* FM 2, 266 no. 128: 14, the first finite D-stem form.
2. OB lit. *mu-bi-ra-at mātāti* CUSAS 32, 59 i 8 (goddess) "who catches the countries".
3. SB *šumma surdû ina bīt amīli bu-ʾ-u-ra īpuš* SAA 8, 237: 4 "if a falcon hunts in a man's house". *bu-ʾ-u-ra* ib. 6.

+ N 1. OB *[rīm]am i-ba-ar-ru-ma* ⸢*ina*⸣ *bītišu ikallû* [...] *ib-ba-ar-ru-ma* KUŠ! *ana ekal[lim] ubbalū inanna mimma rīma[m] ul i-ba-ru ... serramī i-[b]a-ar-r[u] ... maškī serramī ša kīma ib-ba-ru ana ṣēr bēlija ušabbalam* ARM 27, 51 r. 1'–10' "they will catch an [aur]ochs and hold (it) captive in his house [... (which)] will be caught, (its) hide they will bring to the palac[e]. Now they have not caught any aurochs ... They will catch onagers ... the hides of the onagers that will have been caught I will bring to my lord".
2. SB (if a falcon and a raven fall tangled together on to the king's chariot) *[l]a ib-ba-ʾ-ir* CUSAS 18, 36 r. iii 23 "but are(!) not caught". S. also stative G (or mistake for pret. N?) ⸢*ba*⸣-*ʾ-ir* ib. 19.

MPS (G, D, N), NR (G)

bâru II, OA *baʾāru* "to stir up a revolt, to fight"

G *a-ba-a-ri-kà* KTS 1, 1a: 24, for context s. CAD P 210 *pâru*, prob. belongs here.

Gt Cf. Veenhof 2015b:
1. *merʾū mētim nēnu lá ni-ib-ta-ar* AKT 6a, 229: 4 "we are inheritors (lit. sons of a dead person). Let us not quarrel with each other".
2. *anāku mera mētim u attunu merʾū mētim lá ni-ib-ta-ar* AKT 7a, 34: 17 "I am an inheritor and you are inheritors. Let us not quarrel with each other". Cf. also ib. 30: 13; 58: 15; 59: 15; KKS 499: 4.

D 1. *merʾū mētim nēnu lá tù-ba-ar-ni-a-tí*? AKT 6a, 217: 22 "We are inheritors. Don't fight us!"

2. *[l]á tù-ba-a-ra-ni* AKT 6a, 85: 14 "don't fight against me!"

MPS (G, Gt, D), NJCK (Gt)

bâru III "to appear, turn up; be durable; to stay firm, stable, in good health"

G 1. OB *ma-a-tum ka-lu-[ša a-na] be-lí-ia bu-ur be-lí i-ta-ás-si* ARM 26/2 p. 96 no. 327: 3' "the entire land will be calling out, 'Stay in good health, my lord!'" (Heimpel 2003, 304).
2. OB *ma-at* GN *ka-lu-ša a-na* PN *bu-ur be-lí iš-ta-si* ARM 26/2 p. 197 no. 383: 8 "the entire land of GN called to PN, 'Stay in good health, my lord!'" (Heimpel 2003, 331).
3. Deller 1966, 309: PN TA IGI DN *[i]b-tu-ar* AfO Beih. 6, 54 no. 106: 11 "PN has established (it) before Adad".
4. On PN with element *li-bur*, *lil-bur/bir* s. AHw 108, 522 and 1547a (*bâru* III and *labāru*) and CAD B 126 *b.* 2a1', b 1' (reading LIL li_x,). Borger 2010b, 360 no. 544: delete li_x.

D 1. *ina bīt Šamaš li-bé-er-ru-šu-n[u-ti]* AbB 13, 41: 21 "they should establish the truth about them in the Šamaš temple".
2. a) OB *inanna bēlī ana bu-r[e-e]* PN *u mārī ālim dannātim lišpuram* FM 8, 84 no. 25: 15 "now may my lord, in order to notify PN and the inhabitants of the town, give firm orders".
b) *šu-tam bu-re-⌜e⌝-š[u-um?]* ib. 10 "notify h[im] of what is his (duty)!".
c) Durand, ib. p. 96, derives both instances from *būru* "well" and translates "aux puits" and "ceux qui font partie de ses puits" (reading *šu-ut*), an interpret. which makes less sense.
3. Deller 1966, 309: NA *bar*!-*ru*! *kan-nu uṭṭurū* AfO Beih. 6, 54 no. 106: 14 "they are proved, established and fully paid" (reading after Deller).

Dt "to be announced" (CAD B 331 has a separate lemma *burrû*): OB *šumma šāpirī iqabbī li-ib-te-er-ri-šu-nu-ši-im-ma ṣibit ṭēmim liršû* AbB 13, 37: 32 "if my superior gives the order, it should be announced to them, so that they will take action". MPS (G, D, Dt), NR (G, D)

bārûtu, + *baruttu* "work, lore of the diviner"

OB *ina ba-ru-ú-tim ša kakkī anāku etmēku* ARM 10, 120: 6 "I am occupied with a divination concerning weapons". S. also *ba-ru-tim-ma* ib. 9 and *ba-ru-ut-t[im]* ib. 11.

+ **basāmu** "to gladden, to please"; OB, Bo., SB

G OB *awīlê bi-si-im-ma warkānum dīnam awīlū iqabbûnim* AbB 14, 41: 14 "humour the gentlemen, so that later the gentlemen will pronounce a favorable judgement". S. Veenhof, ib. p. 206.

D 1. OB *awâtim nu-ba-ás-si-im-ši-na-ti-i-ma banī'ā* AbB 8, 69: 8 "we have pleased (them) with this matter and they are good";

2. OB *kusīt šikkatim ana bu*!-*sú-mi-ša idnī* AbB 9, 16: 38 (with corr. in BiOr 39, 590) "give (her) a *kusītum*-garment with a tassel to please her". Note that CAD Š/2, 432b interprets the last ref. as *pussumiša* "for veiling her". Not in CAD P 217f. *pasāmu* D.
3. *bu-sú-mu* (var. *bu-uš-šu-u*) = *a-aš-šu* (Hitt.) KBo 1, 44 + KBo 13, 1 iv 12 (StBoT 7, 19). After Otten/von Soden, StBoT 7, 22 both equations, *bussumu* "pleasant" and *bušû* "goods", reflect two mng.s of Hitt. *aššu-*.
4. SB *ú-ba-as-sim ṣeḫḫa* Jiménez 2017, 398: 4 "I soothed(?) the wound(?)".

MPS (D 4), NR (G, D 1–3)

basāru s. *baṣāru*.

bāsi "soon"

Deller 1966, 309: NA *ba-si* ŠE.PAD^{meš} *ina pa-ni-šú-nu lu ta-a*[*b-kat*] SAA 1, 14 e. 3 "may the barley at their disposal soon be p[iled]". NR

baskiltu, **biskiltu** "a wooden object; a boil"

1. "a wooden object":

a) OB *bi-us-ki-il-tu* AbB 9, 16: 18 (reading after von Soden 1982, 590).

b) ^{giš}*ba*!*-ás-ki-la-tim liqēʾam* AbB 7, 43: 6' (reading after von Soden 1978, 207) "take *b*.s for me".

2. *šumma awīlum ina pī qinnatišu ba-as-ki-il-tum ittaṣīʾam* YOS 11, 29: 8 "if a boil has grown out in the anus of a man". Cf. ib. 28: 3.

3. Cf. AHw 1547b. CAD M/1, 324 s. v. *maskiltu*. NR

baṣāru "to tear off, divide, distribute"; +MB Emar, Karkemiš, MB Ekalte, + NA

1. a) In legal texts from Emar, Karkemiš and Ekalte *zīzā ba-aṣ-ra and zīzū ba-aṣ-ru* "they are divided, distributed": s. Pentiuc 2001, 34; Ikeda 2003, 270b; PRU 4, 122: 27; WVDOG 102, 20: 22; 90: 9. Cf. Arnaud, AulaOr 5, 238f. no. 16: 17; Wilcke 1985, 311 n. 181.

b) Diff. Huehnergard 1983, 33; Tsukimoto 1991, 297: 9; Mayer 2001, 26 n. 103; Beckman 1996, 118 no 94: 17 (but the latter transliterates ṣ): G of *bussuru* "to bring pleasant news". Pentiuc 2001, 34f.: *bḏr* "to scatter".

2. NA *ma-ga-di ù ba-ṣa-a-ri* SAA 10, 289: 11 "... and harvesting (the grapes)".

3. Cf. *busṛu*. MPS (2), NR (1, 3)

bāṣu, + pl. *bāṣātu* "sand"

1. OB GN ^{uru}*Ba-ṣumki* etc. RGTC 3, 39. *Ša-bāṣi* ARM 16, 31 s. v. Šabazim; ARM 27, 141: 30 and p. 234 n. j "That of sand".

2. OB lit. *šaḫur ina ba-ṣí* RA 66, 141ff. AO 7682: 8 "(the scorpion lies) quiet in the sand".

3. SB KUR *šá ba-ṣa-a-ti šá Elam* SAA 3, 28 r. 14 "land of sand belonging to Elam".

bašālu "to boil, ripen"

G 1. *ištū* MU.4.ŠÈ *tuṣī luqūtī adīnimā lā i-*⌜*ba*⌝*-šál* OAA 1, 17: 5 "you left four years ago: well, is my merchandise not yet ready to be sold by now?"

2. OB *aššum ḫazannū adī lā ba-aš-lu lā napālim* PN *išpuram* AbB 12, 25: 5 "PN wrote me regarding not to dig up the garlic before it is ripe". S. also *ba-aš-lu-ma* ib. 7 and 10.

3. OB *eqlum ... ba-ši-il* AbB 11, 13: 5 "the field is ripe".

4. OB *akalni Adad adīma ba-aš-lu ikki*[*m*?] CUSAS 18 p. 309: 2 "Adad will take away our food as soon as it is ripe".

5. OB *šeʾum ib-ša-al-ma* ARM 14, 69: 13 "the barley has ripened".

6. OB *šamaššammū ... ib-ta-áš-lu* FM 8, 81 no. 25: 8 (wrongly read *ip-ta-ás-lu*) "the sesame has ripened".

Š 1. OA *ú-ša-áb-ša-al-šu*!*-ma* Prag 483: 18 "I will melt it (gold)".

2. OA *ḫurāṣam sāmam ša ša-áb-šu-lim šaʾamma* WAG 48-1462: 17 (Fs. Matouš II 114) "buy red gold for melting!". S. also Dercksen 2005, 31 n. 33.

3. OA also metaphorically of silver: "to make liquid" > "to make profitable, to turn into profit": 190 *ṣubātē* PN_1 u PN_2 *ú-ša-áb-ši-lu-ni-kum kasapšunu bēt mannim ibašši* OAA 1, 21: 32 "PN_1 and

PN$_2$ have turned 190 textiles into profit for you: in whose house is the silver from their sale?" (lit. "their silver", i. e. of the textiles). Cf. Veenhof 2014, 404–407.
4. OB (juniper wood) *ana šu-ub-šu-ul* 3 GAG SAG ARM 23, 514: 2 "for melting 3 best-quality nails".

+ **Štn** OA (silver) *uš-ta-na-áb-ša-lá-kum* Prag 720: 10 "I keep making your silver profitable for you, some 10 minas each time". Cf. Veenhof 2014, 404–407.

MPS (G, Š, Štn), NJCK (G, Š, Štn), NR (G, Š)

bašāmu II "to create, form"; + OB

G 1. OB *šallatum šī ana zitti rēdî ba-aš-ma-at* ARM 26/2 p. 274 no. 408: 24 "those prisoners of war form the shares for the soldiers".

2. OB in the mng. "to set a price" (Kraus, AbB 10 p. 173 n. 192 b; Moran 1987, 134):
a) *tamkārū izzizūma kasapšunu ib-ši-mu-ú-ma kaspam addin* AbB 10, 192: 16 "the merchants took action and set the price and I have paid".
b) *šīmšu ullânumma bi-iš-ma-am-ma* Sumer 14, 73 no. 47: 25 "as for its price, set it immediately!" (s. CAD B 139 s. v. *bašāmu* C). Note, however, that von Soden 1968, 458 (also AHw 1337b and CAD U/W 76b) prefers the spelling *ti*!-*iš-ba*!*-am-ma*.

3. CAD also has *bašāmu* B "to carry away" and C "mng. unc.". According to von Soden 1968, 458 and AHw 1547, the only non-lex. ref. of *bašāmu* B belongs to *balāmu* (AHw 1546), and neither *bašāmu* B nor C exist.

MPS (1), NR (2–3)

bāšītu "(people or staples) on hand, valuables, possessions"; + MB Ekalte

1. OB *tuppi ba-ši-ti-šu* ARM 10, 134: 4 "tablet (recording) his possessions".
2. *ēm ba-ši-ti ibaššû lukšudamma šêm ana bītija lušāmam* ARM 13, 150: 12 "wherever there are staples for me, I will go there and buy barley for my house".
3. *ba-ši-tum* KTT 285: 68; 351: 1.
4. 2 GUD 5 UZU *ba-ši-tum* FM 12, 214 M.18095: 30 "2 oxen, 5 (pieces) of meat, staples on hand". Cf. Jacquet, ib. p. 215 with lit.
5. MB Ekalte *būši ba-ši-ti*, *bušītum u ba-ši-tú*, *būšši u ba-ši-ta-ši* WVDOG 102 index p. 160 "possessions and valuables".
6. EA *u* [*ša*]*-ka-an ina* ÚR : *su-n*[*i-šu*] [*ba*]*-ši-ta*$_5$ EA 196 r. 5' "and [he pu]t in [his] lap (anyone) [pre]sent" (translation after Moran 1992, 274).

MPS (4–5), NR (1–3, 6)

bašlu "cooked, ripe; finished(?)"

1. OB. mng. "finished"(?): *mārakum ba-aš-lum* ... *rupšum ba-aš-lum* AbB 3, 34: 21, 24 "finished(?) length ... finished(?) width" (s. CAD R 413f.).
2. NA Deller 1966, 309: BURU$_{14}$ *ba-áš-lu na-as-qu* Iraq 23, 42 (pl. 22) ND 2664: 8 (s. also CAD N/2, 31 *nasqu* a2').
3. Deller 1966, 309: 1 1/2 MA.NA KÙ.BABBAR *ba-aš-lu* VAT 16564 e: 3 (= Ass. Fd. Nr. 10805).

MPS (1), NR (2–3)

+ **bašlūtu** "ripeness"

OB *ana mīnim ḫazannū la ba-aš-lu-us-sú-nu innappalū* AbB 12, 25: 13 "why should the garlic be dug up before it is in the state of ripeness?"

bašmu "horned viper"

1. OB lit. *ba-aš-mu* MUŠ[meš] *šu-ku-ú ša daltim* CUSAS 10, 1: 27 "horned vipers, snakes are its (the temple's) door poles".
2. OB lit. *šapal šuppātim nadī kī ba-aš-mi* Fs. Wilcke 61f. Sb 12360: 3 "it is lying like a viper under the rushes".

baštu s. *baltu*

bāštu "dignity, (source of) pride"

1. OA with *šakānu*: *ba-áš-tam jâti tašakkinī* Prag 711: 34 "you will make me proud(?)".
2. OB lit. *nišī ba-aš-tim* YOS 1, 24 i 9 "people of dignity".
3. OB lit. *ba-aš-tu unnēnu šēdu u lamassu ... kûmma Ištar* CunMon. 8, 22ff. i 25 "dignity, prayer, genius and protective spirit is yours, Ištar".
4. Deller 1966, 309: NA *ulṣu bal-tu ḫidûtu mēlulu u nummur kabatti ana* LUGAL EN-*ia lū taqīš* SAA 10, 97: 3 "may she present the king, my lord, with rejoicing, pride, joy, jubilation and merry mood". MPS (1–3), NR (4)

bašû "to be (at hand, available), exist"

G 1. SB *ba-šat uznī ša lā i-ba-áš-šu-*[…] Gilg. SB VII 40 "I am attentive, which [you(?)] are not(?)". Cf. George 2003, 844, discarding the reading *ba-lat* AHw. 1546b s. v. *balûtu*.
2. Deller 1966, 310: delete ABL 358: 13 (SAA 10, 227) in CAD B 151b b. m: instead of *li-ib-šú* read *li-*⌜*qi*⌝*-šú* "may they grant".
3. CAD B 151b *b.* 1n1': Wiseman Treaties 605 s. *baʾāšu* G 2 and D, above.

Š 1. Deller 1966, 310: NA *kī ummaka tu-šab-šu-ka-ni* IV2 R 61 ii 21 "when your mother made you come into existence".
2. Deller 1966, 310: NA [md]30-*šab-si* VAT 10467: 7, 10 "Sîn, cause (it) to come into existence!"

N OB *ina libbika lu-ub-ba-ši-ma lā tamaššīʾanni* AbB 3, 22: 36 "may I appear in your heart. Do not forget me!" MPS (G, N), NR (G, Š)

bāšû "remaining, available".

Substantival use, until now attested only with fem. *bāšītu*: OB *ba-ši-a-am ... muḫrīma* AbB 10, 169: 14 "receive the possessions".

bâšu I "to be ashamed, come to shame"

G 1. OA PN hypcor. *Ba-šum* AKT 6a, 75: 48 // 76: 50.
2. Stative in OB PN [m]*Aššum-Marduk-ba-ša-ku* AbB 7, 187: 21f. "I am ashamed because of Marduk". Elsewhere, a stative is attested in OA PN, s. CAD B 6 *b.* 1e1'.
3. Von Soden 1968, 458: BagM 2, 57 ii 6 (CAD B 5b *b.* b) read *ana ša-ba-ši-im lā naṭû* "(tribes) can not be subjected to collection (of tax)" (CAD Š/1, 6b *šabāšu* 2a).
4. SB *la ta-ba-ia-áš* ORA 7, 208: 32' "don't be ashamed!".
5. Borger 1971, 66: NIR.GÁL.ZU-*ka* NU.TÉŠ (CAD B 6b *b.* 2c s. v. D-stem) = syllabic *at-kal-ku la a-ba-aš* and *at-kal-ku a-a-ba-aš* with *bâšu* in G-stem (s. also CAD T 64a *takālu* 1a1').

D 1. OA in the sense of "to prove wrong":
a) *awīlam ina awātim nu-ub-ta-iš* AKT 3, 92: 25 "we proved the lord wrong in the matter". S. comm. ib. p. 158 (also Akkadica 18, 32: 33).
b) *maḫar kārim nu-ba-i-šu* ib. 93: 29 "we proved him wrong before the trading colony".

c) *ana ammīʾātim nu-ba-i-šu* ib. 36 "we proved him wrong regarding those (affairs)".
2. OB lit. *mīnum ú-ba-ša-ka* Gilg. OB IM 21 "what will put you to shame?"
3. Deller 1966, 306: PN ᵐ*Lu-ba-áš-a-na*-DINGIR CAD B 6a *b.* 1e5' is *Lā-ubāšanni-ilu*/*ilī* "the god/my god will not put me to shame". Cf. PNA 2/2, 667.
4. NA PN *Lā-tubâšanni-Aššur*, s. Deller 1966, 306f. and PNA 2/2, 667.
5. NA PN *Aššur-lā-kīnu-ubāša*, s. Borger 1971, 66 and PNA 1/1, 192.

MPS (G, D), NR (G, D)

+ **batabtuḫḫu** "a textile"; Ur III
túg ba-tab-tuḫ-ḫu-um 3-*kam-ús Inana* CUSAS 3, 1028: 31 "3rd-quality *b.*-textile of Inana". For further ref. s. CUSAS 4 p. 25. Reading and interpret. after Waetzoldt 1972, 291; Sallaberger 2011, 357. NR

batāqu "to cut off, divide, tear off"; +OAkk.

G 1. OAkk. *ab-tùq ṣarbatam* MAD 5, 8: 19 "I cut off the Euphrates poplar".
2. In the mng. "to fell":
a) OAkk. *ib-tu-qù* RIME 2, 193: 57 (NB copy of OAkk. inscr.; for context s. *baqīšu*; the spelling is NB orthography for *ibtuq*).
b) [*i*]*b*-⌜*tu*⌝-*qám* ib. 140 r. 10'.
c) OAkk. (the year Narām-Sîn) ... [*erēnam*] *ib-tú-qam* RIME 1 p. 86 year z "cut down [a cedar]".
3. In the mng. "to deduct" (CAD *b.* 1d): OA (silver) *ba-tí-iq* AKT 6c, 560: 32 "was missing".
4. OA with object *awātu* "to settle an affair, to decide a case" (CAD B 164 *b.* 7a), corresponding to Bab. *warkata parāsu*: *awātam bu-ut-qá-ma* ... *awātum ba-at-qá-at* AKT 6c, 665: 12, 17 "settle the affair! ... The affair is settled".
5. OB lit. object enemy: *ib-tu-uq nakram kī kiṣir abīḫim* FM 14, 13 i 24 "he cut off the enemy like the knot of a rope".
6. Object water: *mê ab-tu-uq* FM 1, 94 A.250: 18 "I diverted the water". *mê ab-tu-qú* ib. 33.
7. NA *ūma annûrig assaprakka* ˡᵘA *šiprika* TA *pan Muskāya lū l*[*ā t*]*a-bat-taq* SAA 1, 1: 14 "I am now writing to (tell) you that you should not cut off your messenger from the Phrygian's presence". Diff. Deller 1966, 310 and Saggs 2001, 188: *i*[*b*]*-bat-taq* "(your messenger) should certainly not be cut off (from the presence of the Mushkaean)".
8. NA ˡᵘA.KINᵐᵉˢ*-ni-šú-*[*nu* xx TA *pa-ni*]*-ia la i-*⌜*ba*⌝*-tú-qu* SAA 15, 90: 26 "they should not cut off the[ir] messengers [... from] my [presence". Diff. Deller 1966, 310: N-stem.

D 1. OA PN_1 PN_2 *u ālikī ba-tí-iq* ATHE 30, 28 "dispatch PN_1, PN_2 and the (other) travelers!". Cf. CAD A/1, 348a; Matouš 1964, 137; Hirsch 1961, 50.
2. OB *ašlātum* ... *bu-ut-tu-qa* ARM 28, 152: 19 "the ropes are cut".
3. OB lit. *mīnum ú-ba-ta-kúm*? *qīštam ša iṣim* Gilg. OB IM 21 "what will cut down for you(?) the forest of wood?"

+ **Š** *ina ša libbika ša-áb-tí-iq* AKT 4, 18: 22 "let it be taken away from that belonging to you(?)!"

N OB *mû* ⌜*ib*⌝*-ba-at-qú* FM 1, 94 A.250: 13 "the water was diverted".

MPS (G, D, Š, N), NR (G, D)

+ **bataru** "ravine"; OB, Amor. lw.

bazaḫātūya ina ḫamqim qerbetim ba!*-ta-ri-im u* GN [*š*]*aknā* ARM 14, 75: 24 "my military posts were stationed in the valley, field, ravine and GN". Cf. Durand 1998, 191f.; Streck 2000, 85.

batiqtu "denunciation, rumor, information

1. NA *mā udīni ba-ti-iq-*⸢*tú*⸣ *lā aḫarraṣa* SAA 1, 29: 19 (s. also CAD U/W, 21a) "I do not have the information yet".
2. NA *ba*!-*ti*!-*iq-tú lā niḫarraṣa* SAA 1, 30: 10' "we have not cleared up the information".
3. NA ⸢*ba-ti*⸣-*iq-tú šī assaparakka* SAA 15, 86 r. 9 "I have sent you in[fo]rmation".
4. NA *ammar* GAZ^{meš}-*ni ammar ḫabtūni ba-tiq-tú lā ni-šá-*[*me*] CTN 5, 115 ND 2448: 12 "we have not heard the full details yet, how many were killed, how many were taken prisoner".

NR

bātiqu "express messenger, informer, accuser; an axe or hatchet"

1. NA ^{lú}*ba-te-qu ana* UGU LUGAL [E]N-*ia assapra* CTN 5, 232 ND 2703 r. 5 "I have sent the accuser to the king my lord".

2. SB ⸢^{lú}⸣ *ba-ti-qu iddūk* SAA 8, 567 r. 6 "he killed the informer".

3. An axe or hatchet (lit. "cutter"):
a) S. AHw 115 *b*. 3; diff. CAD M/1, 413 s. v. *matqanu* b. But s. Stol 1983, 299.
b) New ref.: LB 2 *ba-ti-qa-nu* CT 55, 216: 8; 242: 2! *ba-ti-qu* ib. 12. 1-*en ba-*⸢*ti*⸣-*qu* CT 56, 355: 2.

MPS (3), NR (1–2)

+ **bātiqūtu** "function of an informer"; NA

1. [*b*]*a-te-qu-tú ūtuppiš* SAA 16, 124: 6 "he has acted as an informer".
2. *ba-ti-qu-tú* SAA 15, 73: 7 in broken context.

+ **batiʾu** "a reed container"

1. Ur III 1 ^{gi}*ba-ti-um búr* 3-*sìla* CUSAS 4 p. 25 "1 reed container with a volume(?) of 3 liters".
2. CAD P 285f. mentions two other Ur III ref s. v. *pattû* "bucket": *pa*$_{4}$-*ti-um* and *pa*$_{4}$-[*d*]*i-um*.
3. Since the stem ends in /i/, prob. to be distinguished from *pattû* < Sum. *ba.an.du*$_{8}$.

batqu "cut (off), of poor quality, deficit"

1. OA (silver) *ša ina tuppim ba-at-qam laptu* AKT 7a, 40/t: 7 "which is written on the tablet as(?) deficit". *ba-at-qam-ma* ib. 40/z: 7. Cf. *bitiqtu*.
2. OA AN.NA-*ak qātim ba-at-qám* Prag 709: 18 "available cheap(?)/low quality(?) tin".
3. OB *šeʾam ... ba-at-qá-am u maskam* AbB 7, 53: 17 "barley, of poor quality and bad".
4. S. also *badqu*.

battatāya "each of several, individually, from all sides"

NA *ina* ⸢*bat-ta*⸣-*ta-*⸢*a-a upallaḫūn*(*u*)⸣ SAA 16, 128 r. 7 "they are scaring me from all sides".

battu I "side, region around"

1. Deller 1966, 311f.: NA *ina* UGU URU^{meš} *ša ba-ti ammīte ša Zāba azqupūni* CTN 5, 116f. ND 2453: 24 "for the towns which I planted on that side of the Zab".
2. Deller 1966, 311f.: *mā* UN^{meš} ... *igdurū ina bat-*⸢*te*⸣ *ammīte ša nāre ittalkū mā meni*(*m*)*mēni ina* ⸢*bat-ti*⸣ *annīte ša nāre lā rēḫe* SAA 15, 164 r. 5, 7 "the people have got scared and go[ne] to the other side of the river. Nobody is left on this side of the river".
3. Deller 1966, 311f.: [*Ar*]*bāya ina bat-ti amm*[*īte*] *ša* GN *šaknū* SAA 1, 179: 5

"the Arabs are settled on the other side of the river GN". NR

battu II s. *bittu*

+ **bātu II**, *bādu* "night's rest, vigil"; OB, NA

1. OB lit. *adī nūram tu-ka-al-la-mu-šu-nu-ti ay ut-te-er ba-*⸢*at*⸣ *ilī akḫīka* AnSt. 33, 148 BM 78962: 33 "until you (Girra) show them the light, may the night's rest of the gods, your brothers, not be restored".

2. NA *nadbāku ša ba-te* SAA 12, 69: 18, 26 "the expenditure for the vigil". Cf. *nadbāku ša pandugāni ša šarri* ib. 7 "the expenditure for the king's festival *paddugānu*"; *nadbāku ša* UKKIN DINGIR^{meš}*-ni* ib. 27 "the expenditure for the divine council"; *nadbāku ša rimki* ib. 32 "the expenditure for the bath" and *nadbāku ša garmarte* ib. 35 "the expenditure for the *kanwartu* festival".

3. The words NA *bādu* "evening" CAD B 27 = *bâde* "abends" AHw 95 and SB/NB *bajātu* "nocturnal ceremony" CAD B 34 = *bajjātu* "nächtlicher Opferkult" AHw 97 are later variants of the same word. Since we would expect uncontracted forms in OB and NA, the word does not derive from the inf. *bīʾāt/du*, but is a diff. noun from the same root. MPS (1, 3), NR (2)

+ **bâtu** (only Št attested); OB

Št *bittam uš*!*-ta-ba-at-tu-ma*! Iraq 39, 153 A.1285: 47 "they will interweave the weft". For context s. *bittu* II, from which the verb is denominated.

MPS, NR

batūltu, NA *batūssu* "adolescent, nubile girl"; + OB

1. OB lit. *ba-tu-ul-tum māratu awīlim ana rigmiya ana* {*ri-ig*} *šagīmiya* <*lī*>*mqut* YOS 11, 87: 11 "may the girl, a daughter of a gentleman, fall at my cry, at my shout".

2. MA 1 ^{mí}*ba-tu-ul-ta* BATSH 4/1, 17: 7.

NR

batūlu "boy, young man"

1. Deller 1966, 312: NA PN ^{m}*Ba-tu-lu* SAA 15, 168: 1, r. 8, 11.

2. Delete BE 14, 168: 16 (CAD B 174b): read now with von Soden 1968, 458, CAD M/1, 23b and CAD P 134a *ma-du-tu* instead of *ba-du-li*. NR

baṭālu "to cease"; + OA

G OB lex. *ašar ašpuruka lā ta-ba-aṭ-ṭi-*⸢*il*⸣ CUSAS 12 p. 253: 213 "where I sent you to, do not stop!"

+ **Gtn** OA *adī ayyim ūmim ib-ta-na-ṭi-il*$_5$*-kà-ma* Prag 430: 28 "until when will he miss again and again (the payment date) for you?"

+ **baṭṭu** "the sign BAD"; MB, SB

1. MB ([if the "well-]being") *kīma* BAD*-ma elîš/šapliš dilû šapliš/elîš gigurû* CUSAS 18, 33: 34/35 "is like the sign BAD, with the *dilû* (the horizontal wedge) above/below and the *gigurû* (the winkelhaken) below / above".

2. For syllabic spellings *ba-aṭ-ṭu*, *ba-aṭ/baṭ-ṭa* in SB lex. texts s. Gong 2000, 104.

baṭû I "a platter or container"; + OB

1. a) 1 *ru-um-u-um* 1 ⸢*ba?*⸣*-ṭí-ú-tum ú* ⸢*sá*⸣*-na-an* ⸢*sá*⸣ PN KTT 53: 2 "one lance, *b.*s and a pair of shoes for PN".

b) S. also *bá-ṭí-ú-tum* ib. 13 and 1 *ba-ṭí-ʾà-*⸢*an?*⸣ 1 *u-BU-*⸢*šu-um*⸣ *a-na* PN ib. 54:

13 "a pair of *b.*s, one *u.* and one *marḫašum*-container".

c) Krebernik KTT p. 55 and 240, tentatively analyses the word as *pātiḫum*.

2. OB fem. pl. 4 *ba*!-*ṭa-tum* AbB 7, 116: 23. AbB 7 p. 96 reads *ma*-DA-*tum*.

3. OB 2 *ba-ṭi-a-tum* UD.KA.BAR JCS 25, 211 WHM 014146: 14 "2 bronze vessels".

4. LB *ba-aṭ-ṭu-u* UD.KA.BAR AfO 36/37, 23 Nbn. 761: 3 "bronze *b.*". Cf. Roth, ib. with further ref. and comm. in n. 98. MPS (1–3), NR (4)

+ **baʾu** (or *baʾû*)? "a bird"

OB *ba*?(*ma*?)-*ú-um* Edubba 7, 100: 65 (in list of birds). Cf. also *pû* ib. 29.

+ **baʾû**? I "to seek, desire"; LB, Aram. lw.

G *a-ba-ʾ-i* SAA 18, 153: 19 in broken context. According to Parpola, ib. p. 125 possibly a loan from Aram. *bʿʾ*pe. Akk. elsewhere only has D *buʾʾû*.

+ **baʾû II** "to bark"; SB

i-ba-ʾ-i-ma-⌜*a*⌝ *še-el-bi kīma imḫullum* Iraq 60, 204: 3 (proverb) "does the fox yowl like a tempest?". Cf. George/Al-Rawi, ib. p. 206. NR

bâʾu I "to go along, to come"; + OAkk.

G 1. OAkk. *šumma* PN_1 u PN_2 ⌜*la ba*⌝-*a* FAOS 19, 185 Ga 5: 10 "if PN_1 and PN_2 have not come" (stative dual, s. Kienast/Volk, ib.). For the mng. "to come" s. AHw 117 *b.* G 5b, CAD B 181 *b.* 2a (OA).

2. OA imp. *ba-am* Prag 499: 14 "come!"

3. OB lit. *i-ba-a-ú-m*[*a*] *birqu ša Adad ina ṣērišu* ALL 1 i 10 "the lightning of Adad swept over it".

4. OB lit. *ib-ta birqum ša ṣīḫātim elīja* ALL 1 i 12 "the lightning of love-making swept over me".

5. OB lit. OB *itti* GN *mašmaš ilī ba-ʾ-ma.* 33, 148 BM 78962: 34 "pass by with GN, the excorcist of the gods! (subj. Girra).

6. OB lit. *iṭeḫḫē Enlil ana Apišalîm*! // *ib*!-*tu* Westenholz 1997, 185: 5 "approaching, Enlil came to the Apišalian".

7. In OB Mari the participle is well attested. The following passages contain the idiom *qāta bāʾita šakānu*/*epēšu*:

a) *matīmā awīlum ša ina ṣūmim imūtu ina nārim iddûšuma ibluṭ ištū qātam ba-i-tam ippešū warkānūm mītum ul iballuṭ* ARM 26/1 p. 349 no. 171: 15 (Heimpel 2003, 241) "did ever a man revive who died of thirst (and) was thrown in a river? After (= Even if) they take action, thereafter a dead man does not revive".

b) *bēlī ušamriṣanni išpuram qātam ba-i-tam taškunma karpat karānim u šamnim tašām mimma anāku karpat karānim u šamnim ul ašām* A.3362 (MARI 6, 79 n. 202; LAPO 17, 22f. no. 859): 6 "my lord troubled me (and) wrote me: 'You took action and bought jars of wine and oil!' I did not buy jars of wine and oil."

c) ⌜*ūm*⌝ *kašādiya*[*ma*] [*sa*]*gbam a*[*na*! *qātim*! *b*]*a-ʾi-tim* [*ašta*]*kan u ṣābum* [*e*]*niš ul ša mušītim* A.1155: 6 (Wasserman/Ziegler 1994; restorations given here deviate from their edition) "when I arrived I [mobil]ized the patrol-unit but the troop was [w]eak, not (fit) for the night-watch".

d) In broken context: [*q*]*ātu ba-i-*[*t*]*u ina* ⌜*libbi*⌝ [... *šaknat*] ARM 4, 86: 21 (Wasserman/Ziegler 1994 with coll.; restorations given here deviate from their edition) "action [was taken] concerning [...]".

e) Here also belongs the following passage with stative but without *šakānu*/*epēšu*: *šarrū ša mātim elītim ... kâtama inaṭṭalūka* [*inūma*? *t*]*illātiya attama tudammiqam* [*an*]*a dummuqi*[*m*] *qātka ba-ʾì-a-at* ARM 28, 1: 15' "the kings of the upper land look only at you. [When(?)] you have provided generously my auxiliaries, you will be ready to provide generously (troops for them)".

f) Durand, ARM 26/1 p. 350, followed by Wasserman/Ziegler 1994 (not knowing A.3362 and ARM 28, 1), translates "compte" and suggests derivation from *baʾʾītu* "thing sought" (Wasserman/Ziegler: "check-list"). Heimpel 1997b (only knowing ARM 26/1 p. 349 no. 171 and A.3362) translates "to take the initiative" and suggests a derivation from *bâʾu* "to go along, overtake". The mng. "compte", "check-list" does not fit any of the passages well. Moreover, *baʾʾītu* is a noun, not an adj., and an Ass. form cannot be expected in Mari. Lastly, *ba-ʾì-a-at* cannot be derived from *buʾʾû*/*baʾʾû*: the correct form would be **buʾʾât* < **buʾʾū-at*. On the other hand, a derivation from *bâʾu*, indeed the only choice left, poses no formal problems: *bāʾītu* < **bāʾiʾtu* is the fem. participle, bāʾiʾat the stative of the participle. *qātu bāʾītu* lit. means "hand going along/overtaking", *qāta bāʾīta epēšu* / *šakānu* "to make/put a hand going along/overtaking", *qātka bāʾiʾat* "your hand is going along/overtaking".

8. The participle is also attested in other contexts in OB Mari:

a) Used as synonym of *etēqu*: lúTUR^meš^-*ia e-ti-qú-tim ù ba-ú-tim* ARM 28, 68: 16 "my passing and coming servants".

b) *a-*[*n*]*a e-ti-qí-im ù ba-i-*[*i*]*m ma-ṣa-r*[*i-im*!] ARM 27, 116:14 "to the guard passing and coming".

c) S. also outside of Mari: *ētiqu u ba-a-ú imšuḫma* AbB 12, 194: 5 "a passer-by or someone walking along had stolen (wood)". The spelling renders the form *bājiʾ/yu* < **bāʾiʾu*.

9. S. also the stative (of the participle?): *anāku ba-e-ku* ARM 28, 24: 9 "I am on the way(?)".

10. SB *ina pîka dannatī li-ba-aʾ* Or. 62, 320 BMS 12: 80 "on your command may my distress pass by".

+ **D 1.** OB lit. *mû ú-ba-ú-nim* CUSAS 10, 1: 24 "waters pass by". Cf. George, ib. p. 9.

2. With George 2003, 337, two further forms are:

a) [*šēnu munaššikat šēp*] ⌜*mu*⌝*-be-ʾ-i sūqi* Gilg. MB Emar$_2$ 18' "[a shoe that bites the foot of] one passing the street".

b) *rebīt āliya ú-ba-ʾ-ú* (var. *a-ba-ʾ*) *nēḫiš* Oshima 2014, 464: 291 (note that Oshima on p. 166 has, by mistake, *a-ba-ʾu-ú*) "I used to pass the square of my city quietly".

c) Both *mubeʾʾi* and *ubaʾʾu* look as if derived from *buʾʾû* "to search", and the latter form has indeed been translated accordingly in AHw 775 s. v. *nēḫiš*.

Š OB lit. *kī ša* ... ⌜*sūqam*⌝ *ša nišī ummaka tu-uš-bi-ʾ* OECT 11, 2: 8 "instead of ... letting your mother go along the people's street".

+ **Štn**? OB *ištū* MU 5^kam^ *uš-ta-na-ba-a-ni-a-ši umma šūma* AbB 10, 171: 17 "for 5 years he has been heaping(?) on us the following words". Transferred use of AHw 117 *bâʾu* 4 "übergießen, überfluten"? Prob. not *nabû* (no Š, text writes elsewhere double consonants) or *šubeʾʾû* (no *e*-umlaut).

Disc.: AHw 117b and 1547b proposed two words *bâʾu* in Akkadian, *bâʾu* I with *ā*-vowel and *bâʾu* II with *ū*-vowel, the latter a loan from "Canaanite". However, there is no definitive argument to separate the two verbs from each other, and *bâʾu* II is hardly a loan from Amor., s. Streck 2000, 85: Semantically, the alleged *bâʾu* II "to come" well fits *bâʾu* I, and the *ū*-variant is prob. archaic and genuine Akkadian, primarily attested in OB Mari (*i-bu-ma* ARM 26/1 p. 187 no. 6: 18; *li-bu-a-am-ma* ARM 26/1 p. 465 no. 224: 15) and Shemshara (*bu-ma* Shemshara 1, 2: 27), but also in EA (CAD B *bâʾu* 3c) and perhaps also in OAkk. (*ib-tu* ZA 87, 23 ii 19, cf. C. Wilcke, ib. p. 29). The *ā*-variant is prob. influenced by /ʾ/ as third radical.

MPS (G, D, Š, Štn), NR (G 10)

bâʾu II "to come" s. *bâʾu* I

baʾūlu "great, important"

For lex. *baʾūlu* = *kabtu* s. now AOAT 50, 301 I 19 (Malku).

bayyāru "hunter"; + OB; + SB

1. OB *a-ab-bu ba-ia-ru wāṣûšu* FM 14, 20 iii 11 "numerous(?) were the hunters going out with him".
2. SB *ba-ia-ru* KAL 3, 77: 8.

bayyātu s. *bātu*

bazaḫātu "military post"

Disc. of alleged Amor. etym. in Streck 2000, 85f. S. also *buzzuʾu*.

bazāru s. *baṣāru*

bazāʾu s. *buzzuʾu*

+ **baZiḫītum**? "an object(?)"; OB *šapilti ṣābiya ba-zi-ḫi-tam [pe]ḫḫazam anzūtam ša* ^{gi}PISAN$^{didli.ḫi.a}$ *[išš]û* ARM 26/1 p. 128 no. 18: 24 "the rest of my troops carried the *b.*, the *[peḫḫazu]*-metal and the eagle-emblem(?) in several reed boxes". Durand, ARM 26/1 p. 130 n. d connects the word with OB *baziḫtu* "claim" (hapax, s. below) and translates "le strict minimum". Heimpel 2003, 185 does not give any translation, but in his comm. p. 186 speaks of "provisons". The orthography does not fit the word *baziḫtu* entirely, and the context might also point to an object as part of merchandise transported from Mari to Ḫalab.

+ **baZku** "quacking (of ducks)"; SB *ba*-aZ-*ki* ALL no. 11 r. 5, s. *paspasu*.

+ **bazūšānu**? "?"

NA *lā ina ba-zu-*⸢*šá*?⸣*-nu-u-a ana šarre bēliya ašpura* SAA 10, 187 r. 1 "did I not write in my ... to the king, my lord?" Read *ba-ṣú-*⸢*ṣa*?⸣- from *baṣāṣu* "to trickle"?

bed/ṭû "to dispose of(?)"

G 1. OB *makkūr mātim elītim u šaplītim te-bé-ed-di maḫīr-ka ul imaṭṭi* MARI 5, 258 FLP 1674: 17 "you will dispose of the riches of the upper and lower country. Your economy will not diminish".

2. For the mng. of this verb s. AHw 1547. There seems to be a second verb *beṭ/dû*, s. below. Cf. a. *padû*.

MPS, NR

beʾēšu "to stir"

For OA ref. s. *bêšu* (Veenhof 2015a, 229–232).

+ **bēlānu** "power, force"; OB

1. *ḫiblātika ša ina bé-la-nu-um ukallu luwaššerakkum* ARM 26/2 p. 280 no.

410: 16' "I will release to you your losses that I am keeping by force".

2. *assurri bēlī kêm i[qabbī] ummami ina be-la-ni u[šadbabš]unūtii mimma ul uš[ad]ba[bšunūti] šunuma idabbubū* ARM 26/1 p. 435 no. 207: 36 "I am afraid my lord will s[ay]: 'She [makes] them [speak] by force.' I absolutely do not make [them sp]eak. They speak by themselves".

3. *bēlī idninamma ina be-la-ni ušēṣûninnima attalkam* ARM 26/1 p. 436 n. b M.8512: 14 "my lord pressed me and they drove me out by force and I went away".

4. *ina* GN [PN] *ina be-la-nim iklûma* ARM 1, 91 (= MARI 5, 179) 4' "they kept [PN] in GN by force".

5. (PN has given land in exchange for a plot) *annûm ṭūbu ula be-la-nu* ARM 8, 8: 5 (cf. MARI 5, 180 n. 27) "this was voluntarily, not by force".

6. *salim be-la-nim usallamšunūti* ARM 2, 16: 16 (s. Durand 1998, 93) "I will have them conclude a peace treaty by (lit. of) force".

7. *inanna ina mīnim qišti* GN *ana* PN *ittūr bēlī ina be-la-nim qišti* GN *ana* PN *ittadin* FM 8, 40 no. 3: 27 "now, why has the forest of GN returned to PN? My lord has given the forest of GN to PN by force".

8. *ina be-la-nim* FM 9, 151 no. 32: 12 (in broken context).

9. Note instead of *ina* rather *ištū* ŠÀ-*ba*: *ištu* ŠÀ-*ba* [*b*]*e-la-ni ašaddadš*[*u*] FM 8, 157 no. 44: 32. "I will remove i[t] by force".

10. OB apart from Mari:

a) *šumma awīlum ina* ⌜*be*!⌝*-la-a-ni eleppam lā šattam iṣṣabat* LE § 6 A i 27 "if a man by force seizes a boat which does not belong to him".

b) *kīma ina be*!*-la-ni nīš ilim* [*lā*?] *ušazkir*[*u*] " IM 49238+49543: 13 "that they did [not?] make me take an oath by force".

11. a) Durand, MARI 5, 180 n. 27 was the first to recognize the adverb *ina bēlāni* in OB Mari. Previously, part of the references were listed in CAD N/2, 333 s. v. *nullānū* "evil, fraudulent intention". However, the spelling *i-na bé*(BI)*-la-nu-um* ARM 26/2 p. 280 no. 410: 16' proves that instead of *nu-* we have to read *be-*. Note than none of the altogether four OB references listed in CAD is written *nu-ul-*.

b) Durand derived the word from "*bîlum*" (WBL) "moyen de transporteur" in the transferred mng. "moyen de faire se mouvoir quelqu'un contre sa volonté". S. also Durand, ARM 26/1 p. 436 and Durand 2000, 322 ad ARM 26/1 p. 435 no. 207 "par astuce", Durand, ARM 26/1 p. 436 n. b ad M.8512 "l'on m'a fait sortir sur une civière", ib. ad ARM 26/2 p. 280 no. 410 "contre mon gré", Durand 1998, 93 ad ARM 2, 16 "*toute à notre avantage*". Durand is followed by Joannès, ARM 26/2 p. 281 "malgré moi" and Heimpel 2003, 257 ad ARM 26/1 p. 435 no. 207 "She helped them [speak]" with comm. "literally, 'made them speak with a carrying pole'" (but Heimpel 2003, 351 ad ARM 26/2 p. 280 no. 410 leaves the translation open). Durand, FM 8, 157 n. c. derives the word from an unattested word **pêlum* and proposes the translation "agir avec astuce". In the same volume on p. 40, however, he translates "par échange" (s. also the disc. ib. p. 41 n. f).

c) The orthography with *be-* does not favor a word **bīlu*. It is also dubious that a noun of the pattern *PiRS* could have the mng. "means of transport".

Furthermore, the metaphor "means of transport" > "trick, deceit" or "against my will" is unconvincing. Lastly, none of the contradicting translations does seem to fit all the references. Therefore, the etym. and mng. given by Durand have to be rejected.
d) The orthography with *be-* favors a derivation from *bēlu* "lord". Whereas the suffix *-ān* mostly derives concrete nouns, usually designations for persons, from other nouns (Streck 2014a, 46 § 135), *bēlānu* seems to have an abstract mng. "power, force". A mng. "by force" for the construction *ina bēlāni* (genitive) or (*ina*) *bēlānū* (locative) fits all the ref. well. Only in ARM 2, 16 *bēlānim* is found after a noun in the construct state.

bēltu "lady, mistress, proprietress (of)"

Deller 1966, 312: NA *ginû ša* RN *ana Bēlat-Nipḫa* GAŠAN *rabītu irkusuni* Parfümrezepte 34 r. 23 "regular offerings which RN established for The-Mistress-of Nipḫa, the great lady".

NR

belû II, *balû* "to be extinguished, come to an end"

G ABL 1368 r. 1 (CAD B 73a *b.* 1b) s. *balāṭu* II.

D 1. OB *išātum ... ina danna ú-ba-al-lu* ARM 26/1 p. 500 no. 244: 10 "fire ... they extinguished it with difficulty".
2. Object "battle": OB lit. *bu-ul-lu tuqmātim kûmma Ištar* CunMon. 8, 22ff. i 20 "extinguishing wars is yours, Ištar".
3. LB *ub-te-lu imatka* AMD 1, 237 no. 14: 2' (inc. against a scorpion) "they have nullified your venom!"

MPS (D), NR (G, D 3)

bēlu "lord, proprietor (of)"

1. OAkk. Beydar:
a) ITI.SAR/UD.SAR ^{d}*Be-lim* "month of Bēlum", ITI.SAR (^{d})*Be-lí* GN etc. "month of Bēlum from GN" Subartu 2 p. 180, Subartu 12 p. 124.
b) In PN: *Be-la-ma*-DINGIR Subartu 2, 5 v 4 "God is lord". *Šu-be-lim* ib. p. 190 "He of the lord".

2. OB *be-el mar-ṣa-tim* ARM 26/2 p. 337 no. 434: 35 "victim" (lit. "lord of painful things"), s. Joannès, ARM 26/2 p. 338 n. i and Heimpel 2003, 217 n. 130. Cf. *bēl marušti* "enemy" CAD M/1, 318b *maruštu* 1e.

3. Deller 1966, 312: Negated: NA A. ŠÀ.GA *ša pāḫat* GN *šumma ramû ša lā* EN-*e šū* Iraq 20, pl. 38 ND 2734+ 2416+2457: 49 "if the field in the province of GN is abandoned it is owenerless"; cf. CTN 5, 210.

4. SB *lā bēl ili* "unkucky person" s. Borger 1971, 66 and CAD I/J 103b.

5. LB *bēl ḫanšê* instead of normal *rab ḫanšê*: EN 50-*ú* "commander of 50" Bēl-rēmanni p. 252: 9.

6. *bēl sūti* instead of normal *rab sūti*: PN_1 PN_2 *u* PN_3 $^{⌜lú⌝}$EN^{meš} ^{giš}BÀN^{meš} *šá* $^{⌜d⌝}$[UTU] Bēl-rēmanni p. 221 BM 42646+43612: 3f. "lords of the *sūtu*-taxes of [Šamaš]".

MPS (1–2, 5–6), NR (3–4)

bennu I "epilepsy"

NA Borger 1971, 66: ^{d}LUGAL. AMAŠ. PA.È = *be-en-nu* CT 16, 2: 61f. NR

+ **bennūtu** "epileptic fit?"; NA

adu bé-nu-ti-šú BAM 234: 6 "(he is filled with anger ...) until his epileptic fit". Cf. Stol 1993a, 29 n. 56. NR

+ bērâ "per double mile"; OA

šumma ayyēma udappir be-ra-a u 1 GÍN.TA *tuggaršuma* TPAK 156a: 17 "if he goes somewhere else, he can hire one (other employee) for 1 shekel per double mile". S. comm. in Michel/Garelli, ib. p. 215.
NJCK, NR

****beriʾu** CAD B 207a; CDA 43a

1. For OB Lu MSL 12, 194 C3: 13 s. DCCLT OB Lu$_2$-azlag$_2$ (2006): *lú na-ĝá-aḫ = nu-ḫu-ú-um* "stupid one".
2. For *bi-ri-e-em* ARM 3, 79: 8' s. *berû* II "to be hungry" (AHw 123a; von Soden 1968, 458; Durand 1998, 595).
NR

+ berkabtu "charioteer"; SB

SB lex. *lú-en-*^{giš}*gigir = bé-er-kab-tú/tu* (< *bēl narkabti*) OIP 114, 119: 12; 121: 12. Cf. comm. Cole, ib. p. 248: *lú-en-*^{giš}*gigir* in NB/LB to be read *berkabtu* instead of *bēl narkabti*?
NR

berû II "to be hungry"

G 1. For Cop. 10055 (CAD B 119 *b.* B 1c) s. FAOS 19, 163 Di 8: 5.
2. OB *[k]urummatī ana bé-ri-ki [l]ā ipparras* AbB 12, 110: 18 "may my food provision for your hunger not be cut off!".
3. OB add *bé-re-e-em* ARM 3, 79 r. 9; cf. the lit. s. v. ***beriʾu*.
4. OB said of field: *eqlum ul be-ri ... eqlum inanna šeʾam mali* AbB 9, 228: 12 "the field has not been hungry ... The field now is full of barley!".

Št$_2$ 1. "to be made hungry": OB *qēmam nu-uš-te-bé-r[e]* ARM 26/2 p. 62 no. 306: 10 "we are made to hunger for flour".
2. For other ref. s. *barû* III, above.
MPS (G, Št$_2$), NR (G)

bēru II, *beʾru* "selected; choice; elite troup"

1. OA an official (AHw *b.* II 1b):
a) *inūmī kaspam ašqulu* PN$_1$ *u* PN$_2$ *be-ru-ú* AKT 5, 35: 27 "when I weighed thesilver, PN$_1$ and PN$_2$ were the *b.* officials".
b) (figurines of gods have been deposited as pledge) *ilū ik-kunuk* 3 *be-re-e kankū* ib. 46: 14 "the gods have been sealed with the seal of 3 *b.* officials".
c) *inūmī weriʾam ilqēʾūni* 3 *be-ru-ú ... iš-šaḫātišunu izzīzū* ib. 36 "when they received the copper, 3 *b.* officials stood at their side". S. also *be-ru-ú* ib. 17.
d) *bé-ru* TPAK 26: 5, 13, 14, *bé-ri* 18. Cf. Michel/Garelli, ib. p. 93. *bé-ru* PIHANS 75, 80 n. 272 Kt n/k 204: 18.
e) The ref. show that, pace CAD B 213, there is prob. no *bērūtu* "a collegium of officials"; rather, the form in *-ūt-* is an adjectival pl. This means, in turn, that a derivation of the word *bēru* from the adj. *bēru* is likely. According to Veenhof, AKT 5 p. 135, the *b.* officials act "for and by the order of the Assyrian authorities" and serve "the financial interests of the City, especially in the collection of debts".

2. OB A.ŠÀ *bé-er-tam* ARM 26/2 p. 386 no. 462: 17 "choice field-area" (Heimpel 2003, 378).

3. OB $^{\text{lú.meš}}$*bi-ḫi-ir* [DUMU]^{meš} *um-me-ni* ARM 22, 13 iv 15 "elite of artisans".

4. 1 ^{túg}GUZ.ZA *bé-rum* ARM 22, 139: 7 "1 choice ...-cloth".

5. OB lit. *ina bé-eḫ-ri-im wāšibūt aḫ Purantim* FM 14, 18 ii 35 "by the elite troop, sitting at the bank of the Euphrates". Pace Durand 1998, 362, Heimpel 2003, 593f., Charpin/Ziegler 2003, 217 n. 430 and Guichard, FM 14, 48 not *piḫru* "assembly" (note the spelling with *be* in lex. texts, CAD B 211; correct in CAD P 369).

6. SB *gada-i-ri ka-ad-i-⸢ri?⸣* = *ka?-te bé-⸢re⸣-tum* Emar 6/4, 556: 50, s. DCCLT MB Ura 10 "hatcheled flax = choice flax". For the process of hatcheling s. Waetzoldt 1980–1983b, 585 § 4c. Cf. CAD B 207 *bēru* A lex. sect. for *bērētum*, said of *siki* "wool".

7. No Amor. etym., s. Streck 2000, 86. Cf. Ugar. *biḫīru*, below.

MPS (1–7), NR (1)

bēru III "double hour, league"

In the adverbial acc., s. von Soden 1967, 335a; 1968, 459; Veenhof 1981–1982, 66:

1. OB *ina eqlim bé-ra-am šakin* ARM 4, 26: 28 "(the city) is situated at a distance of one double hour". Cf. CAD B 246 *bīram*.

2. *ù eqlum ana* GN *bé-ra-am ù zu-[uz/za-am]* ARM 2, 42: 7 "and the distance to GN is one double hour and a half". Cf. CAD B 208b s. v. *bēru*.

3. OB *pirṣum bé-ra-am irtapiš* AbB 3, 52: 29 "the breach is a mile wide". Cf CAD P 414a.

4. LB *zibbat* ^{id}EDIN.NA *bé-ra-am* A.ŠÀ KI PN$_1$, PN$_2$ *u* PN$_3$ *gerram ušēṣû* CT 8, 8c: 2 "PN$_2$ and PN$_3$ rented from PN$_1$ the road along the rear part of the Edin Canal over a distance of one double hour". NR

bêru I, *ba᾿āru* "to choose"

1. OA TÚG *ni-be-er-ma* AKT 2, 34: 5 (s. also 23) "we chose the cloth".

2. OB *aššum* ^{f}TUR^{meš} *šiṭrim ... bé-ri-im ...* ^{f}TUR^{meš} *šiṭram lā i-bé-er-ru ...* ^{f}TUR^{meš} *ana šiṭrim e-bé-er-ra-am-ma* ARM 10, 125: 6, 11, 20 "about choosing the girls for the *š*.-song ... they must not choose the girls for the *š*.-song ... I will choose the girls for the *š*.-song". Note two diff. constructions, one with *ana* and one with double acc. ^{f}TUR^{meš} *šiṭrim* is not a genitive construction (thus ARM 10) but reflects the construction with double acc. with case attraction in the inf. construction (cf. Streck 2014 § 209a).

3. By-form *ba᾿āru* in OB: *ṣābam yalūtam ... [l]u-ub-ḫa-ar-[ma* FM 5, 109 n. 276 A.3594+: 35, "let me select alliance troops".

4. "to examine" also NA: *anāku dibbīšu a-bé-á[r]* SAA 13, 3: 8 "I will personally examine his matter".

MPS (1–2, 4), NR (3)

berûtu "hunger"

OB *bé-ru-ta-am ša šê u kaspim* AbB 12, 66: 16' "hunger(?) for barley and silver".

bêšu "to go away, withdraw"

G 1. Cf. Veenhof 2015a, 229–232, with new OA ref., concluding a mng. "to declare, give information"; however, the semantic connection with the mng. "to go away", remains unclear.

2. OB *ṣābam aṭrudma itrûniššunūti aššum pa!?-ni bēlija la i-bi-šu usanniqšunūtima ḫūrassu ēkim* ARM 27, 66: 15 "I sent troops and they brought them here. I checked them and took the sumach away from them so that they can not flee from(?) the presence(?) of my lord". Birot, ARM 27 p. 131 "afin que mon seigneur ne soit pas *irrité*, je les ai interrogés", thinking of *ba᾿āšu* with subject *panū* "to look bad, to be angry". However, *ba᾿āšu* is only attested in LB (CAD B 5 *ba᾿āšu* A 2) and the supposed *pa!-ni* is in oblique case. Furthermore, *ba᾿āšu* always has a strong aleph. Birot, ib. in his comm. also

quotes a translation of J.-M. Durand: "je les ai réprimandés de s'être montrés sans vergogne envers mon seigneur". However, *baʾāšu* B "to come to shame" is not *i*- but *a*-class.
3. SB *ina asīdū šēpīšunu qaqqari i-bi-iš-šú ina sârišunu uḫteppû* GN₁ u GN₂ Gilg. SB V 133 "at the heels of their feet the earth divided; as they whirled about they shattered GN₁ and GN₂". Diff. AHw 1547: *bâšu* II "(Erde) stampfen", followed by CDA 41a.

MPS (1–3), NR (3)

bēšu "distant"

SB *bé-eš-tú* : *rūqu* : *aḫû* SpTU 1, 84 ed. 3 "distant : remote : strange".

beṭ/dû "to cheat(?)"

G 1. OB *i-bé*-DU-*né-ši-ma* AbB 10, 111: 4 in broken context, uncertain. Sommerfeld 1990, 143: *bedû*.
2. MB *ib*-TE-*e* MBLET 42: 14 in broken context. Uncertain.

D *ú-ba-aṭ-ṭi-a-ni-ma šê im-ta-ša*!-*aḫ* AbB 6, 220: 17 "he cheated me and stole my barley". Diff. CDA 42: "to delay".

Disc.: There seems to be a second verb *bed/ṭû*, s. above. Cf. also *padû*.

MPS (G, D), NR (G, D)

bīʾātu, *bīʾādu* "to spend the night, to be safe".

G 1. OA said of silver and goods. Cf. Hecker 1966, 64f.: "'Übernachten des Silbers' (ist wohl) seine sichere Aufbewahrung im Hause". Larsen 2002, 24 ad. 13: "to be available, active".
a) *šīmam lašʾamma lutaʾʾerakkumma* KÙ.BABBAR 1 GÍN *li-bi-it* OAA 1, 15: 13 "I shall make purchases and return that to you, and the silver, 1 shekel, shall be safe".
b) *šīmam lašʾamma lušēbilakkumma li-bi-ta-am* OAA 1, 17: 23 "I shall make purchases and send the (goods) to you, so that they may be safe".
c) KÙ.BABBAR 1 GÍN *li-bi-tám* OAA 1, 38 r. 9'.
2. OB lit. [*in*]*a* MUL *li-bi-it-ma* YOS 11, 29: 6 "let (the medication) spend the night under the stars".
3. OB [*šamaššammū k*]*īma tanappaṣu ina kīdim lā i-bi-tu* AbB 10, 93: 12' "after you have crushed the sesame, it should not stay overnight outside".
4. The form with *d* is also attested in OB Mari: *i-bi-du* ARM 26/1 p. 187 no. 42: 9.
5. SB *lū īdēma lū lā uṣṣāma lū a-bi-it ina ḫurriya* FAOS 22, 42 II iii 42 "had I known, I would not go out, I would stay safe at my burrow".
6. SB said of an animal: *irtappud serramu i-bit ina ṣēri* Westenholz 1997, 46: 58 (Sargon Birth Legend) "the onager ran about, stayed overnight in the steppe". Pace Westenholz, ib. not *i-biṭ* "he twitches".
7. Deller 1966, 312: NA *umā šarru bēlī annaka bé-e-d*[*e*] *illakūnu ušallumū* SAA 15, 223 r. 10 "now that the king my lord is staying overnight here, they will come and comp[lete] (their work)".
8. Deller 1966, 312: UD 15-KÁM *ina bēt ili ni-bi-ad* SAA 1, 134 r. 4 "we shall spend the night in the temple on the 15th".

Gtn OB *ina ekallimma ib-ta-na-ia-at* ARM 26/2 p. 433 no. 495: 17 "he kept staying overnight in the palace".

MPS (G, Gtn), NR (G)

bibbu, + *bību* "wild sheep"

1. SB lex. *bi-i-bu* Emar 6/4, 551: 47 (Ḫḫ XIV 142; MSL 8/2, 17).

2. As demon: SB *bi-ib-bu murtappid*[*u*] AulaOr. Suppl. 23, 19: 2 "ever running *b.*" (in list of demons).
3. The names listed in AHw and CAD s. v. *bibû* "baby(?)" may belong here. S. the spellings *Bi-ib-bu-ú*(*-a*).

bibbulu, *bubbulu* "flood; day of the disappearance of the moon; juggling"

Juggling (with weapons): OB 50 *ṣābam damqam ... ana bu-ub-bu-lim ušērib* FM 1, 138 A.486+M.5319: 37 "I made 50 good soldiers enter for juggling".

bibēnu, + pl. fem. *bibinnātu*, *bibēnātu* "temple; a hair-style designating slaves"

Also attested OAkk., OA, both instances in the fem. pl., designating a hair-style given to enemies in order to make them slaves:
1. OAkk. *bí-bí-in-na-at-su-nu ugallib* RIME 2, 105 ii 4 "I shaved their *bibēnu* hair-style(s) (= I shaved their hair to give them a *b.*-hair-style)". Cf. Gelb/Kienast 1990, 241.
2. OA *bi₄-be-na-tim qaqqadātīšunu aškun* OA Sarg. 52 "I applied *b.* hair-style(s) to their heads". MPS, NR

bibinnu s. *bibēnu*.

biblu "bringing; things brought; invisibility of the moon"

Invisibility of the moon (cf. *bibbulu*): SB Ugar. *ina pī bi-ib-li ina rēš arḫi* AulaOr. Suppl. 23, 65: 1 "at the day of the invisibility of the moon, when the month starts".

+ **bibnu**? "a bird"

OB *bi*/*pí*-⸢*ib*/*p*⸣-*nu-um*^{mušen} Edubba 7, 100: 28 (in list of birds). Black/Al-Rawi 1987, 124 read, with the copy, *bi*-⸢x⸣-*nu-um*, but Al-Rawi/Dalley, Edubba 7 p. 105 ⸢*a-ta*⸣*-nu-um*.

bibû s. *bibbu*

bidalu, pl. *bidalūm*/*na* "substitute, deputy, assistant"; Ugar., Ugar. lw.

Del Olmo Lete/Sanmartín 2004, 217 (with previous lit.), on the base of the alphabetic ref. of the word: "substitute, reserve personnel". Cf. Dietrich/Loretz 2008, 288f.; Tropper 2012, 180 with previous lit. *b.* in ^{lú}DAM. GÀR^{meš} : *bi-da-lu-ma* is not an equation for *tamkāru* "merchant" but rather qualifies the word. NR

+ **Bigû** "a piece of jewelry"; OB

1. B*i-gi-i-im* ARM 32 p. 344 M.10532: 3.
2. B*i-gu* KÙ.GI! ARM 32 p. 464 M.8153: 8'.
3. S. Arkhipov, ib. 74. Related to the plant *pigû* (CAD P 359f.)? NR

biḫirtu "levy"

SB *šumma ina araḫ Šabāṭi šarru lū ana bi-ḫir?-t*[*u*? *l*]*ū ana* ^{d}DI.KUD *īrub* CUSAS 25, 229 K.7079 r. ii 1 "if, in the month of *Šabāṭu*, a king enters either for levy(?) or for Mandānu" (serie *Inbu bēl arḫi*; reading after Labat 1960, 168). Cf. the reading BI SAR x [x] in CUSAS 25, 229. NR

+ **biḫīru** "a soldier", lit. "chosen"; Ugar., Ugar. lw.

$^{[lú.]meš}$*b*[*i*]*-ḫi-ru* ^{uru}*u-g*[*a-ri-it*] PRU 6, 71: 5' "*b.*-soldiers from Ugarit". Cf. Sivan 1984, 171 and 211; Huehnergard 1987, 112f.; Tropper 2012, 175f. Cf. *bēru* II, *beʾru*.

billatu "mixture"

OB in transferred mng.: *ištūma awātum bi-il-la-at alkā māpalīku<nu> nīš ilim ina* GN$_1$ *ūlūma ina* GN$_2$ *šuzkirāšunūti* ARM 27, 116: 42 "because the matter is a mess, go (and) make your spokesmen take an oath in GN$_1$ or GN$_2$!" Pace J.-M. Durand apud M. Birot, ib. p. 203 note n, there is no need to correct the text to *bi-il-la-tum*. For OB Mari "alloy" s. Arkhipov 2012, 25.

billu I, + *bīlu* "(ad)mixture, alloy"; + OB

1. OB 6 SIMUG.GAL *šu bi-lim* ARM 19, 342: 3 "6 experienced smiths for (making) an alloy".
2. OB 39 1/2 MA.NA ZABAR *bi-il-li* 7-ÀM ARM 21, 274: 2 "39 1/2 minas of bronze, an alloy of seven (to one)". Cf. *bi-l*[*i*] ib. 276: 2, [*b*]*i-il-l*[*i*] ib. 285: 8. S. Durand, ib. p. 312f. n. 12.
3. *bi-il-li* 7 GÍN-ÀM ARM 22, 203 ii 8 and passim in this text. S. also Arkhipov 2012, 24f.
4. MA [*b*]*i-i-*⸢*la*⸣ *ana šiltāḫī* BATSH 4/1, 16: 18 "(iron), an alloy for arrows".

bilṣu "squint-eyed(?)"

SB PN *ḫibtu nīku akī* 2-*ma maḫḫu akī* 2-*ma bil-ṣu akī* 2-*ma* SAA 3, 30: 1 "PN raped captive(?), doubly so, runny-eyed one, doubly so, squint-eyed man(?), doubly so".

biltu, *bīsu* "load; talent; yield; rent; tribute"

1. Deller 1966, 313: NA *ana šēṭišu* PN *bi-lat lušātera bi-lat lumaṭṭi* SAAB 5, 20: 9 (s. also notes on p. 53) "for his carelessness, PN will give one bundle extra, or reduce one bundle (of his part)".
2. NA by-form *bīsu* (cf. AHw 1548; or *bissu*): *bi-si* ^{giš}KIRI$_6$ StAT 3, 32: 25 "yield of the orchard".

MPS (2), NR (1)

bīltu s. *bīštu*

binītu I "creation; shape, appearance, structure"

1. OB 3(b) *bi-ni-a-tum* AbB 7, 141: 3' "3 seah of eggs".
2. OB *bi-ni-a-tim ina a-la-al-li* AbB 3, 4: 14 "fish roe in an *alallû*-container(?)".
3. Beaulieu 2003, 196f.: LB 1 GÚ KÙ.GI *šá* ZIZNA 65 *bi-ni-tú* YBC 4174: 24 "1 gold necklace of fish-roe-shaped beads (comprising) 65 beads".
4. Von Soden 1968, 459: SAG.DÙ KU$_6$ BAM 124 i 25, ii 43 =(?) *binīt nūni* "fish roe".

MPS (1–2), NR (3–4)

binītu II "a type of crossbeam(?)"; Ur III

1. 20 ĜURUŠ [*bí-n*]*i-tum* GÍD.DÈ CUSAS 4 p. 289 "20 workmen to tighten crossbeams (for construction of the brewery-kitchen-mill complex)".
2. 10 ĜURUŠ *bí-ni-tum* GÍD.[DÈ?] ib. *bí-ni-tum* IM SUMUR AKA CUSAS 4 p. 249 (5 references) "(workmen) having plastered crossbeams".
3. The word is already known from other Ur III texts (CAD B 238). Heimpel 2009, 180–182 suggests the reading *bi-ì-tum* "a container", lit. "house". S. also Sallaberger 2011, 357, who considers the interpret. "a type of crossbeam" as unsubstantiated.

bintu, *bittu* "daughter"

1. *bittu* in MB: adverbial expression in absolute state: *bi-*⸢*it*⸣*-ta-at bukur* HS

1893: 4 "daughters (and) son(s)" (courtesy E. Zomer, s. forthcoming publ. TMH 11).
2. *bittu* in Ug: ^{f}*bi-it-ta rabīti* AnOr 48, 11f. RS 1957.1: 6, 10 "daughter of the Great Lady". ^{f}*bi-it-ti* ib. 18, 21. ^{f}*bi-it-*[*ti*] MRS 9, 128 RS 17.348 r. 4. Pace Kühne 1973, 177 and Sivan 1984, 212 *bittu* is not necessarily a WSem. cognate of Akkadian *bintu*. NR

bīnu I, *binnu* "son"; + OB

1. *lu-lu bi-in* YOS 11, 17: 3 "the primeval man is a son(?)", s. also *bi-ni* ib. 1 (incant. childbirth).
2. Von Soden 1968, 458f.: SB *ṣa-bi-tu*! *bi-in-na tu-na-kap* CT 14, 50: 72 (word square) "the gazelle knocks the child down". Cf. CAD B 217b, disc.

MPS (1), NR (2)

bīnu II "tamarisk"

1. OB *paššūru ša aḫâ*[*tušu*] *ša* ^{giš}*bi-nim* FM 8, 46 no. 6: 7 "a table whose sides are of tamarisk".

2. OB *kīma bi-nim šumqutū qarrādū* FM 14, 16 ii 15 "the warriors had been struck down like a tamarisk".

3. Unusual spelling OB GIŠ$^{ḫi.a}$ *bi-ia-ni* ARM 26/2 p. 533 no. 541: 5, 18 (letter from Karkemiš). Cf. Streck 2013, 322f.: uncontracted spelling /baynī/.

4. For OB Mari s. also Kupper 1992, 164.

5. a) SB *itti* ^{ĝiš}ŠINIG *aḫî u kušāri ēdi šēpēki arakkas* Lamaštu ii 47 (Farber 2014, 168f.) "I will bind your feet to a free-standing tamarisk and a lone reed stalk".
b) SB *itti* ^{ĝiš}ŠINIG *aḫî u kušāri ēdi rukussima* (note the inverse order in some duplicates: *itti* ^{ĝiš}ŠINIG *ēdi u kušāri aḫî*) Lamaštu ii 146 (Farber 2014, 176f.).
c) S. already Borger 1971, 66f., and correct CAD K 598b *kušāru* a and CAD A/1, 38b *abāru* III.

MPS (1–4), NR (5)

+ **bīnu? III** "a type of garment"; OB

ŠU.NIGIN 20 ^{túg}*bi-nu-um* ARM 30 p. 30 T.158: 8' (summary of diff. textiles).

NR

binûtu, MA *bunûtu* "creation, creature, product, form"

binût amīlūti "child; human being":
1. MA *bu-nu-ut* LÚ.U_{18}.LU *luṣṣâ līmur* IZI.GAR Iraq 31, 31: 49 "may the human being come out, may he see the light".
2. SB *āšib ekleti bi-nu-ut amīlū*[*ti*] *ammīni lā tabkī ina libbi ummi*[*ka*] MesCiv 2, 110 § 39: 16 "you (embryo), living in the darkness, human being, why did you not cry in the womb of your mother?" S. also Farber, ib. p. 139.

NR

binzurru s. *bunzerru*

+ **biqlu** "sapling"; OB

1. GIŠ$^{ḫi.a}$ *bi-iq-lam ša taskarinnim* ARM 26/1 p. 134 no. 21: 11' "trees, sapling(s) of boxtree".
2. For *biqlu* instead of *piglu* s. Zadok 1993, 321: BQL, etym. Syr. *bqlʾ* "sprout", Ugar. *bql* "groats". Also Heimpel 2003, 188, who connects the word with *buqlu* "malt". The lemma *biqlētu* (AHw 127 "Malzkeime", CAD B 244 "malt in one of its stages of germination") is the pl. of this word. S. also Stol 2008, 353 (with the spelling *piglu*). Disc. of Amor. etym. Streck 2000, 86f.

bīram (CAD B 245) s. *bēru* III

birbirru, + *mirmerru* "luminosity"

1. The word is also attested in the sg. (cf. also Mayer 2016, 197):
a) OB lit. *lišānāšu bi-ir-bi-ir-ru-um* VS 17, 4: 4 "its two tongues are luminosity".
b) OB lit. *šinnāšu mi-ir-me-er-ru-um* CUSAS 32, 27: 5 "its teeth are luminosity". Cf. *mermerru* AHw 1575.
c) Stative sg. fem.: OB lit. *bi-ir-bi-re-et* UET 6/2, 404: 1 "she is a shining light" (diff. Mayer 2016, 197: nisba).

2. Instead of *bīt bír-bír-ri-im* ARM 10, 38: 10 read prob. É.BABBAR-*ri-im* = *Ebabbarim*.

+ **birīdu?** "a jewel"; OB

1. *bi-ri-di* ARM 22, 237: 5 among other items delivered for the goddess Dērītu.
2. *bi-ri-du* ARM 32 p. 475 M.12299: 7'', qualifying the garment *mudû*. S. Arkhipov, ib. p. 74.
3. Form of the word unclear: *b/pirīdu*, *b/piriddu*? NR

biriḫḫu "string, bundle"

OB ref. Stol 1987b, 74 n. 108: 12 bi-ri-ḫi ša šūmim AbB 10, 201: 19 "12 strings of garlic"; cf. also CBS 408.

birīt, *berte* in MA and NA "between, among"

1. OB *ana ḫârim qatālim bi-ri-it Ḫa-nameš ù* GN ARM 2, 37: 7 "in order to kill a donkey (= to establish peace) between Ḫana and GN".

2. *birīt- u birīt-* (CAD B 252 *birīt* 4) in the adv. acc.: OB *salīmim bi-ri-sú ù bi-ri-it* PN ARM 26/2 p. 280 no. 410: 5 "peace between him and PN".

3. Deller 1966, 313: NA PN [*ina pa-n*]*a-tu-u-a ina bi-*[*r*]*i-tu-uš-šú-nu madaktu* CTN 5, 22 ND 2717: 8' "PN [has set up] a camp in [front] of me in the midst of them".

4. Deller 1966, 313: with assimilation of r: NA *šulmu ana bi-ta-šu-*<*nu*> Iraq 16, 54 ND 2079: 5.

5. Deller 1966, 313: with connecting vowel *a*:
a) *ina ber-ta!-šú-nu* MCS 2, 19: 7.
b) *ina ber-ta-šú-nu* SAAB 5, 66: 9, 12; ib. 16: 10.

6. Deller 1966, 313:
a) NA *dēnu ina ber-tú-šu-nu iptaras* StAT 3, 102: 6.
b) NA [*dē*]*nu ina ber-te-šú-nu iptarsa* SAAB 9, 97: 12 "he decided the case between them".
c) Without *dēnu*: *ina ber-ta-šú-nu iptarsu* SAAB 5, 66: 9 "(PN) gave a decision between them".

7. LB Cf. Jursa 1999, 89 with n. 361 for *ina* GN *ina bi-rit* BÀD^{ki} VS 5, 103: 2 "in GN within the city wall" and KI-*tì bi*!-[*ri*]*t* [BÀD]^{ki} CT 55, 128 obv. 2 "a plot with[in] the city [wall]".
MPS (2, 7), NR (1, 3–6)

birītu I "space between, distance"

1. Lex. *be-ri-tum*/*ti* Emar 6/4, 542: 219–221 (Ḫḫ I).
2. OB: Unusual plene spelling in OB *bé-e-ri-i-tim* AbB 13, 2: 9.
3. Pl. in SB 4 *ina ammati bi-rat tu-li-šú* AulaOr. Suppl. 23, 42: 35 "the middle parts of his breast were 4 cubits (big)".

birku, *burku*, + *barku* (OA, MB Emar) "knee"

1. OA *ba-ar-ke-a qallil* Innāya 240: 17; AKT 7a, 41: 25 "make my knees light", hence "make things easy for me, ease my burden". The same expression is found in Early OB: *birkīya qú-li-il*$_5$

Sumer 23 pl. 16: 15; for corresponding G, s. CAD Q 55b s. v. *qalālu* 1b end.
2. OA PN *Bu-ur-kà-num* Innāya 152: 37 "The one with knee(?)". Michel, ib. p. 207 *Bu-ur-qá-num*. *Bu-ur-ki-a* ib. 273: 11.
3. OB lit. *urruk* ⸢*bir*⸣*-ki* AMD 1, 215ff. BM 79125: 1 "he is long as relates to the knees".
4. OB lit. *urruḫ bi-ir-ki-i* ib. 218f. BM 79938: 1 "he is swift as relates to the knees".
5. Lex. *šar* DÙG *bá-ar-ku* Emar 6/4, 537: 276.
6. SB [*i*]*mtanaqqutū ištū bur-ke-šu* AulaOr. Suppl. 23, 43: 4 "fall constantly to(?) (text: from) his knees" (unclear).
7. NA a piece of meat as temple offering: 24? ᵘ[ᶻᵘ]*bu-ur-*⸢*ki*⸣ *ša* 14 *alpī* SAA 7, 200 r. 6 "24(?) 'knees' of 14 oxen". [*bu*]*-ur-ki* ib. 202 r. 8.

MPS (2–4, 6–7), NJCK (1), NR (5)

birmu I "multicolored cloth"

1. a) OB *kisal bi-ir-mi* ARM 23, 494: 14 "courtyard of (the workshop for) multicolored cloth".
b) *bīt bi-ir-mi* ib. 574: 6 "house (= workshop) for multicolored cloth". Cf. CAD *b.* A a.

2. NA GÙN SAA 7, 104 r. 3.

3. NA [x ᵗᵘ́]ᵍ*bir-me* JCS 7, 169 Bi 71: 5'.

4. 2 ᵗᵘ́ᵍ*qa*[*r*]-⸢*aru*(PA)⸣ *bir-me* StAT 3, 1: 9 "2 multicolored bedspreads".

MPS (1), NR (2–4)

birqu "lightning"

OB *bi-ir-qum ša ṣīḫātim* ALL 1 i 12 "lightning of love-making", s. *ḫašḫūru*.

birru "lattice, grill"; + Ur III(?)

4 ᵗᵘ́ᵍ*bu-ti-um*? ᵍⁱˢ*be-rum* SIKI ᵍⁱˢGARIĜ AKA CUSAS 3, 807: 2 (CUSAS 4 p. 30) "4 *butiʾum*-cloths for a lattice(?), made of combed wool". However, Sallaberger 2011, 359, tentatively assumes the spelling BAD.AŠ = *zara*₆ "a textile" for *be-rum* here.

birṣu "a luminous phenomenon"

NA *šumma ina šubat amēli bir-ṣu ib-ru-uṣ marušta immar* ZA 71, 114: 23 "if a light flashes in a man's house, he will experience trouble". NR

biršu "felt(?)"

Deller 1966, 313:
1. NA ⸢6⸣ ᵗᵘ́ᵍ*na-ṣa-bat* [...] *bir-še* SAA 7, 119 r. ii 3' "6 straight garments [...], felted".
2. NA ᵗᵘ́ᵍ*ma-qa bir* ZAG GI₆ [n] ᵗᵘ́ᵍ*ma-qa bir* ZAG SA₅ SAA 7, 95: 1f. "gowns, felted, the front black; [n] gowns, felted, the front red"; cf. ib. 98: 4f.
3. [x ᵗᵘ́ᵍ*u*]*r-nat bir* NÍGIN SAA 7, 102: 2 "[x *u*]*rnutu*-garments, felted, the edging [...]". NR

birtu I "fort, castle"; + OA

1. OA *ina bi*₄*-ir-tim ša* GN TPAK 1, 100: 9 "in the fort of GN".

2. OB Plene spelling: [ER]IM *bi-i-i*[*r*]-tim AbB 13, 24: 8 "soldiers of the fort".

3. Appositional construction of *ṣābum birtum* already attested in ARM 2, 39: 62: *ṣa-ba-am bi-ir-tam* "garrison" Shemshara 1, 12: 10; 21: 15; 30: 13. *ṣa-bi-im bi-ir-tim* 30: 8.

4. *eqel bi-ir-tim* ARM 10, 134: 6 "fenced(?) field".

5. Pl. *bi*/*erētu*:
a) OB *ṣābam ša bi-re-tim ... wašbū* ARM 27, 148: 9 "the troops who occupy the fortresses".
b) MB Qaṭna ˡᵘ́·ᵐᵉˢUGULA.10.KUD *be-re-ti mariyannū* QS 3, 20: 1; cf. ib. 26:

1 "decurions of the forts of the *mariyannū*".

c) lú.mešUGULA.10.KUD *be-re-ti* lú.meš*ḫu-up-še-na* ib. 25: 1 "decurions of the forts of the *ḫupše*".

d) S. the disc. in QS 3 p. 100.

6. Deller 1966, 313: Since *birāti*/*birāte* and *ḫal-ṣu*meš seem to be interchangeable in NA letters, ḪAL.ṢU is an Akkadogram for *birtu*. See, e. g., *šulmu ana bi-ra-ti* CTN 5, 194 ND 2372: 8 and *šulmu ana* ḪAL.ṢUmeš ib. 195 ND 2409: 7. Cf. SAA 16 p. 181: uruḪAL.ṢU-*ú-te* = *birtūtu*.

7. Deller 1966, 313f.: *rab birti* "commander of a fortress": NA *mār šipri ša* lúGAL *bir-te* SAA 5, 204 r. 4 "messenger of the fort commander".

MPS (1–3, 5–6), NR (4, 6–7)

bīru I "divination"

LB prob. fem. pl.: *bi-re-e-tu*4 *šá* UDU.NÍTA Bēl-rēmanni p. 177: 2 "extispicies(?) of a ram".

bīru III "ridge"

Ad CAD *bīru* C 2: OB *ina bi-ri-i ... mê lirdē* AbB 8, 133: 8 "let him flow water in the ridges (between the furrows)".

bīru IV, *bēru* IV "hunger"

MB Ekalte *be-ri-im ana šu-zi-bi-im* WVDOG 102, 28: 4 "to save (him) from hunger(?)" (construction and form of the inf. seem to be wrong; for context cf. *tišû*).

****bīru** E in *ša bīrišu*

Delete *bīru* E (CAD B 267): *Ša-bīrēšu* is a geogr. name, "(That) of its wells(?)", and not a designation of an official. Cf. Radner 2006–2008, 474f.

NR

birûtu II "mound, commemorative stone(?)"; + OB

1. S. the disc. by Durand 2005, 191–200. He concludes that the word designates a "commemorative stone" and suggests an *-ūt*-derivation from *barû* "to see, look at". However, although a derivation of *barû* makes sense, the assumption of an *-ūt*-suffix does not, since this suffix never has a concrete meaning. Therefore rather nominal pattern *PiRūS* (s. GAG § 55j: occurs with roots III infirmae instead of *PiRiSt*, e.g., *minûtu*, *ṣibûtu*). For ref. in the dict. s. AHw *bērūtu* (AHw 123 "Untergrund", AHw 1548 with lit. "ein Hügel") and CAD B 213 *berūtu* "foundation pit" and 267f. *birūtu*.

2. OAkk *ḫirītam iškun u bé-ru-tám ibnī* FAOS 7, 341 Ur 5: 13 "he dug (lit. established) a trench and heaped up (lit. built) a mound".

3. OAkk. KI.GAL *išpuk* RIME 2, 129 iii 3 "he heaped up a mound", cf. Kienast/Sommerfeld 1994, 191.

4. + OB (mathematical text): [*b*]*é-ru-tum* 30 GAM AfO 42/43, 103 B2: 8'. For comm. s. Jursa/Radner, ib. 104f.

MPS (1–3), NR (4)

bis "then, afterwards"

1. Deller 1966, 314: NA PN *ša issišu šēbilanni bi-is anāku ilīkunu lušēbilakkunu u sulummû laškun* JCS 54, 82 BM 132980 r. 16' "send to me PN and those with him, and then I myself will send your gods to you and make peace".

2. *bi-is ša* MN *bīt-salā-mê neppašuni* SAA 10, 219: 10 "then, (is it that[?]) we shall perform the (ritual) *bīt-salā-mê* of month MN?"

3. Spelled *bi-si* SAA 10, 189 r. 4.

MPS (2–3), NR (1)

bisru, *bišru* "leek"

1. *bi-si-ir saḫ-le-e lā ikkal* MSL 9, 109 IM 50964: 5' "he should not eat *bisru*-leek".
2. *bi-šir saḫ-le-e* MSL 9, 107 and 108 note D K.8068+: 21.
3. Instead of *biš-ra* CAD B 268 (KAR 147: 25 and dupl.) read *bi-iš-ra*. NR

+ **bisrû**, *bissû* "from the Ǧabal Bišrī"; OB

1. *aššum kalbī bi-is-sé-e bēlī išpuram kalbū bi-is-s[ú-]ú mādūtum ibbašû* ARM 26/1 p. 571 no. 271: 5, 7 (cf. Heimpel 2003, 280) "my lord wrote me about Bissean dogs. There existed many Bissean dogs".
2. *tuppum ša bēliya aššum kalbī bi-is-re-e illikam* ib. no. 272: 6 (cf. Heimpel 2003, 281) "a tablet of my lord about Bisrean dogs came to me".
3. Note that the expected pl. would be *bisr/sûtu/im* instead of *bissû* and *bisr/sê* (or are these forms of the sg.?).

bissu, *bīsu* s. *biltu*

****biṣḫu** Pentiuc 2001, 39

Read with Tsukimoto 1998, 185 *úr-ḫi/ḫu* instead of *bi-iṣ-ḫi/ḫu*:
1. *panūšu úr-ḫu* HANEM 2, 7: 6 "its front is the road".
2. *ina úr!-ḫi ša bāb* GN Emar 6/3, 171: 2 "(a field) at the road (leading to) the gate of GN".

biṣinnu s. *buṣinnu*

biṣṣūru, *piṣīru* "female genitals, vulva"

1. OB *[b]i-i-ṣú-ru-um [š]a lā i-ka-[l]u* AbB 12, 181: 7' "a vulva, which (he?) does not use (lit. eat)" (in broken context, but the text speaks of sexual activities).
2. OB (if a foetus) *šārat bi-iṣ-ṣú-ri-ša īlûnim* "the hair of its vulva is sprouting" CUSAS 18 p. 317: 7.
3. OB *bi-ṣú-ri ilput išaršu ana bi-ṣú-ri-i[a] ul īrub* ARM 26/2 p. 423 no. 488: 36 "he touched my vagina, (but) his penis did not enter my vagina".
4. OB *u ašar abu u ummum panīka ittaplasū u ištū bi-iṣ-ṣú-ri-im tamqutamma annânum bi-ṣú-ru-um imḫurka* FM 1, 117 A.1146: 36 "and atthe (same) place where father and mother used to look at your face and you had fallen out of the vulva, here a vulva has received you".
5. Of animals:
a) OB lit. *[b]i-iṣ-ṣú-úr ṣerri* AMD 1, 235 no. 11: 2 "vulva of a snake".
b) *bi-ṣú-ur kalbatim* ib. 258ff. H 72: 4 "vulva of a bitch".
6. For *piṣīru* KAR 466: 7 s. Böck 2000, 164f.

MPS (1–5), NR (6)

bišru "baby"; + OA, + OB

1. OA lit. *tašaqqīʾame mê bi-iš-ri-im* Or. 66, 61: 16 "she gives (them) to drink the amniotic fluid (lit. water of the baby)".
2. OB lit. *mê bi-iš-ri* YOS 11, 20: 12.
3. For the interpret. of *mê bišri* as "amniotic fluid" s. Michel 1997, 63f. See, however, Farber 2014, 204 and. n. 20: *mê pí-iš-ri-im* "water/liquid of dissolution". NR

bīštu, *bīltu* "evil"

SB *ana têlte u bil-te ina pī nišī ittaškin* SAA 3, 29: 9 "he was put as proverb and evil in the mouth of the people". Derives from *baʾāšu*, other ref. are found in the dict. under the adj. *bīšu*, but in fact belong here.

bīšu "bad; malodorous"

Lex. [*túl a*] ⌜*ur₅*⌝? = *bi-iš-tum* Emar 6/4, 559: 128 (Ḫḫ XXII; for Sum. s. DCCLT MB Ura 13) "stinking (restore *būrtu* 'well')".

+ **bitaḫwa** "to gore(?)"; Hurr. foreign word?

OB (the king's vassals) *kīma*! *rīmim bi-ta-aḫ-wa* CUSAS 18, 19: 24' "who will gore like an aurochs", cf. George, ib. p. 121.

bītānu "in the house, inside"

1. Deller 1966, 314: NA *dibbē annûti* TA ŠÀ GN *ina bit-a-nu-uk-ka esip* Langdon Tammuz pl. 2 ii 23 "collect these words from GN in your inside!"
2. Deller 1966, 314f.: NA ^{lú}*ša* UGU *bit-a-ni* Iraq 25, pl. 19 BT 101b: 14.

NR

bītānû "inner, interior"

Deller 1966, 315: Ebeling Stiftungen p. 19: 3 (CAD B 276 *b.* b) read ^{uzu}*bit-a-ni-a*^{meš}. NR

bitiqtu "damage, loss, deficit"; + NA

1. OA *bi-it-qá-at* AN.NA AKT 2, 55: 16 "outstanding amount of tin".

2. *kaspim bi-it-qá-tim ša naruqqišu* AKT 7a, 52: 6 "silver, deficit of his investment capital".

3. *iṣṣēr bi-tí-iq-tí-ni šakin* ib. 276: 10 "it is added (lit. put on) to our loss".

4. *bi-it-qá-tim* ib. 259: 24.

5. OB *ina bi-it-qa-ti-im išaggum* ARM 26/1 p. 413 no. 192: 5 (cf. Heimpel 2003, 248) "he shouts because of(?) the losses" (unclear context).

6. Deller 1966, 315:

a) NA: *bi-tiq-tú* Iraq 23 pl. 11 ND 2386+ r. i 24'.
b) *bi-ti-*[*i*]*q-tú* [*ša*?] Ú^{me} [*lā*?] *taddana* CTN 2, 182, no. 181 r. 18 "[but do not(?)] give the loss on plants(?)".
c) Note that contrary to CAD B 277a *b.* disc. sect., these Assyr. ref. use the sg.

MPS (1–5), NR (6)

bitqu "break(age), cutting"

1. Stol 2008, 354: OB IGI 6 GÁL UKU.UŠ *ša aššum bi-it-qí-im* (cf. CAD P 441b *pí-it-qí-im*) *illikam* UET 6, 481:31 "one-sixth (barley ration for) the soldier who came here on account of the breakage".
2. NA GN *Bāb-bit-qí* SAA 15, 186: 8; 45: 11; 194 r. 7; SAA 1, 94: 9, r. 4, 12.

NR

+ **bitru**? **I** "a garment"; OB

1. OB TÚG$^{ḫi.a}$ [...] *bi-it-ri damqūtim lišābil*[*am*] ARM 26/2 p. 540 no. 549: 8' "may he send [me] cloths (and) good *b.*-garments".
2. ARM 22, 164: 10 and in unpubl. texts ^{túg}*bi-it-rum* (ARM 30 p. 54 and 99).
3. Since the last vowel is not written plene in ARM 26/2 p. 540 no. 549, prob. does not derive from *bitrû* "outstanding" (pace Durand, ARM 30 p. 99). Hardly to be connected with *bitru* CAD B 279 "mng. uncert.". The first consonant may be *b*/*p*, the second *d*/*t*/*ṭ*.

+ **bitru II** "cutting, sluice; section, half"; SB, MB Emar, WSem. lw.

1. Lex. AN.KUD = *bi-it-ru ša ša*[*mê*] Emar 6/4, 567: 5' "section of the sky". CAD P 449 has this ref. s. v. *piṭru*.
2. SB ^{d}EN *bi-ta-ri* Emar 6/3, 448: 19' "lord of the sections(?)".
3. MB Emar *qarnu* ZÚ.AM.SI AN *bi-it-ru ša* PNf HANEM 2, 37: 20 "a horn of

ivory is the (inheritance) portion of PNf".
4. Cf. Pentiuc 2001, 39f. NR

bitrû II s. *barû* III Gt

bittu I "daughter" s. *bintu*

bittu II, + *battu* "weft"; OB

1. *ṣubātum šū kīma ṣubātim Tuttubêm šutâm u bi-it-ta-am damqiš lū nasik u lū kaṣir ... assurre ana ṣubātim šâtu [ša]têm u bi-it-tam uš*!*-ta-ba-at-tu-ma*! *u ina zunnātim šakākim zunnātum ikabbitāma u ṣubātum uštarraṭ* Iraq 39, 153 A.1285: 40, 47 "this garment should be well woven and knotted of warp and weft (yarns), like a Tuttubian garment. Under no circumstances, in order to weave that garment, should they interweave the weft. Nor, when attaching the ornaments, should the ornaments become heavy, should they allow the garment to become unraveled". Cf. Durand 2009, 30; Wasserman 2013, 265.
2. New by-form *battu*: 5/6 MA.NA *ba-tù-um* 3 1/2 MA.NA *nīdu ša* 1 ^{túg}*ḫalī šiknim* 1/2 MA.NA *ba-tù-um* 2 MA.NA *nīdu ša* 1 ^{túg}*ilbum* 1/2 MA.NA *ba-tù-um* 1 1/2 MA.NA *nīdum ša* 1 ^{túg}*saq burē šēʾim* 2/3 MA.NA *ba-tù-um* 3 MA.NA *nīdum ša* 1 ^{túg}*kap lurmîm* 1/3 MA.NA 5 GÌN *ba-tù-um* 1/2 MA.NA *nīdum ša* 1 ^{túg}*saq burē daqqum* ARM 30 p. 29f. T.263: 8, 10, 12, 14, 16 "5/6 mina of weft, 3 1/2 minas of warp for a (double-sided) blanket; 1/2 mina of weft, 2 minas of warp for a *i.*-garment; 1/2 mina of weft, 1 1/2 minas of warp for a (tightly) woven fabric for a mattress pad of a (stuffed) mattress; 2/3 mina of weft, 3 minas of warp for a 'wing of ostrich' (-garment); 1/3 mina 5 shekels of weft, 1/2 mina of warp for a fine(?) (tightly) woven fabric for a mattress pad".
3. OB lit. *ana bi-it-tim ... kīma šu-tu-*⌜*um*⌝ ... "to the weft yarns ... so that the warp yarns ..." UET 6/2, 414: 11 Cf. Wasserman 2013, 265 and 274. CAD P 443 quotes this passage under *pittu* A "side".
4. For disc. of the term s. Durand, ARM 30 p. 29–31 (*bittu* "warp", *nīdu* "weft"); Wasserman 2013, 265 (*bittu* "weft", *šutû* "warp"). NR

bītu "house"

1. Ur III: Spelled *bi-ì-tum* in Ur III Garšana (Heimpel 2009, 180–182)? S. *binītum* B.
2. OA É*-tum ana lā bé-tim itūʾar* AKT 6c, 647: 7 "the firm will be ruined (lit. becoming a not-house)".
3. OB: The expression *bīt eqlētim* prob. belongs to the ref. CAD B 292 *b.* 5 "place, lot, area, region": *ana* É *eqlētim ... šūšibšu* Shemshara 1, 50: 22 "settle him in a region with fields!". Eidem/ Læssøe, ib. p. 120 translate "farm".
4. Shelter of animals: OB *bi-it imērī* AbB 13, 58: 14 "house of donkeys".
5. Deller 1966, 315: NA É *epšu adi gušūrēšu adi dalātešu* É *dannu* É ZAG *ina libbi* 3 É NÁ*-šat* ^{meš} x[ ] É *šanie* É *šaḫūru* UŠ É NÁ É *šid-d*[*i?*] É *kisalli* É *rēdûte* NIM? É *ubsāte* É KUR*-ru ina libbi* 2 SIG₄ *ina libbi* SIG₄ *šá* É *abi igārātešu gammurūnišu* A^{meš} *ša tarbaṣi ina* É *ešši* Donbaz 1999, 50 no. 30: 6ff. (Ass. 13955gl; house sale contract) "a built house with its beams and doors, main building, the building of the front side with 3 sleeping rooms inside; servants' quarters, a subsidiary building near the house of the bed, house of the long side, a building in the courtyard, upper(?) succession house, storehouse, a ... house with two walls in it, one of which belongs to the paternal house, its

walls encompass it, (and) water is in (lit. of) the yard in the new house".

6. Deller 1966, 316: *ša bīti šanî* "palace servant": NA (lú)*ša* É 2-*e* Iraq 23 pl. 18 ND 2498: 17; ib. pl. 30 ND 2803 r. i 20.

7. Deller 1966, 316: *ša muḫḫi bīti* "palace supervisor": NA lú*šá* UGU É Iraq 19, pl. 28 ND 5448: 20. VAT 8270: 1. VAT 8232 r. 10. SAA 12, 92 r. 7. Parfümrezepte 37 ii 18 (s. also CAD R 220a *rāṭu* c); ib. 38 iii 17.

8. LB *bīt rēdûti*: d30 ⌜É⌝ *re-du-ú-tu* Bēl-rēmanni p. 177: 4 "Sîn of the residence of the crown prince".

MPS (1–4, 8), NJCK (2), NR (5–7)

+ **bi-TU-ru-um** "a building?"; OB

bi-tu-ru-um ARM 19, 258: 4, s. 10. The text lists flour for diff. buildings (storehouse[?], workshop, temple, palace, prison, kitchen), hence the suggestion of a composed noun with *bīt* "house" as first element. In ARM 6, 12: 11f. a *bīt* (É) TU-*ur-ri* is attested, read in CAD R 96 *rakāsu* 2e as *bīt turri*, but in CAD Ṭ 165 *ṭurru* B "an architectural feature, perhaps a courtyard or enclosure" as *bīt ṭurri*. This word designates a construction made of reed used in irrigation, prob. the cladding of a canal (s. also Durand 1998, 635: "coffrage"), a mng. which hardly fits the ref. in ARM 19.

bīʾu, *bību* "opening, outlet"

Deller 1966, 316: NA Pl. *bībī* (also *bībānu*): *bi-bi … kupru kaprū* CTN 5, 215 ND 2666: 11 "the outlets are smeared with bitumen". NR

bû "a bird" s. *pû* III

buʾāru "happiness, health, prosperity"

1. OB lit. *bu-a-ar maštaki kûmma Ištar* CunMon. 8, 22ff. i 44 "the happiness of the chamber is yours, Ištar".

2. SB *qīt bu-ḫa-ri-šu* AulaOr. Suppl. 23, 29: 10 "the end of his happiness".

+ **būʾāʾu**(?) "to intimidate, trump, defeat"; OA

Cf. Veenhof 2015a, 234f. with OA ref. Also the first two ref. in CAD P 472 *puāgu* a belong here. However, the etym. of the verb remains unclear.

bubû "a topographical feature"

Stol 1988, 175: OB (a field of the) *bu-bi-im* CT 48, 90: 4, cf. *bu-bi-im qablim* ib. 6 "lower *b*.". NR

bubūtu I "hunger, sustenance"

OB lit. *bu-bu-ti-iš nišī* Atra-ḫasīs I 339 // CUSAS 10, 2: 4 "for the sustenance of the people".

bubūtu II "axle"; + OB

1. OB *ana … bu-bu-a-tim šupur* AbB 3, 73: 7 "send for axles!"

2. OB [n] *bu-ba-at narkabtim* FM 7, 114 no. 30: 17 "[n] axles of a chariot".

3. giš[*b*]*u-ba-tim ša yašibim* ARM 27, 8: 6 "axles of a battering-ram". S. also ib.: 13.

4. giš*bu-ba-tum* ARM 32 p. 475 M.12348: 2. S. also Arkhipov, ib. p. 153.

5. OB lit. *ana ereq šamê bu-ba-a-tim talâṭ* CUSAS 10, 15: 48 "you shackle the axles for the wagon of the sky". Cf. George, ib. p. 116f. in favor of the mng. "axle".

6. Moran 1992, 57 and 60 n. 53 (s. also CAD M/1, 351): EA 22 iv 37 (CAD B 302 *b*. a) read 10 [giš]*bu-bu-*[*t*]*um* instead of 10 GAR *bu-bu-*[*tu*]*m*.

MPS (1–3, 5), NR (4, 6)

buddudu "to waste, dissipate"

1. NA É EN^{meš}*-ni pāḫutū* ⸢*ub*⸣*-ta-di-du* SAA 16, 42: 9 "the governors have squandered the household of our lord".
2. *tu-ub-ta-di-id* SAA 15, 62: 13 "you have squandered (the barley)".
3. ⸢*lā ú*⸣*-ba-du-du* ib. 55 r. 7 "they should not squander".

budê "a fruit confection or sweet sauce"

1. LB [*šikar*]*u duššupu Bu-du-ú šumšu* OLA 40, 160 no. 18 (Nippur Compendium) vi 11 OLA 40, 160 "sweet [bee]r which is called *b.*".
2. CAD G 65 and AHw 287b list the word as *giddê*, CDA 47 as *Budû*, SAA 12 p. 129 as *budê*. Since we never find a spelling *gi-id-* the reading budû (or *pudû)* is more likely.

MPS (2), NR (1–2)

būdu II "shoulder"

1. Lex. *murg*[*u*]*-sa-ĝu*10 = *bu-da-a* CUSAS 12 p. 150: 36 (Ugumu) "my shoulders".
2. OB 1 *ṣubātam u naḫlaptam ša ēpušu bēlī ana bu-di-šu liškun* ARM 10, 17: 12 "may my lord put the cloth and the coat which I made on his shoulders".
3. OB lit. *šadî bu-di-ni* PRAK 1 B 472 i 10 "the hills of our shoulders".
4. OB lit. *ina bu-di-ia ēmidam šadîʾam* CUSAS 10, 5: 5 (Gilg.) "with my shoulder I leaned against a mountain".
5. Of snake: OB lit. *rapšā bu-da-šu* CUSAS 32, 48: 1 "broad are its shoulders". Cf. George, ib. p. 107 n. 1: cobra?
6. Of scorpion: OB lit. *bu-da-šu libittum* ib. 49: 7 "its shoulders are brick".

būdu III, *budû* "a sacrifice or cultic ceremomy"; + LB

1. Lex.: *lú-bala* = *bēl bu-di-im* MSL 12, 170: 407 (Talon ARM 24 p. 215) "man on duty = lord of the *b.*". Note also PSD B 72 *bala* C "shoulder", which might indicate that *būdu* III is in fact identical with *būdu* "shoulder".
2. OB *inūma šarrum bu-da-a-am ša* PN *ša* U4 30^{kam} *imḫuru* ARM 24, 65: 12 "when the king received the *b.* of PN on the 30th day".
3. OB DN *bēl bu-di-im* ŠU.NIGIN 14 DUMU^{meš} *bu-di-im ša ana puluḫti kaṣrū* ARM 23, 436: 1, 31 "DN the patron of *b.* ... Altogether 14 members (= responsibles[?]") of *b.*, assembled to venerate DN".
4. OB 5 DUG GEŠTIN ša DUMU^{meš} *bu-*⸢*di-im*⸣ ARM 23, 494: 6 "25 wine pots of members of *b.*".
5. OB 5 GUR *ana bu-*⸢*di-im*⸣ *ša* DN ARM 23, 462: 12 "5 gur of grain for *b.* of DN".
6. OB 1 1/2 GUR *ana bu*!*-*[*d*]*i-im ša* É DN ARM 24, 19: 1' "1 1/2 gur of grain for the *b.* of the house of DN".
7. 1 GÚ.È.A *kitītum ana* PN inūma bu-di-im ša PN *ina bīt mayyāli* ARM 25, 17 "1 linen coat for PN in the time of the *b.* of PN in the bedroom".
8. 1/2 SÌLA *ḫazannu ana bu-di-im ša šarrim ina bīt* DN ARM 24 p. 214 "1/2 sila garlic for the b. of the king in the temple of DN".
9. OB *a-na* LÚ.TUR PN *ša šarrum ana* ⸢*bu*⸣*-di uterra*[*m*] Vincente 1992, 77: 4 "(1 garment) for the boy PN, whom(?) the king returned to the *b.*".
10. LB *udê erî ša ana bu-du* OIP 114, 111: 17 "copper utensils, which are for the *b.*".
11. LB 19 UDU *bu-ud ina pānīšu* AUWE 5, 9 edge 1 (s. also AUWE 5, 11 r. 3) "19 *b.*-sheep at his disposal".
12. AHw *p*/*būdu* II "?", CAD *būdu* B "mng. uncert.", CDA *būdu* III "a festival?" and *pūdu* "design. of sheep". Further lit.: Sasson 2001, 416f.; Jacquet

2011, 57f.; Talon ARM 24 p. 213–215 with unpubl. ref.

MPS (1–2, 10, 11), NR (3–9, 12)

budūḫu (mng. unkn.)

Note that the only ref. *bu-du-ḫi-im* occurs in AHw 117b under *bedû* D. Durand 2002, 34 n. 103 connects the word with *būdu* III, above, and derives both words from *padû* "to spare". However, the spelling with *ḫ* does not favor this derivation. NR

budulḫu, *bidurḫu* and var. "(resin from) bdellium-tree"

1. New LB ref. in Jursa 2009, 158:
a) ^{šim}*bi-du-ur-ḫu* BM 64588.
b) ^{giš}*bi-du-ur-ḫu* NCBT 853.
c) ^{šim}*bi-du-ḫu* Iraq 59, 123 no. 40: 12.
d) *bid-lu-ḫu* BM 65030.
e) ^{šim}*bi-du-uḫ-ḫu* YBC 4173.

2. Gum of *Commiphora mukul*, s. Jursa 2009, 158 n. 51. NR

+ **buggu**? "a bird"; OB

OB *b/pu-ug?-gu-um*^{mušen} Edubba 7, 100: 52 (in list of birds). Not **buqqum*, since the next line of the text has *qa-qú-um* with *qú*.

buginnu, *bukinnu* "bucket, trough"

1. OB lit. *bu-ki-na-am* CUSAS 32, 31 iii 4.
2. NA 9 ^{giš}[*b*]*u*!-*kín*(ḪAR)-*ni* SAA 7, 126 r. 2.

+ **b/puḫdinnu** "part of a chariot"; OB, Hurr. word(?)

OB 1 BU-*uḫ-di-in-nu ša šinni pīri bābušu ḫurāṣam šaknu* ARM 21, 254: 7 "1 *b.* of ivory, its 'gate' is laid with gold". Durand, ib. p. 285f., compares *b/putinnu* (AHw 144 "Knopf des Schuhs", CAD B 356 "button of a sandal") and *puḫtu* (AHw 877 "ein Kupfergerät", CAD P 493 "a tool") and translates "shaft" ("timon").

+ **buḫratum** "an offering of warm dishes"; OB

1. *aššum bu-uḫ-ra-tim ana* DN$_1$ *n*[*aqêm*] *bēlī išpuram* [*i*]*na panītimma aššum bu-uḫ-ra-t*[*im*] *šuttum innamerma ... bu-uḫ-ra-tam ana* DN$_1$ *u...* DN$_2$ *liqq*[*û*] *... adī ebūrim 3-šu-*[*ma*?] *bu-uḫ-ra-tum* ARM 26/1 p. 470 no. 231: 5ff. "my lord wrote me about [offering] warm dishes to DN$_1$. Previous to this a dream about an offering of warm dishes had been seen ... They must offer a warm dish to DN$_1$ and ... DN$_2$ ... 3 times an offering of warm dishes until the harvest".
2. S. the disc. of Durand, ib. p. 471 n. a. Similary Heimpel 2003, 265. Cf. *buḫru*, below. Durand 1989b, 35 n. 26 (s. also Durand 2004b, 189 n. 424; Stol 2008, 354), based on the idiom *puḫram nadānum* "to hold an assembly" (s. *puḫru* here), reads *pu-uḫ-ra-tim ... n*[*a-da-nim*]. This is, however, unconvincing, because a) the same word in the same text is used with *liqq*[*û*], b) the mng. "to make an assembly for a god" would remain unclear, c) there is no other occurence of a fem. (pl.) **puḫra/ātum* (note, however, a single ref. for *puḫurtu* in CAD P 502 in broken context). Disc. of etym. (not Amor.!) Streck 2000, 87. MPS, NR

buḫru "cooked state, cooked food"; + OB

1. Lex.: *li-im* : NE : *bu-úḫ-rum* CUSAS 12 p. 9: 35 (Ea).
2. OB *bu-uḫ-ri-im ša* ^{d}*Da*[*g*]*an* FM 8, 81

no. 23: 8 “offering of warm dishes for Dagan”.
3. Cf. *buḫratum*, above.

bukānu “(wooden) pestle”

1. OB lit. [*zi*]*bbatāšu kī bu-ka-nim* Fs. Wilcke 61f. Sb 12360: 5 “(the snake’s) two tails are like a pestle”.
2. Edzard 1970b: *bukānam šūtuq* (CAD 308f.) “man hat ihn/es am *b.* vorbeigehen lassen”: the Akkadian expression implies that a *bukānu* was set up and the person (the seller) passed it (and did not stride over) to conclude a sale. Cf. also Malul 1985, 66ff. MPS (1), NR (2)

+ **buk(k)u**? I “a bird”; OB, SB

1. Lex. [*u*5]-*bi*mušen = *b*/*pu-ku*/*qú*-[ ] Emar 6/4, 555: 118’ (Ḫḫ XVIII).
2. OB *b*/*pu-ku*/*qú-um*mušen Edubba 7, 100: 64 (in list of birds). For l. 18 s. *būṣu*.

bukku II “to dance”; foreign word(?)

OB lex. *bu-uk-ku* = MIN (*raqādu*) MARI 5, 412 BM 38590: 14.

bukru “son, child”

SB *bu*12(U)-*kúr* PN SpTU 2, 28: 19; AOAT 2, 48 no. 115: 2 (colophon) “son of PN”. S. Oelsner 1996, 443 n. 32. NR

buku s. *buk*(*k*)*u* I

būku s. *pūku*

bukurtu “first-born daughter”

NA lit. *ištartu* ⸢*bu*⸣-*kur*-⸢*tú*!⸣ SAA 3, 8: 21 “(Irnina), first born goddess”.

+ **bulālu** “goo”; SB

qēm KUR-*nu*-DIB *kīma bu-la-lim īnīšu taptanaššaš* SpTU 3, 83: 2 “you repeatedly smear his eyes with a powder of *šadânu-ṣabītu*-stone as if with goo”. Cf. *balālu*. Hardly the *bulālu* plant, as von Weiher, ib. p. 112 suggests.

bullu I “to throw down, cast away”

1. SB [*ṣeḫru*] *u rabû ú-ba-al-lu dulla* STC 1, 220: 6, 8 Reschid/Wilcke 1975, 61 “[young] and old cast away the work”.
2. The form *ubtīl* derives from *bullu* (AHw 137a; von Soden 1966, 358; 1968, 459; Reschid/Wilcke 1975, 60f.) and not from *abālu* (CAD A/1, 17b and 29a). NR

bultu “a textile”; + LB

Disc. by Zawadzki 2010, 421. LB 1-*en bul-tu*4 ib. 423 BM 61528: 4.

bulṭu “life; cure, healing”

1. Pl. (cf. AHw *b.* 5) also OB, mng. “life”: *bu-ul-ṭú ana māt bēliya iššaknū* MARI 8, 327 A.3394: 9 “life was established for the land of my lord”.
2. Deller 1966, 316: NA *ina bu-ul-ṭi gabbu akī an-ni-ie-e qabi* “in all prescriptions it is said as follows” SAA 10, 326: 3. MPS (1), NR (2)

+ **bulṭūtu** “life, health”; MB Ekalte

PN *ina bu-ul-ṭú-ti-šu aḫḫē ušēšibma šīmti bītišu* ... *išīm* WVDOG 102, 19: 2; 54: 2; 65: 2; 92: 2 “PN, in full command of his mental faculties, let the brothers enter and drew up a will of his estate”.

bulû “dry wood”; + NA

1. OB lit. MUŠ *bu-li-a*-⸢*tim*⸣ CUSAS 32, 27: 20 “snake of the dry wood”. Note *bulī*- instead of *bulā*-.

2. Pl. NA *ša dullu annê gabbi bu-le-e memēni lā iddinannâ*[*še*] SAA 16, 40: 12 "for all that work, nobody has given u[s] dry wood".

būlu "animals, livestock"

Mayer 2016, 197: Usually masc. For fem. s. *bu-lim ṣeḫḫertu* MSL 14, 366: 290 (Ea IV, s. CAD B 313 *b*. lex. sect.). *kīma bu-lu elī šamkānī ḫabrat* RA 36, 10: 9 "as the animals(?) are superior to the servants".

bunbullu "cone(?)"

For the mng. "cone" cf. Kwasman 1999, 5f.; Cherry apud Luukko/van Buylaere 1987, 61, citing Neo-Aram. *banbūl gelīdi* "icicle". Diff. Jursa 2009, 164 n. 82: "tuber". MPS, NR

bunna(n)nû "physiognomy, (facial) features"

von Soden 1968, 459: IVR 24 no. 1: 34 (CAD B 317b) read *bu*[*-ni*! *š*]*u-un-na-ta* "you are different with respect to (your) appearance". NR

bunnû "beautiful"

A bird: OB *bu-nu-um*[mušen] Edubba 7, 100: 61 (in list of birds).

buntu "daughter"; + OB

a-bu-un-ti luštuḫma CUSAS 10, 12: 8 "let me grow long for the daughter".

būnu II, *bunnu* "goodness; features"; pl. "face"

1. OB *bu-né ša* GN ARM 26/2 p. 23 no. 293: 5 "face of GN".

2. OB *ṣubātam ana bu-ni-ka ul ēpuš* AbB 13, 103: 7' "I did not make the garment for your good appearance".

3. *ša būnī epēšu*:

a) OB *ša ... ša bu-ni-ni ippušu u pānīni ana ṣalāmi lā inaddinu* AbB 10, 147: 10 "who does that of our favor (lit. countenance) and does not let our face become black".

b) *ša bu-ni-ia li-pu-uš* BMS 19: 26 "may he do that of our favor".

c) Kraus apud Walker 1973, 124f.: the idiom means "to read every wish from somebody's face"; cf. already AHw 138 *b*. 2b: "was in meinen Mienen liegt".

4. OB *bu-nu namrūtum ša* DN *ili ālika limḫurūka* AbB 13, 140 r. 4' "may theshining countenance of DN, the god of your city, welcome you".

5. NA *ṣalmu šarri ... ina muḫḫi bu-un-ni ... aqabbâššunu* SAA 13, 34: 9 "The royal image ... I could speak with them about (its) features".

6. NB *ina bunnī* "before" synonymous to *ina panī*: *šandabakkū maḫrūte ša ina bu-un-ni-ka* SAA 18, 3: 5 "the former *šandabakku*s who were there before you". Cf. comm. ib.

7. SB *ša būnīšu* synonymous to *ša panī* + suffix: *ša bu-ni-šú ippalis* CTMMA 2 no. 5: 15' "he looked at that which was in his sight". Cf. Maul, ib. p. 53 ad 15'. MPS (1–3), NR (3–7)

bunzerru, + *b/pi/enzurru*, + *pezzurru* "web, enclosure, trap"

1. New by-form *b/pi/enzurru*, *pezzurru*:

a) Lex. *bi/pi-in-zur-ru* = *ṣulūlu* AOAT 50, 347: 194 (Malku) "web = shelter".

b) Cf. also CAD P 326 *penzurru* (in AHw "ein Funktionär"); s. Civil 2006, 60.

2. Related is also CAD *pizzir* "cobweb" = AHw *pizzer* "a plant". A connection with *bisṣūru* "vulva" (CAD P 452f. s. v.

pizzir; Civil 2006, 60; Hrůša, AOAT 50, 219), is doubtful.

3. ^{kuš}*kin-tur* = *bu-un-zi*!-*ir*!-*ri*! Ḫḫ 11: 144 (Civil 2006, 59). MPS (1–2), NR (3)

buppānu "face"; + OB

1. OB *têrētum* ... *bu-up-pa-na-am abkā* ARM 26/1 p. 349 no. 171: 10' (Heimpel 2003, 241) "the extispicies ... are turned on their face (= are perplexing)".
2. Mayer 2016, 197: OB lit. *abikma ina epri bu-up-pa-ni-šu* UET 6/2, 397 i 12'f. "he is thrown into the dust, on his face".
3. Cf. AHw 139 *buppānī*- and *buppāniš*, CAD B 322 *buppāni*.

buqāmu "lamb ready for plucking"

OB *kupram bu-qa-ma* n *šamaššammī idnāniššu*! AbB 13, 118: 25 "Give him bitumen, a *b.* lamb(?), (and) n sesame!"

buqāru "(young) cow"; + MB Emar

1. MB Emar (sheep for Dagan) *bēl bu-*[*q*]*à*(KA)-*ri* Emar 6/3, 373: 39 "the lord of bovines".
2. MB Emar ^{iti}*marzaḫāni ina* UD 14 *bu-qá-ra-tu* Emar 6/3, 446: 85 "month M., at day 14, (rite of) cows(?)". Diff. Pentiuc 2001, 141: *pugarātu* "funerary rites".
3. For further ref. and disc. s. Pentiuc 2001, 36f. Cf. *baq*(*a*)*ru*. NR

buqlu "malt, vegetables"

1. OAkk NUMUN *bu-uq-lu* RA 55, 94 no. 407: 3 "seed of *b.*".
2. OA *bu-uq-lam* AKT 2, 26: 17, s. *bappiru*.
3. OA *ištū ša bu-uq-*[*lá*]-*tím ana ša bu-uq-lá-tím*!(ed.: *tim*) *išaqqal* AKT 7a, 149: 4, 5 "he will pay from the (time of) malt until the (time of) malt(?)".
4. OA *ana bu-uq-lá-tim išaqqulū* Prag 500: 6 "they shall pay at (the time of) the malt".
5. OB *šeʾum ša a-na* MÙNU *rubbê* ^{lú}MÙNU^{meš} *imḫurū* CUSAS 9, 188: 1; s. also 200: 2 "barley, which the maltsters received for risen malt". Dalley, ib. p. 124 comm. on the mng. of *rubbû*: "Might it refer to stimulating fermentation with a new batch of malting barley?" However, *rubbû* is the terminus technicus for making the soaked malt rise, s. Stol 1987–1990, 324 s. v. Malz § 4. *rubbê* is prob. the verbal adj. rather than the inf.
6. Borger 1987, 145f.: SB *pagrī nuballišu u Aḫlamê* ... *kīma* MUNU$_5$ (ŠE. BÙLUG) *áš-ṭe-e-ma* Iraq 16, 186 vi 49 "I spread out the corpsesof his vanguard and of the Arameans like malt" (cf. CAD Š/2, 343b *šêṭu*). Note the incorrect reading *kīma pu-ṣu-di-e-ma* in CAD P 541.
7. For *buqlu* s. Stol 1987b, 65 and 1987–1990, 323: not always "malt", but also "vegetables". MPS (2–5), NR (1, 6–7)

+ **buqqumtu** "a plant(?), (lit. plucked)"; LB

1. 1/2 GÍN *bu-qu-ma-tu*$_4$ (// *bu-qu-mat-tu*$_4$) Fs. Lambert 149 no. 1: 2 "1/2 shekel of *b.*".
2. 2 GÍR-*e bu-qu-ma-tu*$_4$ Fs. Lambert 151 ad. 2 BM 132097 r. 4. NR

buqūmu, *buqūnu* "wool plucking, wool yield"; + OA

1. OA 6 GÍN KÙ.GI *ana paḫār bu-qú-nim išaqqal* AKT 7a, 190: 14 "he will weigh 6 shekels of gold at (the time of) collecting wool".
2. OB *bu-qú-um* GN *libbaqimma* MARI 8, 387 A.2459 r. 3' "may the plucking of GN be carried out".

bur s. *buru*

burāšu "juniper"

1. Lex. *kur a-u*₅! = MIN (= *šadū*) *bu-ra-ši* Emar 6/4, 559: 15 (Ḫḫ XXII) "juniper mountain".
2. OB 5 SÌLA *bu-ra-ša* AbB 12, 94: 17 "5 liters of juniper (berries)" (s. comm. in Charpin 1993, 88).
3. OB 5 SÌLA *karšum* 5 SÌLA *bu-ra-šum* Fs. Garelli 289 BM 97079: 15 and passim.
4. For OB Mari s. Kupper 1992, 164.
5. MB 1 SÌLA NUMUN LI *bīt* G[N] MBLET 78: 6 "1 liter of juniper seeds, house of G[N]". MPS (1, 4–5), NR (2–3)

burbānu "foal(?)"; NA, Aram. lw.

1. *sissê ga-mu-zu lipšuḫū bur-ba-a-ni* SAA 5, 64 r. 6 "the horses have been heavily pressed; the foals(?) should rest out".
2. *bu-ur-ba-ni* SAA 10, 239 r. 9' in broken context.
3. Lanfranchi/Parpola, SAA 5 p. 56 n. 64 consider *ga-mu-zu* and *bur-ba-a-ni* as Aram. lw. (< Aram. *bar bānā* "calf"). Cf. AHw 1549. NR

burbillatu "an insect"; LB

LB *qaqqassu ša*⸣ [*bur*]-⸢*bi-il*⸣-*lat* BabA 1, p. 219f. BM 55551: 5' "his (god's) head is a *b*.-insect's". S. comm. Reynolds, ib. p. 220. NR

burḫiš s. *burṭiš*

burmāmu "piglet; a striped or speckled mouse (lit. speckled, multicolored)"

1. Lex. *péš-giš-gi-a* = *burmāmu* Ḫḫ XIV 190a "mouse of the marsh reed = *b*.".
2. Weszeli 2011–2013, 49f.: not the porcupine (AHw, CAD) but the piglet with striped back and speckled legs and shoulders. This identification is proven by the equation with *šaḫû* "pig" in Malku V 48, because there is no reason to assume that the porcupine was considered a pig as in Europe. Also lit. texts rather point to the pig instead of the porcupine.

burmu "color(ed) part"

1. OA *bīt bu-ur-mi* ARRIM 9, 13: 9. S. Charpin 1991.

2. OB lit. <*ina*> *bu-ur-mi-*⸢*ni*⸣*-ia dīmatum izannun* CunMon. 8, 110: 18 "a tear rains out of the iris of my eyes".

3. OB *bīt birmī*/*burmī*:
a) *ki-sa-al* É *bu-ur-m*[*i*] ARM 26/1 p.214 no. 74: 25 "courtyard of the house with colored decorations".
b) S. already CAD B 257 *birmu* A a for É *bi-ir-mi*/*bu-ur-mi*. The expression refers to the Ištar temple in the palace of Mari (Durand, ARM 26/1 p. 608). MPS (2–3), NR (1)

burru I "a cereal"

1. OB *bu-ra-am ištū* GN *ublūnim* KTT 142: 4 "(who) brought *b*. from GN". S. also *bu-rum*, *bu-ri* ib. index p. 234.

2. OB *bu-rum* ARM 21, 189: 1; 190: 1; 192: 1.

3. OB 6 1/2 GUR *bu-ur-rum* ARM 12, 17: 2 (between ZÍZ "emmer" and *ḫallūru* "peas") and *bu-rum* passim in ARM 12.

4. S. *bu-rum* passim in ARM 23, 586.

5. a) Women in the harem of Mari, summarized as *lāqitāt bu-ri* FM 4, 137 no. 3 vi 5' "gleaners of *b*.".
b) S. the disc. by Ziegler, ib. p. 104f., with corr. of CAD B 339 *burû* A a 1'. Ib. p. 105 n. 625 ref. for this expression in the OB Chagar Bazar texts, among

them *lāqitāt bu-rum* Akkadica Supp. 10, 86: 34.

6. OB ⸢50⸣ ^giš^*parīsī bu-rum* CHANE 75, 325 AlT 56: 15. MPS (1–5), NR (6)

+ **burru II** "tin(?)"; Ugar., Ugar. lw.

⸢1⸣ GÚN *bu-ri* GAL PRU 6, 158: 14: "1 large talent of *b.*" Cf. Huehnergard 1987, 115 and del Olmo Lete/Sanmartín 2004, 240: =(?) alphabetic Ugar. *br*(*r*) "tin". NR

burrû "a temple servant(?)"

Von Soden 1968, 459: MB Bo. MUNUS^meš^ *bur-ru-tim* KUB 10, 91 ii 7. NR

burrumu, *barrumu*, + *burramu* "multicolored, pied, speckled"; + OAkk.

1. Ass. by-form *barrumu* also lex.: *nēbeḫu bar-ru-mu* Emar 6/4, 556: 60 (Ḫḫ XIX) "multicolored belt".
2. OAkk. *bu-ra-ma-ti ēnēki* MAD 5, 8: 13 "your multicolored eyes".
3. OB *naḫlaptu bu-ur-ru-um-tum* FM 1, 140 A.486+M.5319: 41 "multicolored coat", cf. ib. 60, 63, 69.
4. Read the logogr. in EA 22 iv 14 and EA 25 iv 50 GÙN+A = *burrumu*, not U+GÙN = *iḫzētu* (so CAD I 46 and AHw 367). S. Adler 1976, 166 and 202; Moran 1992, 60 n. 45 and CAD S 390a.
5. For ABL 1077 (CAD *b.* e) s. SAA 7, 89 r. 2: *kur-kur-ru*! URUDU *bar-ru-mu* "2 *k.* containers of copper, speckled". MPS (1–3, 5), NR (4)

burruqu "sparkling"

Lex. [... *lú-igi-s*]*i*12-*si*12 "man with sparkling eyes" = *bu-ur-ru-qu* SpTU 4, 190 obv. i 15. NR

burrušu "with hair growing in patches"

Lex. [x *z*]*é*-⸢*zé*⸣-*a-ĝu*10 = [*bu-ú*]*r-ru-šu-ti* CUSAS 12 p. 154 ii 24 "my patches of hair".

+ **buršānu** "servant"; lex., Sum. lw.

bur-saĝ = *bur-šá-nu* Secondary Proto-Lu Fragment II 11 (MSL 12, 83; s. also PSD B 188 ad *bur-saĝ*). NR

būršašillu (or *pūršašillu*) "a bowl"; OB

1. OB *bu-ur-ša-ši-lu*! (ed.: *-ku*) ARM 22, 206 ii 7 in broken context. The text deals with metal, hence the bowl is prob. made of metal and not of stone (s. CAD B 333 *buršušallu* "a stone bowl").
2. OB 1 ^na4^*bu-ur-ša-ši-lum* ARM 24, 84: 6.
3. OB 2 *bu-ur-ša-ši-lu* ib. 95: 1.
4. OB [n] *bu-ur-ša-ši-il-lum* KÙ. BABBAR ib. 97: 30.
5. 1 GAL *bu-ur-ša-ši-lum* KÙ. BABBAR *bābušu u išissu* KÙ.GI MUL ^na4^ZA.GÌN *ina išdišu* 1/2 *mana* 7-*su* KI.LÁ.BI ARM 31, 34: 11' "1 *b.*-bowl (made of) silver, its opening and base are (covered with) gold, on the base (is fixed) a lapis lazuli star, its weight is 1/2 mina".
6. For further ref. s. Guichard, ARM 31, 188f.
7. The syllabic ref. above show that pace MSL 10 p. 25 ad l. 277 the entry in CAD B 333 is correct. *b.* is prob. a substantivation of the genitive construction *b*/*pūru ša š*/*sīli*. MPS (1–3, 6), NR (4–5)

būrtu I "cistern, well, fish pond, source (of river); hole, pit"

1. Lex. *túl kù-ga* = *bu-ur-tum ellatum* Emar 6/4, 559: 121 (Ḫḫ XXII) "clear well".

2. Lex. *túl* ^{d}EN.ZU = *bu-ur-ti* Sîn ib. 122 “well of Sîn”.
3. Lex. *túl* [*lugal-gi*]-*na* = *bu-ur-ti Šarrukī* ib. 123 “well of Sargon”.
4. Lex. *túl* GIŠ.TUK.MAŠ = [*b*]*u-ur-ti* Gilgameš ib. 124 (cf. DCCLT MB Ura 13) “well of Gilgameš”.
5. *túl a kùm-ma* = *bu-*[*ur-*]*ti mê emmūti* ib. 125 “well with hot water”.
6. Lex. *túl a šed*$_{10}$ = *bu-ur-ti mê ki*!-*ṣú-u* ib. 126 “well with cold(!) water”.
7. *túl a du*$_{10}$-*ga* = *bu-ur-ti mê ṭābūti* ib. 127 “well with sweet water”.
8. OB 8 GI$^{ḫi.a}$ *bu-ur-t*[*a*]-*am ept*[*ēma*] *mê ušēlīma* ARM 26/2 p. 307 no. 419: 11’ “I opened a well 8 reeds (= 24 m) (deep) [and] brought up water”.
9. OB *Sūtû bu-ra-ti-ni ... ṣabtū* FM 8, 101 no. 31: 25 “the Sutians have seized our wells”.
10. OB lit. *bu-ur-ti elletum munassiḫat murṣi* CUSAS 32, 54: 3 “pure well that uproots the disease”.
11. Deller 1966, 306: MA PÚ 1 LÚ *šaplat iltaḫlū mû maʾdū* NABU 2013/28 VAT 9968: 13’ “the well was ‘one man’ deep. They filtered (the water). The water (was) much”.
12. SB *ina rēš* [*eql*]*ika* [*b*]*u-u-ur-tá* // ⌜PÚ⌝ *lā teḫerrī* Šūpê-amēli 92 (s. also 93) “do not dig a well at the head of your [fiel]d!” MPS (1–12), NR (11)

būrtu II “cow, she-calf”

1. OB *itti* ÁB.GA *šināti* AbB 9, 89: 17 “with those suckling she-calves”.
2. 1 ^{amar}*bu-ur-ti ši*!-*iz-bi* YOS 12, 447: 1 “1 milk calf”. For *amar* as a determinative here to distinguish between *burtu* “she-calf” and *būrtu* “cow” s. Stol 1995, 179 and 203 n. 42.
3. 2 ^{áb}*bu-ra-tum* 1 ^{gu4}*bu-ru-um* BiMes 3, 38: 1f. “2 she-calves and 1 he-calf”.
4. LB 1-*it* ^{gu4}*bu-ur-ti* CT 55, 691: 2.
5. LB *bu-ur*!-*tum šaddittum* BM 74482 “draft cow” (van Driel 1995, 234 n. 14).
6. LB *bu-ra-tum* BM 50028 (van Driel 1995, 234 n. 14).
7. LB ^{gu4}*bu-uš-ti mit-tum* CT 55, 673: 1 “a dead cow”.
8. LB 1-*it* ^{gu4}ÁB … ^{gu4}*bu-uš-tum* CT 55, 686: 1, 4 (van Driel 1995, 235 n. 14). NR

burṭiš “yak(?)”

NA 6 *bur-ṭiš* StAT 2, 10: 4 “6 yaks(?)”. The spelling shows that *bur*-ḪI-*iš* has to be read *bur-ṭi-iš* and not *bur-ḫi-iš* (AHw, CAD). NR

+ **buru** “son”; NA, Aram. lw.

NA PN$_{1}$ *bur*! PN$_{2}$ SAA 6, 173: 6 “PN, son of PN$_{2}$”.

burû I, OA *burāʾu* “a garment; (reed) mat, mattress”

1. OA *adī bu-ra-im ša litabšika šatašpuranni bu-ra-am lā našʾakkum* AKT 6c, 543: 25, 28 “concerning the *b.* for your dress that you have written about, he will not bring you a *b.*”.

2. OA *bu-ra-am ša Akkedē* ib. 537: 14 “a *b.* from Akkad”.

3. OA 4 TÚG-*té ša Akkadē* ŠÀ.BA 1 *bu-ra-u*[*m*] AKT 2, 44: 5 “4 Akkadian garments, among them 1 *b.*”.

4. OA 1 ^{túg}*bu-ra-ú-um ša Akkadē* Prag 709: 24 “1 *b.* garment from Akkad”.

5. OB mattress padded with diff. fabrics:

a) *ṣubāt bu-re-em* ARM 22, 325: 1 “mattress pad”.
b) 2 *saq bu-ri-im*!? ARM 21, 257: 18 “2 *saqqu*-cloths for a mattress”.
c) ^{túg}*namaḫuš bu-re-e-em* ARM 30 p. 549 M.12479: 5’.
d) *ḫurrur bu-re-e-em* ARM 9, 97: 1.

6. LB: *bu-ra-né-e* CT 56, 744: 6; 294: 24.
7. Disc. of OA ref. by Michel/Veenhof 2010, 232, with further ref. Disc. of OB ref. Durand, ARM 30 p. 31 with further ref.; pace Durand, the OB Mari form is *burûm* < *burāʾum* and not uncontracted ***burēʾu*. MPS (1–4, 7), NR (5–7)

būru I "cistern, well, pool pit; source"

1. Lex. [*túl gí*]*d-da* = *bu-ru ar*[*ku*], [*túl lu*]*gud-*[*da*] = *bu-ru* [*kurû*] Emar 6/4, 559: 130f. (Ḫ̮ḫ̮ XXII) "long / short cistern". Var. [*bu-u*]*r*!*-ti arku* and [*bu-ur*]*-ti kurû* ib. 130f. with wrong gender of adj.
2. OB *bu-ri eperī tumallā* CUSAS 18, 25: 9' "you will fill the wells with earth".
3. OB lit. in transferred mng.: *ali bu-ur sīḫ̮iki* CUSAS 10, 10: 26 "where is the source of your trouble-making?"
4. Deller 1966, 316: All references in CAD B 343a *b.* 2b belong to *pūru* "lot"; s. also Radner 1997, 257 and n. 1374.
MPS (1–3), NR (4)

būru II "calf"

1. Epithet of scorpion: OB lit. *bu-ru-um ekdum munakkipu šamru* RA 88, 155ff. M.15289: 2 "furious calf, goring, raging".
2. LB [gu4]*bu-ra-a-ni* CT 55, 662: 1. S. van Driel 1995, 222. MPS (1), NR (2)

burubalû, + *parbalû* "ruin, unimproved land; a snake"

1. Kraus 1984a, 43 n. 111: Note KI.BUR.BALA CT 8, pl. 44a: 1 // KISLAḪ̮ (= *turbalû*?) CT 48, 31: 1.
2. *b.* is not a regional variant of *kislaḫ̮* or *ki-gál* (so CAD B 343), since all three words occur in Sippar and Dilbat together (Edzard 1970b, 22 n. 41).
3. Snake: OB *amḫ̮aṣ pa-ar-ba-la u pa-ra-ku-ul-la* AMD 1, 224: 10 "I smote the *b.*-snake and *p.*-snake". NR

burullu "a commercial police official"

For OA ArOr. 24 (CAD *b.* a 4') s. Prag 491 with comm.

burūmū, + *burû* "heaven, sky"

1. SB *bu-ru-me* // *bu-ru-ú* Or. 59, 461: 9.
2. SB *e-di-lat bu-ru-ú* SpTU 3, 75: 12 "who closes the heaven".
3. SB *mar-ka-su bu-ru-u*! ib. 19 "bond of heaven".
4. Mayer, Or. 59, 465: *burû* < *burūwū* < *burūmū*.
5. Plene spelling: SB *šiṭir bu-ru-me-*⌜*e*⌝ KAL 3, 34: 3 "writing of the firmament". MPS (2–3, 5), NR (1–4).

burzibandû "a vessel"

1. Deller 1966, 317: NA [dug]BUR.ZI. BÀNDA[meš] Parfümrezepte 33 r. 7.
2. Sallaberger 1996, 110: "ein kleines, verschließbares Gefäß". NR

\+ **burzisallû**? "a vessel"; SB; Sum. lw.

1. *pēndu ina* [dug]⌜BUR⌝.ZI.SAL.L[A] BaF 18, 133: 74 "charcoal in a *b.*-vessel".
2. Maul, ib. p. 149 n. 153 (s. also Sallaberger 1996, 11): read *burzisallû* instead of *pursītu raqqatu*. S., however, Ḫ̮ḫ̮ X 273 (CAD R 171 *raqqu* lex. sect.): [dug]BUR.ZI.SAL.LA = (*pursītu*) *raqqatu*. NR

burzisilagallû "a pot holding one sila"; + NA

5 BUR.ZI.SÌLA.GA[L] CTN 1 pl. 38: 14' (as a subdivision of the *šappu*-container, s. Postgate 1976, 69 § 6.4.2). NR

+ **b/puskatu?** (mng. unkn.)

OB (on the gall bladder) *bu-us-ka-⸢tam?⸣ peṣûti* CUSAS 18 p. 296: 19 "white *b.*"

+ **bussanû** (mng. uncertain); LB

1 GÚ *šá bu-sa-né-e* KÙ.⸢SIG$_{17}$⸣ YOS 17, 246: 5 (Beaulieu 2003, 195; list of jewelry of Nanāya) "1 gold necklace with *b.*". NR

bussuru "to bring, send a message"

1. CAD B 347b *b.* 2a: ABL 1166 r. 9 read with Deller 1966, 317 and SAA 10, 286 (s. also CAD P 311b) *ú-pa-za-ru-ú-[ni]* "I do not conceal [anything]".
2. For an alleged G-stem s. rather *baṣāru.* MPS (2), NR (1)

+ **būsu** (or *bussu*) "a bird"; OB

As piece of jewellery:
1. (gold) *ša* MUŠEN *bu-si-im* ARM 24, 133: 4.
2. (gold for) 1 MUŠEN *bu-si-im* GAL KÙ.GI ib. 122: 3 "1 big golden *b.* bird".
3. Talon, ib. p. 122 connects the word with *būṣu* "hyaena; a bird", but the shift from *ṣ* to *s* would be difficult to explain.

+ **buṣāru** "struggle, quarrel"; OB

1. *ina birīt* GN$_1$ *[b]u-ṣa-ru šakin ḫaziyannam ana* GN$_1$ *ḫaziyanna ana* GN$_2$ *[bēlī l]išpuramma [… m]uškēnim liṣṣurū [akkī]ma mātum ina qāt bēliya [lā uṣṣ]û* ARM 28, 45: 6 "between (diff. parties of) GN$_1$ a struggle has broken out. [My lord] may send a mayor to GN$_1$ and a mayor to GN$_2$, that they protect the [...] of the poor [so tha]t the land does not [get out of] control of my lord".
2. *bu-ṣa-ru-um i-a* GN <*it*>*taškan* ARM 2, 38: 18 "in GN a struggle broke out".
3. CAD B 346 has a word *busāru* "announcement", derived from *bussuru*, for which only the ref. ARM 2, 38 is mentioned. AHw does not list such a word. Durand 1997, 521 proposes a word *buṣāru "rupture"* instead, a proposal accepted by Kupper, ARM 28 p. 61 with translation "dissension". Durand 2000, 547 offers the translation "divergence d'opinion/fracture sociale" and derives the word from *baṣāru* "zerbeißen" (AHw 110), "to tear off" (CAD B 134).

buṣinnu, *bi/eṣinnu* "lamp wick, lamp"; +OA

1. By-form *bi/eṣinnu* also OA:
a) *be-ṣí-nam* Kt d/k 38 b: 13 (Balkan 1986, 3 n. 4).
b) *bi-ṣí-nu ana bīt* PN *šakin* Kt 88/k 1070: 9 "the lamp is placed at the house of PN". Cf. also *bi-ṣí-nam* ib. 12 (Donbaz 1993, 148, n. 55).
c) S. also *bi-ṣí-ni* Kt h/k 87: 3, CAD U 282 s. v. *ūsu* A b; Dercksen 1996, 77.

2. OB *bu-ṣi-ni* ARM 18, 32: 27.

3. OB *bu-ṣí-nu* ARM 23, 74: 12.

4. OB (oil) *ana pašāš bu-ṣi-ni ša gizillê* FM 3, 245 no. 95: 8' "for anointing the wicks of the torches".

5. OB 30 *riksī ša bu-ṣí-ni* AbB 7, 13 // 14: 8 "30 packages of lamp wicks".

6. SB *bu-ṣi-ni nūri* KAL 1, 20 r. 5 "wick of a lamp". MPS (2–6), NR (1)

būṣu I "hyaena; a bird"; + OA

1. As PN:
a) OA *Bu-ṣí-ia* AKT 2, 58: 17.
b) OB *Bu-ṣú-um* KTT 15: 10; 48: 4.
c) *Bu-ṣí-im* ARM 24, 132: 6.

2. OB *bu!-ṣú-um*^{mušen} Edubba 7, 100: 18 (in list of birds). For l. 64 s. *buk(k)u*.

3. S. AHw *būṣu* I 2 "etwa 'Steinhuhn'" und CAD B *būṣu* C "a bird". It is unclear whether the ref. for the PN refers to the hyaena or the bird.

4. Cf. *būsu*.

būṣu II "fine linen, byssus; glass"; + OB

1. OB 1 DUG GEŠTIN *ša itti* ^{dug}*bu-ṣí-im ana bīt* PN … *innadnu* AWTL 39: 2 "1 jar of wine which was given to the house of PN together with a glass vessel".
2. NA 1^{dug}*bu-u-ṣú kudimme* SAA 12, 77 r. ii 6, cf. i 6 "1 glass-vessel of *k*.-seeds".
3. LB *dullu bu-ú-ṣu u dullu šīpāti rabû u qalla ulammassu* Persika 9, 204 BM 31803: 6 "he will teach him the work of byssus and the work of wool, big and small".
4. LB [*ša ana*] *bu-ú-ṣu illikūnu* CT 55, 147: 9 "who have gone away to acquire byssus".
5. LB GADA *bu-ú-ṣu* NCBT 597: 2 (unpubl., s. Beaulieu 1989, 71).

MPS (2), NR (1, 3–5)

+ **buṣūtu** (or *b/puṣṣutu*) "an object"; SB

bu-ṣu-tum (after the plant *argannu* before *tamšīlu*) Emar 6/4, 545: 496 (Ḫḫ V–VII).

buʾšānu "bad smell (a disease)"

1. *bu-ʾ-šá-nu dān ṣibissu kīma nēši napšāra iṣbat kīma barbari iṣṣabat nurza iṣbat nu*[*rba*] *iṣṣabat lišāna ina ebbūbi ḫašê ittadi kussâšu* SpTU 1, 44: 55 // BAM 543 iii 43'' (Scurlock/Andersen 2005, 40) "mighty is the affliction of *b*. It seized the uvula like a lion; it seized the hard palate like a wolf. It seized the soft p[alate]; it seized the tongue. It set up its throne in the windpipe (trachea and/or bronchi)".
2. *dān ša bu-ʾ-šá-nu ṣibissu kīma nēši qaqqada i*[*ṣbat kīma barbari iṣ*]*bat luʾḫa iṣbat* KA *iṣbat lišāna ina birīt šinnāti ittadi* [*kussâšu*] SpTU 1, 44: 65 // BAM 543 iii 58' (Scurlock/Andersen 2005, 41) "mighty is the affliction of *b*. It [seized] the head like a lion; [it] seized the throat [like a wolf]. It seized the mouth; it seized the tongue. It set up its throne among the teeth".
3. *šumma* [*amēlu* KA]-*šú bu-ʾ-šá-nu ṣabitma* SpTU 1, 44: 29 (Scurlock/Andersen 2005, 40) "if *b*. has seized [a person's nose/mouth]".
4. *šumma amēlu appašu u pâšu bu-ʾ-šá-nu ṣabitma* SpTU 1, 44: 26 // BAM 543 ii 19 (Scurlock/Andersen 2005, 40) "if *b*. has seized a person's nose and mouth".
5. [*šumma pīšu bubuʾ*]*ta mali u illātūšu illakā bu-ʾ-šá-nu šum*[*šu*] AOAT 43, 357: 87 (Scurlock/Andersen 2005, 41) "[if his mouth] is full of boil(s) and his saliva flows, [it] is called *b*.".
6. [*šumma amēlu pīšu b*]*u-ʾ-šá-nu ṣabit ina rebīt šinnātišu* […] BAM 157 obv. 10' (Scurlock/Andersen 2005, 41) "[if]*b*. seizes [a person's mouth] and in the 'square' of his teeth […]".
7. *šumma amēlu šinnīšu munû u bu-ʾ-šá-nu* … SpTU 1, 44: 80 (Scurlock/ Andersen 2005, 41) "if *munû* and *b*. … a person's teeth".

NR

+ **bušītu** "possessions"; MB Ekalte

bu-ši-tum u bāšītu ... uzazzā WVDOG 102, 36: 17 "possessions and valuables ... they will divide".

bušlu "ripening, (s)melting; molten"; + EA

1 GA.RÍG *ša* NA₄ *bu-u*[*š-lu*] EA 25 ii 62 "1 comb of mol[ten] glass" (s. CAD M/2, 291a *mušṭu* a4' and Moran 1992, 82 n. 20).

NR

būštu, *būltu* "shame, dignity"

1. OB (the army of the enemy's country) *ina bu-ul-ti u lumun libbi iturra* CUSAS 18, 29 §57': 48' "will return in shame and misery".
2. OB *ina qāt bu-uš-tim* ARM 27, 133: 33 "from shame".
3. NB *ina bu-ul-ti-ia anaḫḫis* SAA 17, 27 r. 2 "I return in dignity". Prob. not *bulṭu* "life" because of *-ti-* instead of *-ṭi-*.

bušṭītu "wood worm"

SB *namburbû lumun bal-ṭi-it-ti* SpTU 1, 6: 20 "apotropaic ritual (to avert) the evil (portended) by a wood worm".

būšu "goods, property"

Deller 1966, 306: MA *ba-ši-šu bu-ši-šu* VDI 80, 71: 21. NR

bu'šu, *būšu* "stench; a stinking plant"; +OB

1. OB lit. *erṣetum ulid bu-ša-am bu-šum ulid luḫummâm* YOS 11, 5: 2 "the earth bore the stench, the stench bore the mud".
2. Whether ^{giš}*bu-šu* in ARM 19, 260–264: 4; 265: 5 (early OB), mentioned among beer, groats and barley as a food stuff, belongs to the *bu'šu* plant, as suggested by Limet, ib. p. 23f., is unclear. The *bu'šu* plant, as well as its equation *aktam*, and also the frequently attested *būšānu* plant (mng. "like *bu'šu*") are always written with det. Ú whereas our word has the det. GIŠ. Kupper 1992 does not mention the word in his disc. of trees in the Mari texts.

+ **bušuttu** (or *pušuttu*) "grief, depression"; SB, foreign word(?)

Lex. *nissatu* : *bu-šu-ut-tu*! Emar 6/4, 564: 4' (after the diseases *asakku* : *ḫurḫurru*, *murṣu* and *di'u*); cf. disc. by Pentiuc 2001, 42. MPS, NR

+ **butāqu** "cut (of rush)"; SB

bu-ta-qa ša ašli BagF 18, 140: 142 "cut of a rush". For *batāqu* + *ašlu* s. also CAD A/2, 448. NR

būtinnu, + *bu'tinnu* "button; part of a chariot (drawbar?)"; + OB; Hurr. lw.(?)

1. OB *ana* 2 *bu-uḫ-di-nu ša me*[*šēni*] ARM 30 p. 227 M.12169: 3 "(gold) for 2 buttons for shoes".
2. OB *narkab*[*tu*] ... 1 *bu-uḫ-di-in-nu ša šinni pīri bābušu ḫurāṣam šaknu* ARM 21, 254: 7 "a chariot ... 1 drawbar(?) of ivory, its opening is laid with gold".
3. *b*[*u*]*-ti-in-na-šu-nu ḫilipa* EA 25 ii 42 "their b[ut]ton(s) are of *ḫilibû*-stone" (Moran 1992, 76 and 81 n. 13).
4. Disc.: Durand, ARM 21 p. 285f.; ARM 30 p. 169; Richter 2012, 322f. *puḫdinni* "timon"; Arkhipov 2012, 171 (with further ref.).

MPS (2), NR (1–4)

+ **buti'u** "a textile"; Ur III

4 ^{túg}*bu-ti-um*? ^{giš}*be-rum* SIKI ^{giš}GARIĜ AKA CUSAS 3, 807: 2, s. *birru*.

+ **buttatu** (or *puttatu*) "a rope"; OB

7 *ušpaḫe* GAL 10 *našpanu* 10? ^{eš}*bu-ut-ta-tum* 2 *lû arku* GÍD.DA ARM 30 p. 227 M.9889: 7 "7 big *u.*-cords, 10 *n.*-tethers, 10 *b.*-ropes, 2 long *l.*-ropes". Derivation from *pâdu* "to fasten, affix" CAD P 10 pace Durand, ib. p. 181 impossible. MPS, NR

buṭnānu "terebinth"

Clearly terebinth: *ḫīli* ⌜*allānu*⌝ u ^{giš}*bu-ṭu-na-nu* // [*bu*]*ṭun ša šadî* Lamaštu ii 189 (Farber 2014, 125) "resin of oak tree and terebinth (of the mountains)".

buṭnu, + *buṭmu* “terebinth”

1. OB ^{giš}*bu-uṭ-mi naksūtim* FM 2, 164 no. 88: 8 “felled terebinths”.

2. Deller 1966, 317: NA *gupnī ša* ^{giš}*bu-ṭu-ni* CT 53, 230: 7 “terebinth trunks”.

3. *buṭmu* is a back formation from *buṭumtu*. MPS (1, 3), NR (2)

buṭumtu, + *buṭubtu*(?) “terebinth; green seed (of cereals)”

1. Terebinth and oak:

a) OB *lišsī’aššumma ina bu-ṭù-um-tim lišar’ibaššum ina allānim* CUSAS 32, 48: 16 “may he shout at it in the terebinth, make it tremble in the oak”. Cf. comm. George, ib. p. 109 and CAD B 358 *buṭnu* a for association of terebinth and oak.

b) SB *a-kal al*!*-la-an ù bu-ṭù*!*-um-*⸢*ta*⸣ AulaOr. Suppl. 23, 14: 6 “eat(!) the oak and the pistachio!”

2. OB *ana* KUR.RA GN *ana warkat* ^{giš}*bu-uṭ-ma-tim parāsim awīlī* [...] KUR.RA GN *kalâšu ittalkūnimma* ^{giš}*bu-ṭú-um-tum maḫṣat u annûmma* ^{giš}*b*[*u-u*]*ṭ-m*[*a-t*]*im nisan šattim ša ina pānīšunu ilqûnim ana ṣēr bēli*[*ya*] *ušābilam* ARM 27, 123: 7, 10, 12 “[I sent] men to mount GN in order to investigate the matter of the terebinths. They went through all of GN, but the terebinth(s) had been smashed, and (therefore) I have now sent to my lord the terebinths from the beginning of the year, which they had collected earlier”.

3. OB *bu-uṭ-ma-tim* ARM 27, 53: 7, 10.

4. OB *ana* ^{d}KUR.RA *allikma* ^{giš}*bu-ṭú-um-tam āmurma ul išar maḫṣat* FM 3, 189 no. 19: 7 “I went to the mountain and inspected the terebinth(s). (The situation) was not in order. (The terebinth[s]) were smashed”.

5. *bu-ṭú-ma-tum* ARM 21, 153: 12; 155: 13 (after dates).

6. *bu-ṭù-um-tum* FM 12, 171 M.10593: 5; 192 M.10106: 4; 203 M.11134: 4; 216 M.9994: 4.

7. OB 2 ^{giš}*bu-ṭú*!*-tum* RA 90, 127 NBC 8531: 1 (with corr. in AfO 46/47, 568) “2 (beams of) terebinth”.

8. OB Prob. by-form *bu-ṭub-tum* FM 2, 42 no. 13: 5’, 10’ (in broken context), s. Maul, ib. p. 44.

9. 1 ANŠE ZÍD *bu-ṭù-um-t*[*im*] ARM 10, 20: 8 “1 homer of *b.* flour”.

10. 1 (PI) *nāḫum* 10 (SÌLA) *bu-uṭ-na-tim* ARM 10, 116: 29 “1 (PI) of lard, 10 (liter) of *b.*”.

11. As PNf:

a) OB *Bu-ṭú-um-tum* ARM 21, 403 viii 15.

b) Deller 1966, 317: NA ^{f}*Bu-uṭ-nu-tu* VAT 8674 r. 16; VAT 8689 r. 3’; VAT 8681 r. 7’. S. PNA 1, 357 *Buṭnutu*.

12. On terebinths s. Postgate / Streck 2011–2013 with previous lit. Etym., there is only a single *buṭumtu* (AHw) and not three (CAD B 359f. *b.* A–C; Powell 1984, 52): the mng. “green seeds (of cereals)” is derived from “green nuts of the terebinth” (s. Postgate/Streck, ib. p. 595 with previous lit.). Powell, ib. p. 52: in OB, MB crushed emmer, in NB prob. husked emmer.

MPS (1–3, 5-6, 8–12), NR (4, 7, 11)

bu’’û II “to look for”; + OA

1. Stative:

a) OB (1 ship) *ul bu-uḫ-ḫa-a*[*t*] ARM 13, 95: 7 “has not been inspected”.

b) (2 ships) *ul bu-uḫ-ḫa-a*! ib. 96: 8, s. Durand 2000, 31.

2. Deller 1966, 317: NA *issu libbi šallete ša tūṣânni* [*ub*]*-ta-’i* 30 *napšāte* [*ina lib*]*bi ātamar* CTN 2, 194: 9 “out of the captives who came out I have searched and chosen 30 persons".

3. Deller 1966, 317f.: NA *anāku alpānī qātē manni ú-ba-ʾu* SAA 5, 37: 26 "(I shall show the king) whom I hold accountable for the oxen."

MPS (1), NR (2–3)

buzzuʾu "to encroach on, to loot"

1. OB *gerseqqûka qāssunu išakkanūma šurīpam ú-ba-az-za-ḫu* FM 2, 149 no. 82: 21' "your servants lay claim to and loot the ice".

2. OB *kī ... ālam šêtu taṣbatāma tu-ba-zi-ḫa* ARM 26/2 p. 339 no. 435: 14 "how could you seize that city and encroach on it?".

3. OB ⸢*ú*⸣-*ba*!-*zi-ḫu* ARM 28, 101: 38 "they looted (sheep)".

4. OB PN *ana mātiya iḫḫabtamma* 3 4 *ālānīya ilqē mātī ú-ba-za-ḫa* ARM 26/2 p. 199 no. 384: 27' (Heimpel 2003, 332) "PN made incursions to my land and took 3, 4 of my cities. He was looting my land".

5. OB *awīlam šâtu ina* GN *iṣbatūma ú-ba-zi-ḫu-šu u mimma ša našû īkimūšu* MARI 6, 63 n. 129: 20 "they seized that man in GN and looted him and took away from him all he was carrying".

6. OB *kīma bu-zu-ḫu-um ibaššī ú-ba-az-za-ḫa-an-ni* ARM 10, 77 r. 7', 8' "whenever there is (a possibility) to encroach (on me) he encroaches on me".

7. For ARM 5, 39: 13 (CAD B 185a *b.* 2b; AHw 145b) s. *pasāsu*.

8. a) Heimpel 2003, 332 and 367 translated "to encroach on". Joannès, FM 2, 150 n. c, suggested the slightly diff. nuance "piller", Durand 2000, 547 "agresser qu'un, traiter avec mépris".

b) A short disc. of diff. suggestions (BZḪ, BZʾ/W, BṢʾ) for the etym. of the verb is found in Streck 2000, 85f. s. v. *bazaḫātu*. The verb is perhaps connected with Hebr. BZZ "to plunder, to loot" (HAL I 113, also Arab.; cf. also possible variant BZʾ "to sweep away" HAL I 113) rather than with Hebr. BZʾ/W (AHw 145; cf. Hebr. HAL I 113 "to disdain"). There is no need to postulate an Amor. lw., and a connection with *bazaḫātu* is still semantically difficult.

MPS (1–6, 8), NR (7)

P

****-pa**

Veenhof 2006, 294f. (s. also AKT 6a, 56: 15; 58: 17) postulates the existence of an enclitic particle *-pa* (written BA = *pá*) in OA. However, the mng. and use of this particle as described by Veenhof are similar to that of the particle *-ma*: "used to express surprise or indignation, to give emphasis to a statement, to express a contrast, or frequently in a question ... linked to interrogatives such as *mīnum*, *mannum* and *miššum*". Veenhof connects this alleged particle with Ugar. *-pa*, a conjunction mng. "and (then)" (Tropper 2012 § 83.12). ***-pa* = -BA? is therefore prob. not more than a (graphic or phonetic?) variant of *-ma*. This conclusion is corroborated by spellings of the type *mì-nim*-BA? and *mi-nam*-BA?, that can hardly be interpreted as *mīnappa*, *mīnuppa*(sic) as suggested by Veenhof 2006, 294 but prob. stand for *mīna*/*imma*. For a diff. opinion cf. Kouwenberg 2017, 475–477.

paʾāṣu "to break up, crush"

G "to separate(?)": NA *ip-ta-ṣ*[*u*] SAA 13, 21: 14 in broken context.

D "to separate(?)":
1. NA PN ... *urdē ša* MÍ É.GAL ... *up-te-ii-ṣi ana bēt* PN$_2$ *ittidin* SAA 16, 63: 11 "PN has separated(?) the servants of the queen ... (and) given (them) to the house of PN$_2$".
2. For *ú-pa-ṣi* ib. 127: 21 cf. AHw 807 *p.* D 2a "zerschlagen", CAD P 2 *p.* 2b "he will crush".

padānu, + *padannu* "way, path"

1. Lex. [*gìr*] = *pa*!?*-da-an-núm* Emar 6/4, 537: 486 (Sa Voc.).
2. OB PN ^{d}*I-šar-pa-dan-e-mu-qí* AbB 13, 126: 8 "Išar-adān ('Straight is the path') is my strength". S. CAD P 4 *p.* 1c for similar ref.
3. Mayer 2008, 94: logogr. ŠU + BAR (simplified form of GÌR?) in OB TIM 9, 79: 8, 10 and 14; YOS 10, 17: 38.

MPS (1, 2), NR (3)

+ **pādu** "fetter, handle"

1. Stol 2008, 349: OB ^{giš}*pa-di-im u maškanim* ARM 26/1 p. 283 n. 18 A.3096 "fetter and chain".
2. OB ^{giš}*pa-du ša katappī* FM 7, 114 no. 30: 20 "wooden handles for *k.*-weapons". Corrected in ARM 32 p. 118 to *<na>-pa-du.*
3. Substantivation of the adj. *pādu* "fixed, fastened" (CAD P 7). MPS, NR

pâdu "to confine, imprison"

G OB with two acc. objects:
1. *maškanam i-pa-du-ú-šu* ARM 26/2 p. 70 no. 312: 9' "they fettered him in a *m.*-chain". For *maškanam padû* s. Durand, ARM 26/1 p. 282f. n. a.
2. OB PN *nāšpaḫallam ip-ta-as-sú* FM 9, 270 no. 67: 26 "PN fettered him with a shackle".

D OB with two acc. objects: DUMU^{meš} *šipri* EL[AM.M]A$^{[meš]}$ *maškanam up-ta-i-du-šu-nu-ti* ARM 26/2 p. 165 no. 363: 27 "they put the Elamite envoys in shackles". MPS (G), NR (G, D)

pagālu "to be strong"

D SB ⸢*pu-gu*⸣*-la-ku emūqī* Jiménez 2017, 302: 8 "I am the strongest".

****paggallu**

Stol 2008, 349; Borger 2008, 438: *mušen gal* = *iṣṣūru rabû* (CAD I/J 214b). For MUŠEN.GAL-*lum* s. *mušengallu*. NR

pagru "body; corpse"

1. Labat 1973, 57: Susa logogr. LU. BAD MDP 57, 220 no. 10 r. 5–8.

2. OB *pa-ga-ar-ka e-il* "bind yourself (by a contract)!" AbB 14, 142: 30.

3. Borger 2008, 438: OB *pagra naṣāru*:
a) [*pa-gàr-š*]*a inaṣṣar* CH § 133.
b) [*pa*]*-g*[*à*]*r-ša lā iṣṣurma* CH § 133b.

4. Mayer 2008, 94:
a) *lu-um-ši pa-*[*ag-ri u ṣubātī*] Gilg. MB Emar$_2$ i 8' // [*lu-um-š*]*i*? *pag-ri u ṣubātī* Gilg. SB VI 25 "should I neglect myself and my clothing".
b) *pagar*(LÚ.BAD)*-šú ma-ši* "(if) he has forgotten his body (= if he is not aware of his physical condition) TDP 90: 14 // SpTU 1, 34: 13. NR

pagû, *pagītu*; + *pegû*, + *pegītu* I "monkey"

1. Lex. *pé-gu*, *pé-gi*!*-tum* Emar 6/4, 551: 35f. (Ḫḫ XIV 118f.; MSL 8/2, 16).

2. Stol 2008, 349: OB [*u*] *tamartašunu ša ištū mātim elītim našû* [*šumm*]*a pa-gu*!*-ú šumma sà-ú-um* Amurru 3, 96 A.3297+: 41 "[and] their [pres]ent which they bring from the upper land, [whet]her a monkey, whether a *sà-ú-um*-bird".

3. Representations(?):
a) OB 1 *nūbalim ša pa-gi-i* ARM 25, 160 = ARM 32 p. 219 M.6751: 6 "1 palanquin with (a figure) of a monkey(?)". Arkhipov, ARM 32 p. 148 suggests a sort of wood.
b) OB 1 *ḫullu ... qadum šamnim ša pa-gi-im* ARM 25, 364 = ARM 32 p. 423 M.11392 "1 ring (of silver), together with oil, with (a figure) of a monkey(?)". Arkhipov, ARM 32 p. 148 n. 498 refers *ša pagîm* to *šamnim*; but perhaps it refers to *ḫullu*.

4. SB *mīrānu pa-gi-i ilabbu* JCS 66, 76: 24 (Gilg.) "the young of the monkey used to shriek". MPS (1, 3, 4), NR (2)

****pagû** (AHw *pagû* I 3; CAD P 19 *pagû* B)

Borger 2008, 439; 2010, 289: to be deleted (including logogr. SA.LI). S. already Volk 1989, 202: 87 with comm. p. 250: *mu-mu nar-e*!*-ne sa li-bí-ib-sìg*(PA)*-ge-e-*[*ne*] // *ana šu-mi-ia na-a-ru ina pit-*[*ni*? *ul* ...] "beim (Nennen) meines Namens schlagen die Musiker die Saite(n) nicht an". NR

+ **pāgu** "part of a fish(?)"; SB

Stol 2008, 349: 19 ÙZ Ù.TU-*ma pa-a-ga u* GEŠTU^{ii} *nu-nu* TUK Hunger/Sachs 1988, 198 no. 324B r. 7 "the 19th, a she-goat gave birth and (the kid) has the ... and the ears of a fish". NR

paḫantarru, *paḫattarru* "a blanket or cover"

New spellings:
1. MB Qaṭna \ *pa-ḫa-at-tá-ri* QS 3, 13: 9.
2. MB Qaṭna \ *pa-ḫa-ta-ri* QS 3, 18: 24.

+ **pāḫānu** "responsibility"; MA

1. 5 *ēṣidū pa-ḫa-nu* PN Subartu 14, 9: 9 "5 harvesters (in the) responsibility of PN".

2. Related to *pā/īḫatu* and perhaps also *paḫnu* (for the latter s. CAD P 33), cf. Radner Subartu 14 p. 89.

paḫāru I "potter; a plant"; + LB

1. Relatively rarely spelled syllabically: MA *pa-ḫa-ru* Chuera 60: 5.
2. LB "potter-plant": Ú LÚ.BÁḪAR *ša ḫarru ina ziqqi tašakkan* Fs. Lambert p. 176 no. 21A: 17 (s. also ib. no. 21B r. 24) "you put ... and 'potter-plant' from a ravine in a wineskin". S. also Finkel, ib. p. 177. MPS (1), NR (2)

paḫāru II "to gather"

+ **DRt 1.** OB *up-ta-ḫa-aḫ-ḫi-ru-ma* ARM 1, 69: 15 (s. Charpin/Durand 1988 no. 9).
2. *ṣābum ... ina māḫirim up-ta-ḫa-ḫi-ir-ma* A.396 (RA 83, 30 CC and n. 21) "the troops ... have gathered together against the enemy".
3. Cf. Stol 2008, 349; Kouwenberg 2010, 440.

Št2 OB lit. *uš-ta-pa-aḫ-ḫa-ru ittīka* Gilg. RA 101, 59ff.: 21 "I shall gather with you" (instead of *uštamaḫḫaru*).
MPS (Št2), NR (DRt)

+ **paḫārūtu**(?) "pottery making"; OB

Stol 2004a, 134: BÁḪAR-*ut-tim* VS 29, 20: 7 (or LUNGA-*ut-tim* = *sīrāšûtim* "brewing"?). NR

+ **paḫāttu** "fear"; OB, Amor. lw.

1. *šumma niḫittumma mim-ma ittabšī* [*elī*]*ni*! *pa-ḫa-tu-um* [*lā*! *išš*]*akkan* ARM 5, 68: 18 "if any trouble comes up fear shall [not be] imposed [on] us". Cf. Durand 1998, 98 no. 504 n. e.
2. *šumman ... iša*ʾʾ*urūnim ulāman pa-ḫa-at-tu-um* [*i*]*štētman ittenpeš* FM 2, 113 no. 71: 14' "if they had ... *helped* me, there would not have been a single case of fear".
3. ⸢*ù pa*?-*ḫa*⸣-*t*[*um*? ...] FM 2, 27 no. 6 r. 1'.
4. Cf. Streck 2000, 109; 2007, 151; *paḫādu* AHw 810, CAD P 20.

paḫāzu "to be arrogant"

NB *ip-ḫi-z*[*a*] SAA 17, 109: 17 in broken context.

+ **paḫipʾetan**? "for my sake(?)"; MB Qaṭna, Hurr. word

\ *pa-ḫé-ip-e-ta*!(copy: *ni-wa*)-*an* QS 3, 4: 33, s. the disc. ib. p. 63.

+ **pāḫu** "breathing"; NA, Aram. lw.

1. *ša ḫīṭūšunu pa-a-ḫi bēl šarrāni* [*rēmu*? (xx)] *liškunšu* SAA 10, 118: 5 "let the lord of kings par[don] those whose guilt is (light like) breath".
2. *ša ḫīṭūšunu pa-*[*a-ḫi rēmu*] *liškun-ma* SAA 17, 83: 5' "have [compassio]n on those whose crimes are (lig[ht) like breath]".
3. Dietrich, ib. p. 74 n. 83: lw. from Aram. *pwḥ* "to blow, to breathe", *pwḥ*ʾ breath, breeze". NR

pakku II, + *pikku* "a metal or wooden object"

Lex. *lu-uk-ki-iš* = LAGAB = *pa-ak-ku*, *pí-ik-ku* Emar 6/4, 545: 88f. (Ḫḫ V–VII) (followed by *ḫaṭṭu*).

****pakku** C (CAD P 36f.)

Pace CAD prob. = *pakku* I "reason": "go and collect the rest which to care for (? *nasḫur pakku*, lit. to seek reason) you have been instructed (lit. has been given to you)!" (San Nicolò 1954, 368).
NR

pakuttu "wooden stave"

Stol 2008, 349: logogr. GIŠ.PA. KUD (CAD P 37a) does not belong here but stands for *urû* III "ein Zweig; Palmwedel" (AHw 1435b). NR

palāḫu "to fear, revere"

G Spelling: *I-el-kà-pi*$_4$(KA)*-la-aḫ* Tell ed Dēr II (1978) 26: 4 "Fürchte deinen Gott!" (Stol 2008, 350).

Gt SB *pi-it-lu-ḫ*[*u*?] SpTU 4, 157 obv. 17 (Streck 2007, 151). NR

palāku "to devide off, demarcate"

D Stol 2008, 350: OB *ú-pa-al-li-ik* Amurru 3, 119 n. 34 A.1177: 40. NR

palālu I "to guard, watch over, precede"; OAkk Beydar in PN:

1. *Ip-lul-il* Subartu 2, 74 iv 2.
2. *Ip-lul*-DINGIR ib. 109 iv 5 "The god has guarded".
3. Unlikely *palāsu* (Talon, ib. p. 78).

palālu II "to interrogate"

G 1. OA *alī rābiṣum i-pá-li-lu lutammē* AKT 6a, 135: 25 "wherever the attorney interrogates, he may impose an oath".
2. For the mng. "to interrogate under oath" s. Hertel 2013, 366f.

palāqu I "to slaughter, strike down"

G Mayer 2008, 95: MB *ip-lu-uq-ma i-kul-ma* UET 7, 19: 6 "(cow) he slaughtered and ate". NR

palāsu "to look (at)"

G 1. OB *adī ilum i-pa-la-sú* Shemshara 1, 50: 28 "until the god looks (at us)".
2. OB *ina warḫim annîm ilum ana mātim i-pa-la-às* Shemshara 1, 64: 62 "in this month the god will look at the country".
3. Mayer 2008, 95: OB *pa-li-is-ku-um* YOS 10, 9: 29 not a participle (CAD P 53b *p.* 1b: "strike the one who faces you") but stative: "he (= the enemy) is looking towards you".
4. SB *ul inamdinšuma* [*an*]*a* ⌜*pa*⌝*-la-sa arkassu* Gilg. SB IX 159, 162, 166 "it did not allow him [t]o see what was behind [him]". Cf. George 2003, 867 ad l. 140–1.

D For *pu-ul-lu-ši-im pu-ul-li-iš* Iraq 39, 150 (CAD P 54a *p.* 2) s. *palāšu* D.

Dt 1. Borger 2008, 439; Mayer 2008, 95: the verb in CH § 159 (CAD P 54 *p.* 3) is *balāṣu* D, not *palāsu*.
2. Kupper 1988; Borger 2008, 439; Mayer 2008, 95: Delete CAD P 54b *p.* 4 and read *bu-ta-al-lu-ṭì-im* instead of *pu-ta-al-lu-sí-im*. MPS (G, D), NR (G, Dt)

palāšu "to perforate"

D 1. Stol 2008, 350: For Ì.DAB PN … *pu-ul-lu-šu* JCS 29, 150: 12' (CAD P 61a *p.* 2a) s. Hirsch/Hunger 1980, 428a: "gelocht".
2. Mayer 2008, 95: OB PN *ana eqlim kirîm pu-lu-uš* AbB 14, 36: 4' "'pierce' PNf as to the field and garden!". Cf. Veenhof, ib. p. 213f.: an idiom mng. "unmask his behaviour" or "refute his claims".
3. Stol 2008, 350: *ašar pu-ul-lu-ši-im pu-ul-li-iš* Iraq 39, 150: 29, 36 and *ul tu-pa-la-aš* ib. 33, quoted in CAD P 54a under *palāsu*, belong here. Mng. after Durand 1997, 273f., 275 with comm. f.: "slit (bundles of wool)".
4. SB [*bu*]*šṭītu ana marāqi ú-pal-la-áš lānka* Jiménez 2017, 172 Ic 34 "[the wo]odworm bores through your body to grind it". MPS (2, 4), NR (1–3)

****palatuššu** (CAD P 62)

Mayer 2008, 95: delete, s. LB duplicate *Enlil īḫuzu*? *erṣetam ba-ú-la-tu-uš-šu* Iraq 58, 153: 14 "Enlil occupied earth for his subjects". NR

palgu "ditch, canal"

Mayer 2008, 95:
1. SB *mê palgi*(PA_5) BM 65299 r. 1 (unpubl.) "canal water".
2. SB *ṣalam ṭīd* PA_5 *kirî* SpTU 5, 246 iii 6' "figures made of clay from the garden canal". NR

****palīlu** (AHw 816, CAD P 66) s. *pālilu*

pālilu "vanguard, front-runner; sack, bag; safety catch(?)"

1. OB lex. *pa-li-lum* IGI.ŠÈ.DU.ÉRIN = *illat ṣābim* "group of soldiers", *piqitti ṣābi*[*m*] "muster of men", *aḫum rabûm* "big brother" MSL 15, 16: 127f. (Diri); cf. George, CUSAS 18 p. 197.

2. OA Disc. by Michel/Veenhof 2010, 238, with new ref.

3. Mayer 2017, 23f.:
a) OB lit. *nakru pa-li-li-ia ušerreba* CUSAS 18, 28: 11 "the enemy will cause my vanguard to enter".
b) OB lit. *pa-li-il nakri* CUSAS 18, 28: 14 "vanguard of the enemy".

4. OB "sack, bag" (for storing textiles and wool, lit. "the guarding one", participle, not *palīlu*), for ref. s. ARM 30 p.179, e. g.: 35 *pa-li-lu ša* 10-ÀM TÚG ŠÀ.BA 57 ^{túg}ŠÀ.ḪA *pa-li-lu ša* SÍG ŠÀ.BA *za-am-ra* 2 *pa-li-lu ša* BAR.SI^{ḫá} ARM 22, 321: 2–5 "35 *p.*-bags each of which contains 10 textiles; 57 *p.*-bags (made) of *šaḫḫû*-canvas to keep wool; 2 *p.*-bags for headbands".

5. LB Safety catch(?) after Beaulieu 2003, 179f., 384: *ayyarī* IGI KÙ.GI *ša* ^{d}GAŠAN.ME *u* 4 *šišâtišu ina libbi* 8 *sanḫānū ša pa-li-l*[*e*]*-e maṭû* 3 *ayyarī* KÙ.GI *ša kulūlu ša* ^{d}GAŠAN.MEŠ *ina libbi* 10 *sanḫānū ša pa-li-le-e maṭû* NBC 4503 "16 frontal rosettes of gold belonging to the Goddesses together with their 4 joints(?), from which are missing 8 safety(?) catches; 3 golden rosettes for a crown belonging to the Goddesses, from which are missing 10 safety catches(?)". MPS (1–3), NR (4, 5)

+ **pāliqu** "butcher"; SB

Lex. *gud-gaz* = *pa-li-qú* MIN Emar 6/4, 602: 148 (Lú) "butcher of dito (= a bull)".

palkû "wide, broad"; + OB

šubalkut pa!*-al-ki-i-ši-id kabtati* CunMon. 8, 22 i 17 "to overthrow the broad foundation of the mind".

+ **pallāšu** "stoneborer; piercer"; OB, SB

1. Lex. [*alim*?]*-bu-u* = *pa-la-šu* AOAT 50, 398: 37b (cf. comm. ib. p. 253) "[bi]son(?) = piercer(?)".
2. Stol 2008, 350: OB *pá*!*-lá-š*[*u*!*-u*]*m*! KTT 53: 14, s. coll. Durand 2004a, 123.
3. S. also *pālišu*. MPS (1, 3), NR (2)

+ **pālišu** "drilling stone, stoneborer"; OB, NA

1. OB 5 GÚ $^{na4.ḫá}$*pa-a*!*-li-šu* ARM 5, 13: 10 "5 talents of drilling stones" s. coll. Durand 2004a, 123.
2. OB *innuḫa*[*r*]*am qitmam u šammam pa-li-*[*š*]*a-a*[*m*] ... *liššûnim* ARM 26/1 p. 298 no. 134: 9' "let them bring (white) dye, black dye and a drilling stone".
3. NA ^{lú}*pa-liš* StAT 3, 2: 33 "stoneborer". Same person written logogr. [^{l}]^{ú}NÍG.BÙR.BÙR ib. 3: 22.

4. The ref. ARM 5, 13 with plene spelling *pa-a-* shows that we have to distinguish *pallišu* and *pālišu*. S. also *pallāšu*.
MPS (3, 4), NR (1, 2)

pallurtu s. *išpallurtu*

+ **paʾ(a)lu** "a kind of flour(?)"; MB Emar

1. 4 SÌLA PA-*a-lu* (manuscript K: PA-*ʾa-a-lu*) Emar 6/3, 388: 8 "4 liter of *p*.".
2. Pentiuc 2001, 137: root B/P-ʾ/ʿ/H-L. Watson 2002, 9: cf. Ugar. *pil* "some type of foodstuff", "flour" or "some type of grain". del Olmo Lete/Sanmartín 2004, 658: Ugar. *pil* "a food". MPS, NR

+ **paʾlu?** (*paʾālu?*) "work"; NB, Aram. lw.

NB *aššu lēʾi ša ekurrāti ša šarru išpura umma rēḫti p*[*a*]*-ʾ-lu u lēʾī ... šūbilanni* SAA 17, 43: 8 "concerning the writing-board of the temples, of which the king wrote to me: 'Send to me the rest of the work(?) and the ... writing-boards!'" Cf. Dietrich, ib. p. 41. Lw. from Aram. PʿL.

palû "period of office, reign; staff; a royal garment"

1. OB lit. *u šumum inaššī pa-la ramanišu u alpum inaššī pa-la ramanišu* ZA 75, 204: 112f. "and the garlic plant raises its own staff! And the bull raises its own staff".
2. An insign of kingship (CAD P 74 *p.* 5). With *labāšu*, pointing to a garment: OB lit. *ištēn eṭlum la-bi-*⌜*iš*⌝ [BAL]A-*a-am* Gilg. OB Schøyen₂ 9 "there was a man, clad in a royal [mantle]".
3. The pl. of *palû* is well known from MA and NA in the sense of "regnal year" (CAD *p.* A 1d) but not from OB: *ina* ⌜*pa*⌝*-le an-nu-ti-in* Shemshara 1, 46: 6 "during these regnal years".
4. Mayer 2008, 95: SB *li-te-diš pa-le-e* SpTU 2, 12 ii 23 "may my reign be renewed".
5. CAD P distinguishes *palû* A "reign; an insign of kingship" from *palû* B "rod"; but the connection of *palû* and *našû* in ref. 1 above, also attested with *palû* A, proves that *palû* A and B are in fact the same word, as was already correctly analysed by AHw.
MPS (1–3, 5), NR (4)

+ **palubazḫi?** (mng. uncertain); MB Nuzi; Hurr. lw.

1. 1 BÁN ŠE *a-na pa-lu-ba-a*[*z-ḫi*?] HSS 16, 23: 39 (= AdŠ 3, 114: 40), coll. Wilhelm 1985, 105; s. Richter 2012 v. *palupa*[*zḫi*]. AHw 839 and CAD P 222: *a-na* SIPA *pá-as-pa-sí*.
2. Wilhelm 1985, 106: s. *-a/umbaz/šḫi* in Hurr. from Bogazköy and [*q/p*]*a*?-*lu*?-*pa-aš-ḫi* Hermitage 15344: 4.
NR

pana "previously, earlier; in front"

1. Stol 2008, 350: for *ištū pa-na ana warka* "always" s. OB CRRAI 43, 98 n. 25 A.371: 5.
2. Stol 2008, 350: for *ālik pana* "leader" s. OB CT 45, 48: 24; OLA 21, 22: 3 (*ša* ÉREN.GÌR). Cf. *ālik maḫra*, said of divine emblems (CAD A/1, 344b, 3').
3. SB *ištū ūmī pa-na-a* // *panānū* Ballad of Early Rulers 3 "since days of yore".
4. New spelling: LB *ultu* IGI-*a-am ina Ayyari* [UD] 3^{kam} *ša* MU 148^{kam} BiMes. 24, 25: 12 "earlier, in month Ayyar, 3. [day] year 148".
MPS (3–4), NR (1–2)

panāku, *panāgu* "to mount, cap"

D said of villages, mng. uncl.: NA *ālānū ina libbi a-ḫi-ši pa-nu-gu* SAA 1, 172: 12 "the villages are ... by each other".

panīmu "before him(?)"

pa-ni-mu EA 155: 46 (CAD P 82): Moran 1992, 241 "(the word of the king [g]oes) before him". Therefore *panīhu* > *panīwu* with /w/ spelled *m*? Diff. Sivan 1984, 133 and 257: NWSem. prep. with 3 masc. pl. suffix "before them; in front of them" (**panī-humu* > *panīmu*).

MPS, NR

paniš "in front; in advance"; + OB

Mayer 2008, 95: *pa-ni-iš-ša* VS 10, 214 vii 22 "in front of her" (s. also CAD P 157a, 3b2'). NR

pannaru "a textile(?)"

OA *pá-na-ra-am* AKT 3, 77: 19; 4, 42: 13.

pannigu, *punnigu*, *pinnigu*(?) "a pastry or bread"

1. Lex. spelled *pa-an-ni-gu* Emar 6/4, 560: 91 (Ḫḫ XXIII).

2. Further ref. from Emar not listed in CAD P 83f (cf. Pentiuc 2001, 141f.):
a) ${}^{\text{ninda}}$*pu-ni-gu* Emar 6/3, 472: 78.
b) ${}^{\text{ninda!}}$*pu-un-ni-gi*! Emar 6/3, 367: 3.

3. CAD P 383b considers *pinigu* "cereal product" as a separate lexeme. But Parpola 1979, 30 connects the word wirh *pannigu*. CDA 263a: *pi*(*n*)*nigu* by-form of *pannigu*. Cf. Hebr. *pannag* (Pentiuc 2001, 142). MPS (1–2), NR (2–3)

panu I "front, face"

1. MB Ekalte: plene spelling *pa-a-ni* in WVDOG 102, 20: 12.

2. Note that in stat. cstr. the sg. is used in the mng. "face". OB ref. from Mayer 2008, 96:
a) *pa-an šarrim* KN [*n*]*awrūtim ātamar* OBTR 135: 7 "I have seen the bright face of the king".
b) *pa-an ṣābim ul iṣallimū* ib.1: 31 "will the troops' face not darken?".
c) *pa-an* ${}^{\text{d}}$*Ašš*[*ur*] *petû* MARI 7, 273 M.14895: 17 "the face of Aššur is 'open'".
d) *pa-an bēliya juttun* ARM 28, 98: 5 "the face of the lord is mine" (= my lord was favorable towards me)".

3. Mayer 2008, 96:
a) OB [*p*]*a-ni-ia ṣalmūtim īmu*[*r*] AbB 10, 134 1. e. 2 "PN saw my black face".
b) OB *p*[*a-ni-šu ṣa*]*lmūtim ammarma* ARMT 28, 18: 36 "I will see his black face".

4. Stol 2008, 350: translation Iraq 39, 150: 37 "before I come" (instead of "according to my specifications" CAD P 92a).

5. Stol 2008, 350: *ina pani* "(my/him)self":
a) *ina paniya ana* GN *ērumma* RA 42, 128: 13 "I myself entered GN".
b) PNf *ṣuddīʾamma ṭurdašši ina paniša* ŠE.NUMUN … *lilqēʾamma alākam līpuš* AbB 6, 130: 8 "supply PNf with food and send her (to me); she herself should take seeds and set off on a journey".

6. Stol 2008, 350: *ina pani* "(to take/go) away from":
a) 1 BÁN *ḫašḫūrī ip-pa-ni-ia ilqûma* AbB 10, 169: 23 "they have taken 1 seah apples away from me".
b) *butmātim nisan šattim ša ina pa-ni-šu-nu ilqûnim* ARM 27, 123: 14 "the first terebinth fruits, which they have taken from them for me".
c) PN … *ina pa-ni bēl ḫubullišu ana* GN *illikma* AbB 13, 89: 14 "PN … had fled to GN from his creditor".
d) *kīma iṣṣūri ša ina pa-ni kasūsi ana sūn awīlim īrubu* Sumer 23, 161: 13 like a bird which enters a man's lap (fleeing) from a falcon".

7. Stol 2008, 350: *ana pani* "instead(?)":
a) *ana pa-ni awātim awātam apul* AbB 1, 86: 25 "instead of a legal case settle the matter!".
b) *ana pa-ni alpī itaplusi u naṣāri ana paniya* 1 *alpam amurma* AbB 6, 93: 30 "instead of checking constantly over the oxes and guarding (them), find for me an ox".
c) *ana pa-an gimil dumqi gimil lumni irtībam* ARM 13, 97: 6 "he repaid me with evil instead of good" (cf. CAD R 54b "with evil for good").

8. Stol 2008, 350: *ana pani* "against":
a) *ana pa-an awīl Ešnunna* Akkadica Suppl. 1, 161: 19 "against the ruler of Ešnunna".
b) *mimma nakrum ana kakkim ana pa-ni-ia ul iptinam* ARM 10, 123: 7 "no enemy became strong enough in battle to oppose me".

9. Stol 2008, 350: *ana pan, appani* + subord. "in order to; so that":
a) *ap-pa-ni ḫišeḫti ekallim umallû* FM 7, 105 no. 28: 6 "so that it (the village) fulfills the requirements of the palace".
b) *ap-pa-ni ālam išāmuma* id. 11 "(go and look for a village), so that he may buy this village and (give it at the disposal of the palace)".

10. Stol 2008, 350: *ana pani* + *izuzzu* "to support":
a) *kīma atti ana pa-ni-ia tazzīzī* AbB 8, 102: 5 "as you have supported me".**b)** *mādiš ana pa-ni-šu izīz* AbB 8, 141: 18 "extend your full support to him".

11. Stol 2008, 350: *ana pani* + *izuzzum* "to confront":
a) *kīma ša anāku allikam ana pa-ni-šu izīz* AbB 12, 45: 23 "as if I had come myself, confront him!".
b) *attima lā tadabbubīma ana pa-ni-ki lā tušzazzī-niāti* AbB 3, 2: 17 "you should not complain and force us to confront you".

12. Mayer 2008, 95: *ina pan* NN "at the disposal of NN" also in MB: PN_1 *i-na pa-an* PN_2 *ša-ak-nu* UET 7, 47: 3 "(barley which) PN_1 put at the disposal of PN_2". MPS (1), NR (2–12)

panû I "to move forward"

D "to transfer, turn over": OA *ašar pá-nu-im pá-ni-ši* AKT 6b, 451: 9 "transfer it wherever it has to be transferred!"

+ **panû III** "bow"; LB, Sum. lw.

1. 1-*en širʾam* 1-*en* É *pa-né-e* 1 *ṣallu* 2 *šibbānū* Zawadzki 2010, 422 BM 61345: 3 "1 jerkin, 1 bow case, 1 shield, 2 belts".
2. ⸢túg⸣É *pi?*-⸢*né?*⸣-*e* ib. 61425: 5.
3. Cf. *bīt qašti* CAD Q 155.

pānu "a basket; a measure of capacity"

1. OB 1 *pa-an* ŠE 1 *pa-an* ZÚ.LUM CUSAS 9, 113: 1f. "1 pan of barley, 1 pan of dates".

2. OB 1 *pa-an* ŠE.GIŠ.Ì BÁN ZABAR ib. 139: 1 "1 pan of sesame by the bronze seah-measure".

3. Note the spelling OB 10 ^{gi}*pa*$_{12}$(PI)-*ne-e* AbB 12, 118: 4.

4. Used for the measurement of ribs, s. Powell 1987–1990, 491 § III B:
a) OB (I erected 30 ribs in it) *ša* 1 PI *ikbirū* Finkel 2014, 360: 14 "which were one *pānu* thick".
b) OB (I set up 3600 stanchions in it) *ša* 1/2 (PI) *ikbirūma* ib. 16 "which were (each) half a *pānu* thick".

papāḫu "cella, shrine"

1. Fem. pl. also SB KÁ *pa-pa-ḫat bīt* DN SAA 8, 567: 2 "gate of the cellas of the temple of DN".

2. Mayer 2008, 96: For the mng. of *papāḫu* s. Jahn 2005, 127–131: Originally a "Mitteltürraum/reception room" in the middle or at the rear of a private house, later a chapel in a temple.

MPS (1), NR (2)

papallu, + *pamallu* "shoot, sprout"

1. SB *pa-ma-al-li-ia* Emar 6/4, 783: 12 (ZA 79, 177: 55') // *pa-pal-li-ia*.
2. SB *lamnu ša ina rēš ra-a-ṭu našû pa-pal-lum* Jiménez 2017, 254: 53 "the almond tree, that lifts up its shoot at the source of the ditch".
3. SB *ša lā pa-pal-li-ia ul issekkerū mê nagbi* ib. 168 Ic 11 "without my shoots, the waters from the spring could not be dammed."
4. SB [...] *pa-pal-la ana bērā erēnu* JCS 66, 76: 12 (Gilg.) "the cedar [sent forth] the sapling for one mile".

MPS (2–4), NR (1)

pap(p)ān libbi "part of the body, swelling of the stomach"; + OB

1. OB lit. with double /*pp*/: *pa-ap-pa-al-li-ib-bi-šu agargarum* CUSAS 32, 27: 7 "its belly is fish-spawn".
2. Stol 2008, 350: "the umbilical area" instead of "diaphragm" (CAD P 105b).

MPS (1), NR (2)

papātu "a container"; + MB Qaṭna

1. MB Qaṭna 1 *pa-pa-a-te ša* GIŠ.Ì *malû* QS 3, 13: 23. "one *p.*-container filled with oil".
2. MB Qaṭna ⌜23 ^{na4}⌝*pa-pa-te-na ša* Ì *malû* ib. 18: 21 "23 *p.*-containers made of stone, filled with oil". **3.** The word is already attested once in Alalaḫ (AHw 824 "ein Holzgegenstand", CAD P 106 "a wooden implement or furnishing"). The new ref. make clear that we deal with a container, that the second syllable contains a long /ā/ and that the word is prob. of Hurr. origin (note the Hurr. pl.-suffix *-na*); s. the dicussion in QS 3 p. 89.

****papātu** (AHw 824a; cf. CAD ***papātu*)

Borger 2008, 440: in Weidner Tn. 1 v 24 read after duplicate Görg 1989, 214 vii 22 *ú-šal-pa-tu* instead of *ú-pap-pa-*[...] (Schramm 1989/1990, 123). Wilcke 2010, 438 vii 21–22: C: *ú-šal*!(PAP)-*pa-tu*. NR

+ pappaddû? (mng. uncertain); SB; Sum. lw.

PAD.PAD.DA-*a aqarraš-ka* BagM 10, 112: 8 (s. also Iraq 55, 66) "I can carve off the *choicest cuts* for you", s. George, Iraq 55, 67: *pad* = *qa-ra-šum* (MSL 16, 163: 292). NR

pappāltu "porridge; seminal discharge"; + MA

1. Stol 2008, 350: MA 1 *pasru ša taḫalte* 1 SÌLA *pa-pa-al-tu* SAAB 8, 13 r. 6' "1 container of a foodstuff *taḫaltu*; 1 liter of porridge".
2. Fem. of *pappāsu*: *pappāstu* > *pappāltu*. NR

pappardaliʾu "agate(?)"

1. OB 3 ^{na4}BABBAR.DILI *takpītu rabītu ša* 1 *idušunu* GE$_6${X} *u šanûm idušu* SU$_{13}$.A ARM 32 p. 422 M.11692: 3 "3 big *t.*-beads of *p.*, whose one side is white and whose other side is red".
2. OB 1 ^{na4}BABBAR.DILI *er-bé-et-tum* ARM 32 p. 424 M.10382: 1 "1 *p.* with four (stripes?)".
3. For further ref. from Mari (all written logogr.) and disc. s. Arkhipov, ARM 32 p. 35f.; Frahm 1997, 147f.; Schuster-Brandis 2008, 403f. NR

papparḫītu "a decoration in the shape of the *papparḫû* plant"

1. OB 16 *pa-ap-par-ḫe-et uqnîm* ARM 32 p. 467 M.8509+: 35, 44; ARM 25, 643: 17 = ARM 32 p. 453 M.5153 ii 16; ARM 32 p. 454 M.6495+ ii 8 "16 *p.* made of lapis lazuli".
2. OB 51 *pa-ap-par-ḫe-tum* $^{\text{na4}}$Z[A.GÌN] ARM 24, 130: 1.
3. OB 16 *muššar uqnîm* 65 *pa-ap-par-ḫe-et uqnîm terdītum ana agêm ša ḫurāṣi* 10 *pa-pa-ar-ḫe-et uqnîm* ARM 25, 426 = ARM 32 p. 285 M.10764: 2, 5 "16 *m.* of lapis lazuli, 65 *p.* of lapislazuli, consignment, for a golden tiara. 10 *p.* of lapis lazuli".
4. OB 1 GAL [*K*]*aptarītim ša ina qablītim*! *pa-ap-pa-ar-*<*ḫi*>*-tum* ARM 25, 45 = ARM 31, 184: 4 "1 Cretan cup, a *p.* plant in (its) middle part".
5. Disc. with further ref. from Mari by Arkhipov, ARM 32 p. 52f. s. v. *papparḫûm*. Pace Arkhipov, not all ref. are a pl. *papparḫêtu* < *papparḫīʾātu* of *papparḫû* (cf., e. g., sg. in YOS 10, 56 i 42; ARM 31, 184: 4, above), and there is no doubt that a sg. *papparḫitu* exists.

papparḫû "a herb, perhaps purslane, *Portulaca* species"

Stol 2008, 350: ⌜*bábbar*⌝*-ḫi-a* = *ga-lu-lu-u-pí-iš*; [*numun*] ⌜*babbar-ḫi-a*⌝ = ŠU.SI-*aš* NUMUN-*an* Fs. Hoffner, Jr. 353 § 8' (practical vocabulary from Ortaköy) "*p.* = fingers; [seed of] *p.* = finger's seed". S. disc. in Süel/Soysal, ib. p. 360 ad § 8: *ga-lu-lu-u-pí-iš* is pl. from Heth. *kalulupa-* "finger". NR

papparmīnu "a semiprecious stone"

1. OB 12 *takpīt* $^{\text{na4}}$BÁBBAR.MIN$_5$ ARM 32 p. 447 i 35 "12 *t.* beads of *p.* stone".
2. OB 1 GÚ *takkas* $^{\text{na4}}$BÁBBAR.MIN$_5$ ARM 21, 247: 11 (cf. also ib. 12, ARM 32 p. 473 M.12019: 21 etc.) "one necklace with *t.* ornament of *p.* stone".
3. OB 1 *kišād ša takkas* $^{\text{na4}}$BÁBBAR.MIN$_5$ ARM 32 p. 239 A.4555: 3 (cf. $^{\text{na4}}$BABBAR.MIN$_5$ ARM 32 p. 195 M.11552+: 15) "1 necklace with *t.* ornament of *p.*".
4. OB 1 *kišād tašmēt* $^{\text{na4}}$BABBAR.MIN$_5$ ARM 21, 219: 10 (cf. ib. 4f., 11; ARM 32 p. 195 M.11552+: 17, 20f.) "1 necklace with *t.* ornament of *p.* stone".
5. OB 2 "ŠÁḪ" $^{\text{na4}}$BÁBBAR.MIN$_5$ 1 *šubûm ša* $^{\text{na4}}$BÁBBAR.MÌN ARM 32 p. 456 M.5954 r. 14'f. "2 pigs of *p.* stone, 1 *š.* bead of *p.* stone".
6. OB 1 *nēšu ša* $^{\text{na4}}$BABBAR.MÌN ARM 25, 575: 6 = ARM 32 p. 477 M.12498 r. 7 "1 lion of *p.* stone".
7. The transliteration follows MesZL p. 471: BABBAR = UD, BÁBBAR = UD-UD, MIN$_5$ = AŠ-AŠ. Arhkipov ARM 32 p. 36 inaccurately has BABAR and PAR-PAR, ARM 21, 219 has *pár-didli*. ŠÁḪ transliterated in ARM 32 p. 456 (s. no. 5, above), according to MesZL p. 415 no. 744, only occurs NA.
8. Stol 2008, 350: Black banded agate with two white stripes or any stone made to look like it; Frahm 1997, 147f.; Schuster-Brandis 2008, 404; Arkhipov, ARM 32 p. 36 with further ref. from Mari. MPS (1–7), NR (8)

pappiru s. *bappiru*

pappu I "curl, strand of hair"

1. Constructed as fem.: SB *pa-pa-am qatattam* ALL no. 11 r. 8 "thin curl".
2. On *pappāt īni* "eyelashes" s. the disc. s. v. *epepiʾātu*.

paqādu "to entrust, care for, appoint"

Gt. 1. SB *itʾidā pit-qí-da* "pay attention, be careful!" K.6310+: 33' (Streck 2007, 151; Mayer 2008, 96).
2. NB *lū pu-ut-qu-ud* SAA 17, 63 r. 14 "may he be cautious!"
3. NB *pit-qí-du* ib. 129 r. 20 "be cautious!" (in broken context).

D 1. OB *namrīʾātim ša tu-pa-aq-qá-du-šu-nu-š[i]-im* AbB 13, 48 r. 5' "the fattened animals that you entrust to them".
2. Stol 2008, 350 (s. also ARM 27 p. 40 n. b): "to make an inventory":
a) OB *mimma ša ana mārtišu inaddinu … li-pa-aq-qí-id-ma* (var. *li-pa-qí-id*) *tuppam lišṭurši* NAPR 5, 6: 32 "whatever he will give to his daughter, let him make an inventory (of this) and write (it on) a tablet".
b) (List of objects) *mimma šumšu malī ibaššû ú-pa-qa-du-nu-kum* Amurru 2, 77 n. 444 A.2640 r. 12' "he will make for you an inventory of the (list of objects) and of everything that is there".
c) *bītam ú-pa-aq-qí-⌜du⌝* FM 7, 128 no. 36: 23 "they have made an inventory of (each) household" (s. also ib. p. 83 n. e).

N Mayer 2008, 96: *[mīt]u ul ip-pa-qí-di ana eṭem kimtišu* LKA 155: 11' (= "Šamaš 67", Mayer 1976, 418) "the spirit of the dead will not be handed over to the ghosts of his family".

MPS (Gt, D), NR (Gt, D, N)

paqru, *baqru* "claim"

OB *ba-iq-ru-um* KTT 55a: 6 (in unclear context).

parādu I "to be scared, terrified"

G OA *maḫīrum pá-ru-ud* Prag 598: 8 "the market is disturbed"

Gtn OA *libbī lā ip-ta-na-ri-id* AKT 6c, 606: 23 "my heart shall not become frightful all the time".

Gt 1. SB *šumma … pit-⌜ru⌝-[ud?]* AOAT 43, 155: 85' "if he is very scared".
2. ARM 26/1 p. 321 no. 155: 16 (CAD P 143b, 2) does not belong here: s. *parāṭu* Gt.

Dtn OA *bītī tù-up-ta-na-ra-ad* AKT 2, 33: 9 "you constantly frighten my house".

MPS (G, Gtn, Dtn), NR (Gt)

+ **parʾagal** "mule for riding(?)"; OB

Compound in the absolute state (< *parû* I + *agālu* I) or pseudo-logogr.: 4 ANŠE ^{giš}GIGIR 4 ANŠE.KUR.RA 3 ^{anše}*pa-ar-a-ga-al* 3 ANŠE.LA.GU ARM 24, 5: 8' "4 chariot donkeys, 4 horses, 3 mules for riding(?), 3 donkeys for riding". Corresponds to ANŠE.KUNGA.LA.GU "riding mule" in ARM 9, 149/150. S. van Koppen 2002b, 21ff. (with ref. to further studies); Militarev/Kogan 2005, 233 no. 176.

NR

paraḫšītu s. *paraḫšû*

paraḫšû, *parašû*, fem. *paraḫšītu* "from Marḫaši"

1. Lex. *⌜dìm-ma⌝-mar-ḫa-a-ši = pa-ra-šu/su-u* Emar 6/4, 545: 404 (cf. DCCLT MB Ura 04) "figurine from Marḫaši".

2. Fem. "a musical instrument":
a) OB ^{giš}*pa-ra-aḫ-ši-ti* FM 9, 192 no. 44: 8.
b) [^{giš}]*pa-ra-aḫ-ši-[ta]m* ib. 9.

3. Cf. *paramšītu* (CAD P 161), disc. by Durand 2009, 71.

parāḫu "to ferment" s. *parāʾu* II

parakku "cult dais, sanctuary"

1. Mayer 2008, 96:

a) SB *elī-ma tišab ina kussî* BÁRA *šarrūtu* SpTU 1, 1 iii 7' (Nergal and Ereškigal) "go up and take your seat on the throne, the royal dais".

b) SB *lā lamassi Uruk ina* BÁRA-*šu ušeššeb* ib. 3 r. 5 "he will let a non-protective deity of Uruk take the seat on his dais" (s. also ib. r. 13f.).

2. SB *iḫīṭma mitḫāriš pa-rak-ke-*⌜*e*⌝ AulaOr. Suppl. 23, 42: 5 // Gilg. SB II 5 "likewise he inspected the shrines".

MPS (2), NR (1)

parāku I, NA *parāḫu* "to lie across, obstruct"

G 1. OA *annakam* PN *ina bāb kārim kīma nēšim pá-ri-ik-ma* AKT 6c, 528: 17 "here PN lies across the gate of the colony like a lion".

2. OA With acc. (CAD 158 *p.* 3d): *mamman lā pá-ar-kà-ku* AKT 4, 66: 31 "I am not giving trouble to anybody".

3. OB lit. (*lā*) *ap-ri-ik Ištar ana šibbatu panīki* Ištar Baghdad 21, 23 "I did (not) oppose the wrath of your face".

4. Mayer 2008, 96: OB lit. *kummuskunūšim immerum pa-ri-ku-nu-ši pa*[*trum*?] YOS 11, 23: 139 "the sheep kneels for you, the knife lies crosswise for you".

5. Mayer 2017, 24: OB lit. *ṣābi tillatišu u napḫar qarrādīšu mamman ana paniya lā ip-ri-ku* BagM 34, 142 vii 4 "his auxiliary troops and all his warriors – nobody blocked me".

6. Mayer 2008, 96:

a) OB *šer'am ip-ta-ar-ku* FM 6, 465 no. 67 (// no. 68): 17 "(five plows) have cross-plowed the furrow".

b) *eqlam mala pa-ar-ku kullimaššunūti* FM 6, 468 no. 67 (// no. 68): 34 "show them the field as much as it has been cross-plowed".

7. Mayer 2017, 24: OB *bēlī ḫuṣāba*[*m*] *ina pāni mākaltim ip-ri-ik* FM 9 p. 136 no. 27: 23 "my lord laid a twig across the dish". Cf. also Mayer 2017, 24.

8. Mayer 2008, 96: SB *ša ... kīma šigari māta par-kát* AfO 50, 25 K.4339: 7 // AfO 50, 21 BM 65454+: 7 "(goddess,) who like a door lock blocks the country".

9. Mayer 2008, 96: with *panuššu:* SB *ša ina uzzišu dannu ilu mamma lā i-par-ra-ku panuššu* BagM 21, 341 no. 1: 7 "(Adad), whom, in his violent rage, no god can oppose".

10. Mayer 2008, 96f: *Šamas našêkkum mutqī 7 u 7 ša pirkī šinā ana kâšim* ⌜*pa*⌝-*ar-ku* YOS 11, 22: 43 (CAD P 158a *p.* 3c; s. also CAD P 408a *pirku* B 4) "Šamaš, I bring you 7 and 7 sweet cakes, which are lined crosswise in two rows for you".

11. Stol 2008, 351: mng. "to crumble" (Hurowitz 1989, 69) is uncertain:

a) For *pirkī parāku* YOS 11, 22 s. 8, above.

b) Instead of *par-ka-nu ... ú-par-rak* BM 50350: 6f. prob. read *ú-ḫaš-šal* "he will crush the *p.*s" (Da Riva 2002, 111f. and 113 with comm.).

c) The only ref. left is OB *še'um pirkum* UET 5 60: 14 (cf. CAD P 408a: "obscure").

Gtn 1. OB *šāpir nārī ip-ta-na-ar-ri-ku-nim-ma* AbB 13, 31: 11 "the heads of the river districts are constantly hindering me".

2. *mu-*⌜*up*⌝*-ta-ri-ik bītim* (// *é-a ku*₄*-ku*₄) PBS 1/2, 135: 12' "who constantly passes(?) the temple". Reading follows Cavgineaux 1996, 26. For translation cf. CAD P 158 *p.* 4b. Sövegjarto 2014, 66, without mentioning Cavigneaux's new ed., reads *mu-*[*uš*]*-ta-ri-ik* "the entrusted one of the temple", deriving the form from *šarākum*; however, neither Gtn nor Dt can mean "the entrusted one".

Š Cf. *barāqu* Š.

N 1. NA variant *parāḫu* (AHw 829 *p.* D 2, CAD P 159 *p.* 5c2'): *mannumma lū? lā? isamma lū! lā ip-par-ri-ḫi* SAA 16, 5: 11 "nobody should be undecided and stand in the way". Cf. Luukko/van Buylaere, ib. p. 6.
2. CAD P 160a *p.* 7a: delete with Mayer 2008, 97 KAR 26: 37: *ib-ba-šu-ni-ma*, not *ip-par*(text *-ba*)*-ku-ni-ma*". S. Or 68, 150 (coll.) and KAL 2, 21 (new copy). MPS (G, Gtn, Š, N), NR (G, N)

parāmu "to shred, to rend, to slice through"

+ **N 1.** NA *kī ša* kušE.SÍR *šalqatuni ina qaqqar paqutti* [kušE.SÍRme]š*-ku-nu li-par-ma* SAA 2, 6: 658 "just as this shoe is split, so may your [shoe]s be torn by thorns".
2. Cf. also *pirindu*. S. also Watanabe 1987, 209 ad § 103. MPS, NR

parāqu "to divide off, separate"

+ **D** Stol 2008, 351: LB *ina* túg*širʾam tik-kašu tu-par-ríq* RA 78, 73: 35 "(if she abandons her husband,) she will(!) 'separate' her neck from a tunic" (i. e. will go unveiled)" (s. disc. in Joannès, ib. p. 75). NR

parāru "to be dissolved, broken up"

G SB DIŠ *ip-ru-ur-ma ušḫarrir* TDP 190: 26 "if he became weak and lapsed into silence", with AHw 829b and Stol 2008, 351. CAD B 107a quoted under *barāru* B. Durand 1997, 101: *barāru* "to speak blasphemy".

D 1. OA *bītam lā tù-pá-ra-ar* AKT 2, 31: 21 "don't disperse the house!"
2. OB, said of *muḫḫu* "brain" (George 2013, 283f.): *muḫḫu pu-ru-ur* CUSAS 18, 43: 1, 5, 8 and passim in this text "the brain is jagged". Cf. CAD P 152 *p.* A 2b for *parāru* with body parts.
3. OB lit. *qinnašu ú-pa-ar-ri-ir* FM 14, 13 i 20 "he dispersed his family".
4. MB Ekalte *ṣuḫārta ummiši* [*ú-*]*pá-ri-ru* "the mother released(?) the girl" WVDOG 102, 25: 19.
5. Mayer 2008, 97: LB *lū parsā lū purrusā lū pur-ru-ra gillātūʾa* (var. *saklātūʾa*) *u maskātūʾa* BBR 26 iii 6 // SpTU 2, 12 ii 12 "may my sins (var. my follies) and my wickedness be cut, separated, dissolved".

Ntn Stol 2008, 351: OB *it-ta-pa-ar-ru*, *it-ta-pa-ar-ra-ru* RA 86, 48, n. 73, Di 620: 17, 20 "(the oxen) are running around". MPS (D), NR (G, D, Ntn)

parasu s. *paršu*

parāsu I "to cut (off); decide"

G 1. OA *šumma luqūtka i-pá-ru-sú-ni-ma itabbulūnim* AKT 7a, 260: 15 "if they divide your merchandise and bring it to me".
2. OA With *ištī* (cf. CAD P 172 *p.* 4f1' end): *bāʾam pu-ru-us-ma ... ištī awīlim a-pị-ra-as-ma* Imdilum 278 LB 1290 r. 9'–11' "'Come, decide ...!' I will decide about the man".
3. OB lit. *pa-ar-sà-at Ištar* Ištar Baghdad 18 "you are far away, Ištar".

Gt 1. OB *šumma qaqqadāt rēʾîm še-e-na-ma pí-it-ru-sa* CUSAS 18 p. 301: 15' "if there are two heads on the 'shepherd' (gall bladder) and they are separate".
2. In the sense of "to apportion" (cf. CAD P 170 *p.* 2) said of bitumen, in OB Finkel 2014, 360: 18f., s. *iṭṭû*.

D 1. OB, Stol 2008, 351: *amursāna tu-pa-ra-as* YOS 11, 25: 47 "you divide

the wild pigeon" (recipe, s. Bottéro 1995, 49).
2. SB, Mayer 2008, 97: *šēpu* + *parāsu* (cf. CAD P 169a, li2'): *šē[p l]emutti ina bītiya pur-ru-sa ... šēp lemutti pur-ru-sa* SpTU 5, 246 iii 13'f. "to keep the 'evil foot' away (from my house)".

MPS (G, Gt), NR (D)

parašû s. *paraḫšû*.

parāšu "to flatter"

+ **Gtn**: OB lit. [*pí-ta-ar-r*]*a*!-*as-si pí-ta-ar-ra-si*! (ed.: -*as*!-<*si*>] CUSAS 10, 11: 1 "flatter her, flatter her!" George, ib. p. 67, 69 derives the word from *parāsu* ("keep her apart!"). For the combination of /*s*/ and /*š*/, however, we expect a spelling with *sí*(ZI) (Streck 2006, 231), which the text uses elsewhere in *ḫu-us-sí-ni* l. 8, whereas the combination /*š*/ and /*š*/ may be spelled *si* (Streck, ib. p. 239).

parāṭu "to tear, clear away; flicker" (in astron. context)

G "flicker" in astron. context (Parpola 1993, 89; cf. CAD P 180 "uncertain mng."): *šumma mišḫu* IM.U18. LU *iškun iškun-ma imṣur imṣur-ma* GUB-*iz* GUB-*iz-ma ip-ru-uṭ ip-ru-uṭ-ma issapiḫ* NUN *ina* KASKAL DU-*ku* NÍG. NAM NÍG.GÁL.LA ŠU.2-*su* KUR-*ad* SAA 10, 111: 7 "if a flash appears and appears again in the south, makes a circle and again makes a circle, stands there and again stands there, flickers and flickers again, and is scattered: the ruler will capture property and possessions in his expedition".

+ **Gt** Streck 2003a, 63: OB *iš*[*dā rē*]*ʾîm i*[*mittam*] *p*[*i*]*t-ru-ṭa-ma šumēla*[*m*] [*s*]*armā* ARM 26/1 p. 321 no. 155: 16 "the base of the gall bladder was completely torn on the right and cut on the left". CAD P 143b reads *p*[*i*]*t-ru-da-ma*, Gt of *parādu* "to be confused".

NR

parāʾu II "to sprout"

AHw *parāḫu* I "gären" (= CAD *parāḫu* "to sprout") is in fact the same verb as AHw *parāʾu* II "aufgehen" (= CAD *parāʾu* B "to sprout, flourish"): root PRʾ, the aleph spelled *ḫ* in OB and SB lex. Pace CAD P 182, there is no need to assume a denomination of *pirʾu* "shoot". Note that the verb is *a*-class in OB (*ip-ta-ra-aḫ*) but *u*-class in NA (*i-par-ru-ʾ*).

paraʾuru (mng. uncertain)

Although deleted in CAD P 182a, the word seems to exist. Lauinger 2015, 134: "may Ištar sink the *paraʾurum* into his loins, as with an *assinnum* (adv. acc.)". Frayne 1990, 800 and Zsolnay 2010, 400 n. 35 assume a mng. of *p.* similar to *mutūtu* "manliness": "and may the goddess Eštar, (as with) a eunuch, cause potency to leave his private parts".

NR

pardēsu "garden, park"

1. LB *eqlu ša ina pa-ar-de-e-su* CUSAS 28, 53: 2 "(dates, *imittu* rent of) the field that is in the garden". Cf. comm. Pearce/ Wunsch, ib. p. 186.
2. Stol 2008, 351: ^{kur}*par-an-*[*de*]-*e-zu* Gesche 2000, 629 BM 76478 v 4'f.

MPS (1), NR (2)

pardu "frightening"

Said of a wall: OB Lex. *bàd-kár-dar* = *pa-ar-du-um* ZA 94, 230 i 7. Cf. Krebernik, ib. p. 233.

pargallu "a kind of sheep"; + OB, + MB

1. OB *ma-a-tum ka-lu-ša i-na la b[a-še-e] pa-ar-ga-li ṣa-al-[l]a-at* ARM 26/1 p. 201 n. 9 M.9050 "the entire land lies there for lack of *p.*-sheep".

2. MB Ekalte [1] *līttu* 1 *pár-ga-*⌜*lu*⌝ "[1] cow, 1 *p.*-sheep" WVDOG 102, 19: 17.

pariktu "wall, curtain; injustice"

1. SB *kīma ša bāʾirimma pa-ri-ik-ta šēt* Šūpê-amēli 29 "escape the fence like that of a hunter!"

2. SB *ana šupšuqti ša āl* GN *pa-ri-ik-ti di-ni* ib. 28 "for the difficulty of the city of GN is my(?) injustice (and) my(?) justice" (unclear).

3. NA 3 ^{túg}*pa-ri-kát* ^{siki}ZA.GÌN.NA StAT 1: 29 "3 curtains of blue wool".

+ **parīru** "dispersed troop(?)", MB Emar

In omen apodoses, always in the pl.:

1. *qīt pa-ri-ri-ia* Emar 6/4, 698: 21 "end of my dispersed troops(?)".

2. [*qīt p*]*a-ri-ri nakri* ib. 22 "[end of the dis]persed troops of the enemy".

3. *pa-ri-ri nakri aṣabbat* ib. 32 "I will seize the dispersed troops(?) of the enemy".

4. *pa-ri-ri-ia nakru iṣabbat* ib. 33 "The enemy will seize my dispersed troops(?)".

5. In broken context: [*pa-r*]*i-ri-ia*, [*pa-ri-*]*ri* ib. 701: 6f.

6. Cf. Arnaud, Emar 6/4 p. 323, n. 21–22, and Pentiuc 2001, 138. S. also George 2013, 182. Cf. *barīru* III.

parīsu I "rudder, pole"; + SB, + MB Emar

1. Lex. [...*gi-*]*muš* = *ṣerrat pa-ri-si* Emar 6/4, 545: 542 "rope of the rudder".

2. Mayer 2008, 97:

a) OB [*pa-r*]*i-si ša ṣuppā* 5 *šūši iksam* Gilg. OB VA+BM iv 27 "cut me 300 (lit. 5 x 60) [punting]-poles, each one *ṣuppu* (= sixty cubits)" (George 2003, 280f.).

b) *erid ana qištimma pa-ri-si ša* 5 *nindanā* [5 x 60 *ik-sa*] Gilg. SB X 160 "go down to the forest and [cut me 300 punting-poles, each 5 rods long" (George 2003, 688f.; s. also Gilg. SB X 166, 176–180).

c) *āmur pa-ri-su u ḫišiḫtum addī* Gilg.SB XI 65 "I found a punting-pole and put the tackle in place" (George 2003, 706f.; s. also Gilg. SB XI 276).

d) *ina gipiš tâmti rapašti* ... ^{giš}MÁ.GUR$_8$ *bāʾiri lībukū ina pa-ri-su* Cagni Erra IV 49 "may they lead the fisherman's barge with the punting-pole(s) in the expanse of the vast sea".

MPS (1), NR (2)

parīsu II "a measure of capacity"

The abbreviation *pa*, already attested in Alalaḫ, also occurs in MB Qaṭna, s. QS 3 index p. 185.

parku "harm, problem; clod"

1. LB pl. *parkānū* "clods lying across a field", s. Jursa 1995, 125.

2. SB *šamna šá? erṣeta* SÙ *pa-aš-ka tapaššašma* SpTU 3, 76: 45 (Zgoll 2003, 114 and 119) "with oil, which is sprinkled on the ground, you smear the clod(?)". MPS (2), NR (1, 2)

parkullu "seal-cutter, lapidary"

SB *muḫrī ša* ^{lú}BUR.GUL *sāmta simat kišādiki* RA 18, 163 r. 27 "accept from the gem-cutter carnelian befitting your neck" (Farber 2014, 268ff. and 298f.).

NR

parkullūtu "lapidary's craft"; + OB

Mayer 2008, 104; Stol 2008, 354: OB BUR.GUL-*lu-sú šāninam lā īšû* BagM

34, 148 xiii 6 "(an image) whose stone-cutter's art is unrivalled". NR

+ **parrāṣāyu?** "lying, mendacious, criminal"; MA

DUMU *pár-ra-ṣa-ie-e qí-bi-áš-šu* Chuera 2: 13 "call him 'son of criminals'!"

parratu "young female lamb"

Many MA ref. BATSH 9/3 p. 195 (index).

parru I "(male) lamb"

1. OB 1 ME 83 UDU *pa-ar-ru-tu u pa-ar-ra-tum baqmūtu* NABU 1991/30 M.10431: 2f. "183 shorn male and female weaned lambs".
2. Pace Durand 1991a, *pa-a-ru-um* TLB 1, 184: 10 (CAD P 210a: *pāru* F "mng. unkn."; AHw 836b: *pāru* IV a "ein Rind?"), because of the diff. spelling, hardly belongs here. NR

parsātu *s. parsu*

+ **parsikallu** "big (head)band(?)"; OB, SB; Sum. lw.

1. Lex., equated with *nargītu* "a headband" and *paskāru* "a headdress" (CAD N/1, 352):
a) ^{túg}*bar-si-gal* = *nargītum* MSL 10, 135: 250.
b) [^{túg}*bar-s*]*i-gal* = [*nar*]*gītum* = *pa-ás-*$^{ka-rum}$*kír* MSL 10, 142: 74.

2. OB, ARM 30 p. 82f. (for further ref. s. there). Spellings:
a) *par-si-kál-l*[*i*]*-im* ARM 30 p. 82 T.341: 22.
b) 1 ^{túg}*pa-ar-si-ka-al-li* ARM 30 p. 197 M.6001: 6.
c) ^{túg}*pár-si-kal-li*(*-im*) ARM 22, 175: 5.
d) ^{túg}*par-si-*⌜*kal*⌝*-li-i*[*m*] ARM 30 p. 514 M.18222 ii'10.
e) ^{túg}BAR.SI.GAL ARM 30 p. 83.
f) (^{túg})BAR.SI.KAL ARM 21, 294: 14'; ARM 18, 49: 8.

3. Used as a bandage: OB 1 ^{túg}BAR.SI.KAL ... *ana* PN *inūma imra*[*ṣú*] ARM 22, 145: 2 "1 *p.* bandage for PN when he became si[ck]".

4. Several ref. of *p.* are quoted by CAD P 204b under *paršīgu* "turban". The syllabic spellings above show, however, that *parsikallu* is diff. from *paršīgu* (*rabûm*). MPS (2), NR (1–4)

parsikku s. *paršīgu*

parsiktu II s. *paršiktu* II

parsu I "cut off"

1. OA *pa-ar-sà-ti-kà awâtim ušēṣi*ʾ AKT 5, 18: 5 "he has disclosed confidential matters of yours".
2. *ap-parsāti-* "separately(?)": s. Veenhof AKT 5 p. 111 n. 112; CAD P 192 *parsātu* "mng. unkn."

+ **parsu II** "fraction"; OA, SB

1. Lex. *sa*₉ *ma-na* = *pa-*⌜*ra*⌝*-*[*as* MA].⌜NA⌝ Emar 6/4, 553: 222 "1/2 mina = fracti[on] of the [mi]na", s. DCCLT MB Ura 10. Cf. *parasrab* and *paras-ṣeḫru* CAD P 164f.

2. OA *manāʾum pá-ra-as lā tašaqqal* AKT 6c, 638: 24 "will you not pay one *parsum* per mina?" MPS (1), NJCK (2)

parṣu "office, (cultic) ordinance; a tax"

1. Mayer 2017, 25: OB lit. *išteʾat teppuš pár-ṣa-am ša mutim šipirti zikari* Gilg. OB Schøyen2 = CUSAS 10, 5: 18 "you will do something unique, the custom of a warrior, the task of a man". Cf. George CUSAS 10 p. 34f.

2. OB, said of a city: *ana pa-ar-ṣí ša ālim* FM 7, 127 no. 35: 10' "according to the customs(?) of the city" (broken context).

3. SB *ina pīšu uṣû pa-ra-aṣ ūmī aḫirâti* Šūpê-amēli 5 "from whose mouth came forth the ordinance for days to come".

4. Mayer 2008, 97f. (further ref. in Mayer 2017, 24f.):
a) SB *ša ina kissat par-ṣi kunnât* AfO 50, 21 BM 65454+: 2 "(goddess), who is praised in all rituals".
b) SB *serqī ellūti ana ilī šūt* PA.AN^{meš} CTN 4, 168 ii 2 "(I provided) the gods of the rituals with pure offerings".
c) SB *ilū šūt pár-ṣi likkišū murṣu ša zumriya* id. ii 8 "may the gods of the rituals drive the disease of my body away (from me)".
d) SB 7 *u* 7 *ana* DINGIR^{meš} *šūt pár-ṣi imitta u šumēla ina muḫḫi šammi kirî tašakkan* id. ii 27 "7 and 7 (fruits) you put to the left and to the right on the garden plants for the gods of the rituals".
MPS (1–4), NR (4)

+ **paršīgtu**, *parsīgtu* "turban(?); a part of the rigging(?)"; OB, SB

1. Lex. ^{giš}TAGxTÚG.BAR.SI = *šá par-sik-ti* MSL 6, 31: 303. Cf. Durand 2009, 184. S. the variant *par-sik-ki* CAD P 203 lex. sect.
2. Lex. $^{\text{gada!}}$*bar-si má* = *ba-ar-si-ma-a* = *pá-ar-si-ik*!*-t*[*um ša*] *i-l*[*i-pí-im*] MDP 18, 56 "*p.* of a ship" (reading after Durand 2009, 184). Cf. AHw 836b under *paršīgu*.
3. OB 3 MA.NA *ni-is-qum* KI.LÁ.BI [*pár-s*]*í*!*-ik*!*-tin* ARM 19, 321: 3 "30 minas of *n.* wool, the weight of a *p.*" Cf. ARM 30 p. 83.
4. The word is the fem. derivation of *paršīgu* and diff. from *paršiktu* "a plank, part of a boat" (CAD P 205). Whether AbB 4, 140 belongs here, as Durand, ARM 30 p. 184 assumes, or rather to *paršiktu* remains unclear.
MPS (3–4), NR (1–3)

paršīgu, *parsikku* "headdress, turban"

1. By-form *pars/šīku* or *pars/šikku*: OA *pá-ar-si/ší-ke* AKT 6b, 429: 7. Cf. CAD P 203b *p.* a 2'. Disc. by Michel/Veenhof 2010, 238, with new OA ref.

2. OB s. ARM 30 p. 78–82 with numerous ref.:
a) 6 BAR.SI SAG GAL *ana rakās* 3 PN AWTL 85: 1 "6 big headbands for bandaging 3 PN".
b) x BAR.SI SAG GAL *ana ṣamād šēp* PNf ib. 86: 1 "x big headbands for bandaging the foot of PNf".
c) 12 BAR.SI SAG GAL AWTL 83: 1 "12 big headbands".
d) Cf. *parsikallu*. MPS (1), NR (2)

paršu, *parasu* "excrement"; + MA

1. Stol 2008, 351: OB biling.: [*u*]*zu-šà-maḫ in-gar-bi* [*dú*]*b*?*-ù-ab a luḫ-ḫa-ab* = *karša pa-ra-sú upuṣma mê misī* Fs. Sjöberg (1989) 168: 16 "clear the feces from the colon (Akk. rumen) and wash it in water".
2. MA GN *gabbu kī pa-ar-še da-li-iḫ* BATSH 4/1, 9: 41 "the entire land GN is stirred up like excrement".
MPS (2), NR (1)

parû I "mule"

1. Stol 2008, 351: OB lex. x = *anše-šú-an* = *pa-ru-ú* MSL 15, 61 Ur Diri 26.

2. OB 1 *narkabtum ša* ⸢$^{\text{anše!}}$*pa-re-e*⸣ PN (27 PNN) 27 *narkabātum ša* ^{anše}*pa-re-e* [8] *narkabātum ša ilī* 10 *narkabātum ša sisî* 27 *narkabātum ša* ^{anše}*pa-re-e* ARM 32 p. 452 M.5092: 18-48 "1 chariot of mules PN (27 PNN) 27 chariots of mules, (summary:) [8] chariots for the gods, 10 chariots of horses, 27 chariots of mules".

3. Mayer 2008, 98: The mules of Šamaš: **a)** SB *pa-ru-ú-ka ḫanṭūtu* Gilg. SB III 96 "your swift mules". **b)** SB *ul* ʾ*-da-ru* (var. *lā i-ad-da-ru*) *pa-r*[*u*]*-ka* BWL 128: 41 (hymn to Šamaš) "your mules will not become restless". **c)** SB *pa-ru-ka ezzū šamrū* ib. 134: 150 "your mules are furious, impetuous".

4. Mayer 2008, 98: The mules of Nisaba: SB *ina pa-re-e* ᵈ*Nisaba duššûti* SpTU 4, 141 r. 9 "with the magnificent mules of Nisaba".

MPS (2), NR (1, 3–4)

parû II "to insult"

+ **Gtn** SB *ul tēdē ša šēlebi pi-tar-*⌜*ru*⌝ Jiménez 2017, 391: 3 "you do not know fox's constant slandering".

parû IV "to vomit"

G 1. SB *pa-ra-a ana parāsi* AulaOr. Suppl. 23, 25: 3, 15 "to stop vomiting" (incant.).
2. SB [*šumma*] *šurānu ina* (*apti*) *bīt amīli ip-ru* KAL 1, 22: 23f. (cf. already CAD P 209a *p.* A 1c) "if a cat vomits in (the window) of a man's house".

Gtn 1. SB [*šumma šurānu*] *ina apti bīt amīli* ⌜*ip*⌝*-ta-nàr-ru* KAL 1, 22: 25 "[if a cat] vomits several times in the window of man's house".
2. SB *ip-ta-nar-*⌜*ru*⌝ KAL 1, 22 r. 22.

pāru I "a song"

OB lit. *pa-*[*r*]*u-ú* VS 10, 215: 28a, s. Streck/Wasserman 2012, 193.

pāru II, *bāru* "skin"; + OB

1. OB lex. GA-*kišib-lá-mu* = *ba-ri rittiya* CUSAS 12 p. 156 vii 19 (Ugumu) "skin of my hand".
2. OB CUSAS 18, 19: 41, s. *pi*ʾ*azu*.

pāru IV "a cow"

1. OB ÁB *pa-ra-tu*[*m*] ARM 24, 42: 4.
2. Cf. *parru* I, above.

pâru I "to seek"

G For KTS 1, 1a: 24 s. prob. *bâru* II.
Gt delete, perfect G, s. Streck 2003a, 78 no. 203; 2007, 151. NR

paruktu "sail"

Beaulieu 2003, 385: 2: ^{gada}*šal-ḫu šá pa-ru-uk-ti* NCBT 1069: 8 "two *šalḫu* cloths for a canvas". NR

parūru "malt, porridge"

Stol 2008, 351: a sort of porridge, s. Deller 1985, 327. NR

+ **paruštu** "girdle"; OB, foreign word(?)

Lex. *pa-ru-uš-tum* = MIN (*nēbeḫu*) MARI 5, 412 BM 38590: 5.

parūtu I "a kind of alabaster"; + EA(?)

1. *pa-*[*ru*]*-* ⌜*ti*⌝ EA 13: 31 (Moran 1992, 25f. with n. 13).
2. For Cole Nippur 116: 16 (CAD P 211 *p.* b end) s. *parūtu* IV. NR

+ **parūtu IV** "female mule"; SB

pa-ru-tu OIP 114, 116: 16' after *parû* "mule" in a list on a school tablet. Cf. *šaḫû*/*šaḫītu* "boar/sow" ib. 3'f.). S. Streck 1999, 295. NR

parūtu V, *parītu* "insult"

Mayer 2008, 98:
1. SB *pa-ru-ti* SpTU 3, 58 iii 32, s. *pīštu*, below.
2. SB *pa-ri-tum ay aqbi* Or. 59, 450: 19' "may I not say something mean".

NR

+ **parwatru**, *permatru* "an object"; OB

1. *ana ruššuk* 4 *pa-ar-wa-at-ri* ARM 32 p. 327 M.7018: 11 "(silver) for 'drying' 4 *p.*s".
2. *ana ru-šu-un pé-er-ma-at-ri* ib. p. 338 M.5222+: 55.
3. Cf. Arkhipov, ib. p. 171: object of unclear nature.

parzikku "saddle hook(?)"

Stol 2008, 351: Civil 1987b, 47 interprets the Sum. equation ^{giš}DAG-*si* as "a part of the donkey's harness for hanging leather bags on for transportation", i. e., "some kind of knob, ring, or hook for hanging the bags". *par-zik(-kum)* is a lw. of ^{giš}DAG-*si* = *pàr-si(.g)*.

parzillu "iron"

OA *annuqum ša pár-zi-lim* AKT 3, 97: 21f. "an iron ring".

pasālu "to turn (away)"

Borger 2008, 442: translation Lie Sg. 368 (CAD P 217a *p.* c) with Fuchs 1994, 331: 309 and n. 344 "he (Elamite) turned away, saying to him (Marduk-apluiddina), he (Elamite) would not make the expedition". NR

pasāmu, *pesēnu*, *paṣānu* "to veil"

G NB *mannu ša ummânu ina pānīšu ibaššûma lapā[n šarr]i i-pe-si-nu u [an]a ēkalli [lā iš]apparu* SAA 18, 131 r. 4 "whoever has a scholar in his presence but hides him fr[om the kin]g and [does not s]end him [t]o the palace".
Dt SB *dīšu up-ta-ṣa-na* LKA 15: 2 "the grass is veiled".
+ **N** NB *amāt šarri tap-pe-⌜es-si⌝-i[n]* SAA 18, 131: 21 "the king's word will be suppressed (lit. concealed)"
MPS (G, N), NR (Dt)

pasāsu "to erase"

D 1. OB *[tupp]i bēlija ša* PN *[u]* PN_2 *ublūnim pu-sú!-us-ma šitassâšu ul ele*ʾʾ*ī* FM 8, 166 no. 47 r. 20' (the ed., by mistake, has *-sú-sú-*) "the tablet of my lord, which PN and PN_2 have brought to me, is erased and I can not read it".
2. OB *šumma dīni tu-pa-as-sà-as pu-ús-s[í]-is* RATL 83: 12f. "if you want to cancel my verdict, cancel (it)!"
3. Stol 2008, 351: OB *dīnī u dayyānī ú-pá-sà-as* ARM 5, 39: 13 "he neglects (lit. obliterates) my verdict and neglects my judges". S. Heimpel 1997a; Durand 2000, 248f.
4. Stol 2008, 351: NA *abnu li-pa-sis-su* AMD 3 no. 156: 23'; ib. no. 149a i 23' "may the stone obliterate it" (quoted in CAD P 249a *pašāšu* 3a as Köcher BAM 5, 503 i 23'). MPS, NR

+ **pāsigu** (or *pasīgu*) "a bird"; OB

pa-si-gu-um^{mušen} Edubba 7, 100: 27 (in list of birds).

pasillu "a kind of sheep"

OB 1 UDU *pa-⌜si⌝-l[u-um]* ARM 24, 45: 7.

paslu s. *pašlu*

paspasu "duck"

1. Borger 2008, 443: AbB 1, 113 r. 7 (CT 43, 113; CAD P 222 *p.* a1') read NIMIN *paspasim* "40 ducks" instead of NUNUZ *paspasim* "duck eggs".
2. SB *alālū pa-as-pa-sí-im urriš* ALL no. 11: 9 "the songs of the duck are by day-light".
3. SB ⌜*pī*?⌝ *šulmi baZki pa-as-pa-sí* ib. r. 5 "a word(?) of greeting is the quacking(?) of the ducks".
MPS (2–3), NR (1)

pasru "a wooden part of a chariot"

OB n *ereqqētu* 3 ^{giš}*pa-as-ru* ARM 32 p. 484 M.15106: 16 "n wagons, 3 *p.*s".

****passātu** (CAD P 224) s. *pasūtu*.

pasuttu, *pasuntu* "net(?)"

1. Mayer 2008, 98: SB DN *pa-sú-un-ti pušqi ša erēbša egru* AfO 50, 22 BM 65454+: 18 "GN, the fine-meshed net, difficult to enter".
2. SB *bāʾeru ana pa-as-su-ti-šú ileqqē itannu* Jiménez 2017, 250: 20 "the fisherman takes mesh for his net".
MPS (2), NR (1)

+ **pasūtu**, pl. *pasâtu* "a wooden container"; OB

1. 1 ^{giš}*pa-[su-tum]* ARM 32 p. 246 M.12668 iii 20, cf. ib. p. 365 M.8266 ii 1f.
2. 2 *pa-sa-tum Ya[mḫadêtum]* … 1 *pa-su-tum* … ib. p. 256 M.6260 iii 15, 17.
3. *passātu* (CAD P 224) belongs here. Cf. Arkhipov, ARM 32 p. 166: listed between containers and precious vessels.

pašāḫu I "peace, tranquillity"

1. Mayer 2008, 98: translates *qadu mātika ṭūba pa-ša-ḫa lā šapāra … šūma liḫliq* KBo 1, 1 r. 66' // 3 r. 15' (CAD P 227b) "may he perish together with your(!) land without someone sending (you) prosperity (and) peace".
2. Mayer 2008, 98: SB *pa-šá-aḫ šēbūti lū šīmatk[a]* JRAS 1920, 566: 8' // TIM 9, 55: 9' "the peace of old age is your destiny".
NR

pašāḫu II "to cool down, rest"

D 1. Mayer 2008, 98f.: SB *[bēl]ī* ⸢*ú-pa-aš/áš-ši-ḫa*⸣*-an-ni* BWL 58: 1 // BM 34650: 1 "my lord has given me relief".
2. For TuM 2–3 (CAD P 231a *p.* 3) s. *pašāḫu* III.

Š Mayer 2008, 99:
1. SB *inamdin tê ša šup-šu-ḫi šipat balāṭi* ARBT II 17 r. 25' = JRAS 1929, 15: 27' "she gives the incantation-formula of relief, the spell of life".
2. SB *ina têša ú-šap-šaḫ namrāṣa* BM 75974 r. 25 (unpubl.) "she relieves the complaint with her incantation-formula".
NR

+ **pašāḫu III** "to break, cut off (branches)"; LB, Aram. lw.

D Stol 2008, 352: *pu-uš-šu-ḫu* (*ša gišimmarī*) TMH 2–3, 136: 8; 137: 11 "cutting the palms". S. already AHw 841a *p.* D 7b; Joannès 1989, 146 n. 2. Diff. CAD P 231a *p.* 3: *puššuḫu* "to lie fallow".
NR

pašālu "to crawl"

Gtn OB *ta-ap-ta-na-aš-ši-lam qaqqa[ram]* ZA 75, 204: 109 "you keep crawling towards me on the gro[und]".

pašāqu "to (be)come narrow"

Štn SB UD 1^{kam} *ul-ta-nap-šá-a[q-ma]* KAL 1, 10: 13 "he will continuously suffer for one day".

pašāru "to release, free"

G 1. OA PN *pá-še-er awātim* AKT 4, 27: 13 "PN is the one who settles the case". Cf. CAD P 239 *p.* 4.
2. NA "to convert into cash, liquidate": *[uppiš]-ma* PN … *[ina libbi]* 80 *manê erî* 2 *imārī kurummāti akī pa-ša-[ri] izzirip issiqi* SAA 6, 3: 4 "PN [has contracted, purcha]sed, and bought (the slave) [for] 2 homers of barley (equalling) 80 minas of copper at its current value".

3. The ref. NA *mê nagbi pa-ši-ru-ti* ZA 97, 116: 24, already mentioned in Mayer 2008, 99, is now interpreted by Mayer 2017, 25 as "cleared water of a well": according to Mayer, here and in other ref. of *pašāru* in connection with water, the adj. *paš*(*i*)*ru* and not the participle *pāširu* is used.

Gt OB *mimma e-la-am ša libbišunu ay íp-ta-aš-ru-ú* CUSAS 10, 13: 3 "may they not disclose to each other whatever is pure(?) in their hearts".

+ **Dtn**: Mayer 2008, 99: *pu-taš-šir ruḫîya puṭur iʾiltī* K.256 (IV R^2 17) r. 29 // Ki. 1904-10-9, 108: 7' // VAT 13645 iii 5' (= "Šamaš 43", Mayer 1976, 415) "always undo the sorcery affecting me, release me from my sin!"

N SB "to become calm", said of sheep: *šumma immeru enūma takarrabu ip-pa-šar šubat nēḫtu* Emar 6/4, 698: 1 "if a sheep, when you offer (it), becomes calm: dwelling of peace".

MPS (G, Gt, N), NR (G, Dtn)

pašāšu "to anoint"

G 1. Mayer 2008, 99: SB *anāku asḫar paššāka*(ŠÉŠ-*ka*) *asḫar ramkā*<-*ka*> SpTU 2, 24: 26 "I am anointed with *asḫar*-extract, I am bathed in *asḫar*-extract".

2. Mayer 2008, 99: SB *šaman bālti pa*-ŠÍK (for *paššāk*, var. ŠÉŠ-*ku* and [*pa*]-*áš-sá-ku*) KAR 237: 13 // LKA 105: 1 // LKA 107 r. 5' "I am anointed with the oil of pride".

3. CAD P 249a *p.* 3a: Köcher BAM 5, 503 i 23' s. *pasāsu*.

Gtn with reflexive mng.: Bo. *pí-ta-an-*⌈*ši*⌉*-ša* KBo. 36, 29: 23 "keep anointing yourselves".

Gt For the inf. stat. cstr. *piššaš* in OB s. also MARI 5, 598f.

N Mayer 2008, 99: SB *at-ta-ap-šá-áš šamna ṭāba anāku* SpTU 2, 24: 5 "I have anointed (perf.) myself with sweet oil".

+ **Ntn** SB *it-ta-nap-ša-šu*? SAA 8, 38: 3 "he keeps anointing himself".

MPS (Gt, Gtn, Ntn), NR (G, N)

pašāṭu "to erase"

G Unique spelling in MB Ekalte [*p*]*a*-ZA-*a-ṭa ippuš* "(who) makes an erasure(?)" WVDOG 102, 19: 33.

pašertu s. *pišertu*

pašīšu I "anointed (a priest)"

Stol 2008, 352: syllabic spelling on a cylinder seal: *pa-ši-šu-um ša* ^{d}EN.ZU Collon 1986 no. 205: 3. NR

+ **pašīšu? II** "a garment or piece of jewellery(?)"; LB

kulūlu taškīsu 2 *pa-ši-šá* OIP 122, 118: 5, 30 "a crown, a headband, 2 *p.*"

+ **pašlu** "a cup"; OB

1. 1 ^{gal}*pa-áš-lu* ZABAR ARM 24, 83: 3; 85: 8; 95: 4 "1 *p.* cup of bronze".

2. 1 ^{gal}*pa-áš-lu ma*/*qú-i-tum* KÙ. BABBER ARM 24, 83 = ARM 31, 78: 3 "1 *p.* cup … of silver".

3. 3 *pa-áš-lu papparḫim* ARM 25, 393 = ARM 31, 85: 3 "3 *p.* cups with *papparḫum* plant".

4. 1 ^{gal}*pa-áš-lu ša minêtim* ARM 31, 85: 24 "1 *p.* cup with limbs".

5. For further ref. and disc. s. Guichard, ARM 31 p. 257f.

MPS (1–4), NR (1–3, 5)

+ **pašluzzu** (mng. unkn.); MB Nuzi; Hurr. lw.

MB Nuzi *pa-aš-lu-uz-zu* HSS 14, 247: 28 (palace inventory). Prob. ending

-*ussi* (Wilhelm 1998, 175 n. 10). S. also Richter 2012, 306. NR

+ pašqu II "a stone"; SB

Lex. *gug* LAGAB = *pa-aš-*⌜*qu*⌝ Emar 6/4, 553: 76' "carnelian...". Related to the adj. *pašqu* "narrow"?

pašru s. *pašāru* G 3.

+ pašrūtu "(broth) with crumbs(?)"; OB

Stol 2008, 352: OB *pa-aš-ru-tum šīrum* {*ú-ul*} *izzaz* YOS 11, 25: 23 "(Broth) with crumbs (?). Meat is used". S. disc. in Bottéro 1995, 40. NR

****paššaru** CAD P 259a

Stol 2008, 352: delete and s. *paršu*.

NR

paššūru "table"

1. OA [*p*]*á-šu-ru ša* IGI *ilišu* AKT 6b, 468: 1 "tables in front of his gods".
2. OA 5 *pá-šu-ru ša ammā u uṭā* AKT 7a, 79: 12 "5 tables of one and a half cubit each"; cf. 5 *pá-šu-ru ša ammā* ib. 14 "5 tables of one cubit each"; (similarly 78: 12–14).
3. Mayer 2008, 99: OB lit. *ṣēnū pa-aš-šu-ru-*[x] YOS 11, 21: 24 "[their(?)] tables are loaded up".
4. Mayer 2008, 99: SB ⌜giš⌝*banšur ní-ba íl-íl-lá-ĝu*10 = ⌜*pa*⌝*-áš-šu-ru ša ina ramāni-šu neʾû* BagM 37, 95 BM 38593: 23 "the table that turns over(?) by itself".
5. Beaulieu 2003, 385: LB written logogr. URUxGU (= ŠAKIR) or URU xGA (= ŠÀKIR) instead of URUx URUDU (= BANŠUR).

MPS (1–2), NJCK (2), NR (3–5)

pāštu "axe, adze"

1. *ra-ak-ba-sú*(text: *šu*)*-ú-um ana kuppî pa-aš-tum* CUSAS 10, 7: 5 "for the eel the sickle-sword is riding". Cf. George, ib. p. 44f.
2. (gold and silver) *ša* giš*pa-áš-ti ša Sîn* ARM 25, 467 = ARM 32 p. 213 M.6035: 3 "for the axe of Sîn".
3. (gold and silver) *iḫzu* giš*p*[*a*]*-aš-tim ša Sîn* ARM 32 p. 483 M.14094: 3 "for the mounting of the axe of Sîn".
4. Disc. and further ref. from Mari s. Arkhipov, ARM 32 p. 119f. Since ARM 14, 29 = FM 8, 77f. no. 21 (CAD P 266b *p.* b) mentions *p.*s for cutting (? the verb remains unclear; pace Durand 2000, 149 certainly not *nepû*), there is no reason to assume, pace Arkhipov, ib. p. 119, a clear distinction between a weapon *pāštu* and a tool *pāšu*; cf. also CAD P 266b *pāštu* b for *pāštu* used in the household.

pāšu "axe, adze"

1. OB (bronze, the weigth of) 6 *pa-ás* NA4ḫi.a ARM 25, 419 = ARM 32 p. 426 M.9785: 4 "6 axes for stones".
2. OB 1 *pa-šu Tukrušû* ZAB[AR] ARM 32 p. 246 M.12668 iii 31 "1 axe from Tukriš made of bronze" (after *katappu* and *ḫaṣṣinnu* "axes").
3. OB 1 ÁGA ZABAR *Akkadû* ARM 31, 4: 20 "1 Akkadian axe of bronze".
4. For disc. and further ref. from Mari s. Arkhipov, ARM 32 p. 141.

+ patabāru "outer wall(?), outer side of a wall(?)"; OB, Sum. lw.

1. Lex. *bàd-da-bar-ra* = *pa-ta-ba-ru-um* ZA 94, 230 i 3 (in list of diff. expresions for walls). Cf. Krebernik, ib. p. 232.
2. Lex. DI.IB? = *pa-ta-ba-ar dūrim* ZA 94, 230 i 16 "outer side(?) of the wall". Cf. Krebernik, ib. p. 234.

patāḫu "to puncture, bore through"; +NA

ša KUR *pát-ḫat-u-ni* SAA 16, 5 r. 11 in broken context.

patālu "to twine, twist"; + MB

G 1. OB lit. *li-ip-ti-il-kum iṣ arti pitiltam* Finkel 2014, 359: 11, s. *pitiltu*, below.
2. SB [*šumma ṣur*]*ārû kīma pitilti patlu-ma ina bīt amīli ittanallak* KAL 1, 16 r. 6 "[if liz]ards are entwined like a rope and go(!) around a man's house".

N MB ⸢*ti*⸣*-pá-ti-*⸢*il*⸣ Lamaštu p. 264: 8 s. *pû* II.

patānu I "to dine"

G 1. OB (wine) *inūma sugāgū* [*š*]*a* GN *ip-tu-nu* FM 10, 71 no. 42: 8 "upon the occasion when the sheikhs of GN dined".
2. Mayer 2008, 99: OB *ba-lum pa-ta-an* YOS 11, 4: 8 "without eating".

Š OB *akalam u šikaram ú-ša-ap-ta-an-*⸢*šu*⸣*-nu-ti* FM 9, 39 no. 4: 27 "I will give them bread and beer to eat".

MPS (G, Š), NR (G)

patāqu I, *petēqu* "to shape, create"

G 1. OB *ṣērum ša* PN *ip-tu-qú adī amšalī* PN *īpušma* ARM 13, 210: 10 "the snake that PN was casting, yesterday (lit. until yesterday) PN has finished it".
2. OB *inūma laḫtanam ip-tu*!*-qú*! ARM 21, 130: 8 (cf. ARM 32 p. 27) "when he cast the beer vat".
3. OB *inūma ḫalli ša ereqqim ša* DN *ip-tu-qú* FM 3, 231 no. 60: 40; ib. 227 no. 56: 14 "when they cast the 'thigh' of the chariot of DN".
4. OB *siparrum ballūtum ina pa-ta-qí-im* 1 *manû* 1/2 GÍN *imaṭṭī siparrum lā damqum ištū ballu ina pa-ta-qí-im* 1 *manû* 1 GÍN *imaṭṭī* ARM 25, 714 = ARM 32 p. 227 A.3145 r. 1, 4 "bronze alloyed loses half a shekel per mina in the process of smelting. Bronze which is not good, after it has been alloyed, loses 1 shekel per mina during the process of smelting".
5. SB *ḫaṣṣinnu ni-ip-ti-qu* Gilg. SB II 248 "let us cast an axe".
6. NB *minû ibašši kī itti libbišunu idabbubū* ... *minû ibašši kī itti libbišunu i-pe-et-<ti>-qu-nu* SAA 18, 132: 12 "what is it, that they are plotting (lit. talking to their heart), what is it, that they are planning (lit. creating with their heart)?" Unlikely N *ippetqūn*(*u*).

D OB 12 MA.NA *abārum* ... *inūma ina bīt* DN *ú-pa-at-ti-qú* 10 MA.NA *abārum ina bīt têrtim ú-pa-at-ti-qú* ARM 25, 314 = ARM 32 p. 229 M.18468: 3,6 "12 minas of lead, when they smelted (it) in the temple of DN, 10 minas of lead, (when) they smelted (it) in the house of the administration".

N 1. OB (silver) *itūr ip-pa-ti-iq-ma* 3 GÍN *kaspum imṭī* ARM 24, 123: 6 "was melted again and 3 shekels of silver were lost".
2. (silver) ... *ša ana kakki kaspim ip-pa-at-qú* ib. 94: 20 "was cast into a silver weapon".
3. OB (silver for weapons) *ša warkānūm i*[*p-p*]*a-at-qú* ARM 25, 176 = ARM 32 p. 349 M.7298 r. 1 "which was smelted later".
4. Cf. Arkhipov, ARM 32 p. 27 with further ref. from OB Mari.

MPS (G, D, N), NR (G)

patāqu II "to drink"; + OAkk.

ruʾti kanaktim ti-ip-tá-at-qá MAD 5, 8: 11 "you (dual) have drunk the sap of the incense-tree". Note that AHw 1582 tentatively lists the ref. under *patāqu* I whereas CAD does not have the ref. at all (neither *batāqu* nor *patāqu* I, II).

patarru, *atbarru*? "knife(?)"

Var. *atbarru*(?) in OB lex. *ba-da-ra* = *at-ba-ru* UET 7, 93: 16. Cf. Sjöberg 1996, 225.

patīḫatu "a leather container"

OB ARM 30 p. 179f. Pace Durand, ib. unlikely fem. pl. of sg. *patīḫu*, since the word is attested in lex. texts and in Lamaštu (CAD P 276) in the sg.

patinnu "sash, band"

1. OB s. ARM 30 p. 83–85 with numerous ref.; 162; 169.
2. NB *pa-tin-nu* KÙ.GI *šulmān ša šarri* SAA 17, 58: 5' "a golden sash, a gift for the king".

patīru "a leather bag"

OB 1 [kuš]*pa-tí-ru* ARM 30 p. 416 M.18159: 3 (between *pālilu* and *patīḫatu*). NR

patniš "strongly"

Mayer 2008, 99: SB DN *tukšu allalû ša ana pan kiṣir šašm*[*e*] ⸢*pat-niš*⸣ *izzazzu* AfO 50, 21 BM 65454+: 14 "DN, the strong shield that faces the battle group powerfully". NR

patnu II, *petnu* "strong, sturdy"

LB *ḫuṣṣu pét-nu iḫaṣṣaṣ gušūrē pét-nu-tu ina libbi iṣabbat* OIP 122, 16: 9 "he will erect a resistant reed hut, he will put in solid beams". NR

patru "sword, dagger"

1. Stol 2008, 352: MB Emar 3 GÍR *makkasātu* 3 GÍR ZABAR GAL 3 GÍR ZABAR TUR CunMon. 13, 70 no. 28: 2–4 "3 *makkasu*-knives, 3 big bronze knives, 3 small bronze knives".
2. Mayer 2008, 100: SB *ina pa-tar bi-ni* (*ina* GÍR GIŠ.ŠINIG) + *nakāsu* Walker/Dick 2001, 73: 52 and 142: 86b "to cut with a knife made of tamarisk wood".
3. Stol 2008, 352: LB fem. pl. GÚ.UN AN.BAR *ana pat-ra-a-ta* WZKM 91, 355 no. 7: 2 "one talent of iron for daggers".
4. SB GÍR *siparri ša* 10 GÍN *šuqultašu teleqqēma* SpTU 5, 246 iii 23 "you take a bronze dagger weighing 10 shekels".
5. SB *pat-ri katappê uqnû šikiršu/ muḫḫašu* … *ana Bibbi ṭābiḫ erṣeti* Gilg. SB VIII 175 "a double-edged dagger, its haft/top lapislazuli … for B., the butcher of the netherworld".
6. CAD P 282b *p.* b: delete with Borger 2008, 443 the ref. BBR 2 no. 62 r. 7: *la ma-gír-tú tu-še-ṣa* (instead of GÍR UD. K[A.BAR).
7. Numerous ref. from OB Mari in Arkhipov, ARM 32 p. 120f.
MPS (5, 7), NR (1–4, 6)

pattu "canal"

OB lit. as metaphor for the vagina: *ana pa-ti-i-*⸢*ki mamman*⸣ *ul iṭeḫḫēši*! CUSAS 10, 10: 36 "to your canal no one will come near".

pattû "bucket"

1. OB lex. *gi-bunin*? = *pa-at-tu-um* CUSAS 12 p. 252: 163, s. Civil, ib. p. 255.
2. OB lit. [*p*]*a*!*-at-tu-ú napišti* (// *zi-pàd-dè*) CUSAS 32, 54: 2 "bucket of life".
3. S. also *b/patiʾum*.

paṭāru "to loosen, release"

G 1. OAkk. Beydar in PN: *Ib-ṭur-il* Subartu 2, 5 iii 9 "God has ransomed".
2. OA, object silver (cf. CAD P 290 *p.* 2a):
a) 7 *manā kaspam ip-ṭù-ru-ni-ku-nu-tí* AKT 7a, 279: 29 "they opened 7 minas of silver for you".
b) 3 GÍN.TA *iqabbīʾū ulā i-pá-ṭù-ru* ib. 21 "they promise 3 shekels each, but do not open (the silver?)".
3. OB *ina pa-ṭá-ri-šu* [x] ⌜TA/ŠA⌝ URU[ki] GN ZA 90, 266, no. 3: 8 "if he deserts [from?] GN".
4. OB *ša pa-ṭa-ri in-na-an-di-in* CUSAS 9, 106: 18 "(barley and beer) was given for removal of ritual arrangement".
5. OB *pa-ṭa-a-ar* KI.BI ib. 111: 1 "removal of its (sacred) place(?)", s. comm. Dalley, ib. p. 98f.
6. PN [m]*Pa-ṭe₄-er-e-il-tim* AbB 13, 160: 8 "(god) releasing the guilty". For *eʾiltam paṭāru* s. van Soldt, ib. p. 137 and CAD P 292 *p.* 4.
7. Mayer 2008, 100:
a) OB *ši-in mātim elītim u šaplītim ta-pa-ṭà-ar* MARI 5, 258: 15 "you will loosen the sandal(?) of the upper and lower country".
b) SB *paṭār*(DU₈) *še-e-nu* TCL 6, 20 r. 7 "loosening of the sandal".
8. Mayer 2008, 100: SB *šiptu* DN *a-paṭ-ṭar immera kasâ maḫar-ka kīma anāku immera annâm a-paṭ-ṭa-ru arnu šērti gillat u ḫiṭītu lemnētu ša ina zumriya ina pan ilūti-ka lip-paṭ-r*[*a* SpTU 2, 12 ii 31–33 "Incantation: DN, I release a bound sheep before you. As I release this sheep, so may be released fault, guilt, sin and evil crime, (which are in my) body, in front of your divinity".

Gt Missing in AHw but mentioned in CAD P 287; s. Streck 2003a, 51f. for ref. analysed as G perf. in AHw *p.* G 14a, e.g.: *šalmūssunu*! *uṣû ṣābum tillatum kalûšina ana mātišu ip-ta-ṭà-ar u Ḫanû ištū* GN *ana nawîmma iṣbat* ARM 14, 92: 18 "they safely went out. All the allies departed to their land and the Ḫanû headed off to the pasture".

D OB *ana pu-uṭ-ṭú-ri-ni* 3 *manā kaspam ana ṭātim niddinakkum* VS 29, 2: 9 (ZDMG 156, 183f.) "for our ransom we have given you 3 minas silver as baksheesh".

Dtn *kiṣall*[*āya*] *up-ta-na-ṭa-ra* (var. *up-ta-na-aṭ-ṭa-*[*ra*]) LKA 155 r. 3 = AMD 8/1, 259 no. 8.2: 67) "my ankles slacken repeatedly". Here belongs also KAR 80: 5 (CAD P 299b *p.* 10c2' under D).

Dt SB *ina ūm išartišu up-ta-aṭ-ṭa-ru eʾiltu u annu* Iraq 60, 192: 24 // CTN 4, 201: 24 (Ludlul I) "on his day of justice sin and guilt are absolved".

N 1. Stol 2008, 352: "take apart a precious metal object for reutilization; remove a plating from the object":
a) OB 1 *ḫubūsi* GAL *ezub abnātišu ip-pa-aṭ-ṭà-ar iššaqqal* RA 83, 119 n. 23 "1 big *ḫubūsi*-weapon without its stones must be taken apart and weighed".
b) 2 *muššar* BÁBBAR.DILI *ša ina ḫīšim ippaṭru* MARI 4, 514 no. 2.4.7 "2 *muššar-pappardilû*-stones, which are removed from the headband". S. also Durand 1997, 257 for D with the same mng.
2. Stol 2008, 352: MB Nuzi *šumma* ... *šiprušu ip-pa-ṭar* AdŠ 4, 21 n. 16 "if ... his work will be neglected".
3. Mayer 2008, 100: with *šēnu* "sandal" "to be taken off": SB AN *še-ni* (var. E.SÍR) (NU) DU₈ = *šamû šēnu* (*ul*) *ip-paṭir* Astronomical Diaries 1 p. 33 "it rained (but/and) the sandal was (not) removed".

MPS (G, Gt), NR (G, D, Dt, Dtn, N)

paṭīru "a table"

LB *pa-aṭ-ṭi-re-e* KÚ.BABBAR AOAT 414/1, 309 no. 200: 5 "silver tables".

paṭru "released"

Mayer 2008, 100:
1. LB *ḫi-in-di pa-ṭi-ir-tu*4 ZA 61, 255: 2 "opened money bag"
2. *ḫindu pa-ṭir-ti rakistu u kanikti* NABU 1993/19 no. 2: 1 "money bag, opened, bound and sealed". NR

pāṭu, *pattu* "border; district"

1. OB *pa-ṭú-u-ni ša sanqū irappiš* CUSAS 18, 19: 8' "our border areas that are contracted will expand". Note the disagreement in number, which sometimes occurs in the Tigunanum texts (diff. George, ib. p. 120: monosyllabic stem from a final-weak root).
2. Streck 1995, 47 and n. 59: SB *izzīzūma* ⸢*i-na pa*⸣*-at-tu* // *i-*⸢*nap*⸣*-pa*!*-at-*⸢*tu*⸣ (Sandhi writing) *qīšti* Gilg. SB V 1 "they stood at the edge of the forest". Diff. George 2003, 602f. and 821: "they stood *marvelling* (*napātu*) at the forest". MPS (1), NR (2)

pa'û "a bird" s. *pû* III

+ **paʾurru** (mng. uncertain); LB

NB 1 GÚ *šá pa-*⸢*úr-ri*⸣ KÙ.SIG17 YOS 17, 246: 5 (Beaulieu 2003, 195) "one gold necklace with *p.*". NR

+ **paz** (mng. uncertain); MB Qaṭna; Hurr. word

\ *pa-zu-šu ša*? ⸢uru⸣*Qàṭ-na* QS 3, 1: 13. S. disc. ib. p. 45.

pazāru, *bazāru* "to abscond, to go into hiding, to steal through"

G 1. OB *šumma ana* GN *allak šumma kaṣâmma a-ba*!*-az-za-ar* ARM 2, 120 = ARM 26/2 p. 436f. no. 500: 21 (Heimpel 2003, 392) "if I go to GN, (or) if I steal through(?) the steppe (not *maṣāru* pace AHw 619 and CAD M/1, 329).
2. OB PN ... *ina* GN1 *ūlū ina* GN2 *ūlū ina i* GN3 *kaṣâmma i-ba-az-zi-ir* ARM 26/2 p. 435 no. 498: 12 (Heimpel 2003, 391) "PN is stealing through(?) the steppe from GN1, or else from GN2, or else from GN3".
3. Disc. in ARM 26/1 p. 345 n. g and n. 37; ARM 26/2 p. 435f. n. a. and Durand 1998, 262 ad no. 600 n. b. Durand derives the verb from *pazāru*. In spite of the spelling with BA = *bá* is unlikely to derive from BṢR, "to tear off" (CAD B 134) but rather an assimilation /p/ > /b/ before voiced /z/.

D 1. OA PN *lū pá-zu-ur* AKT 6c, 538: 17 "PN may hide".
2. OB lit. *ezub* 120 G[UR] ⸢*ú-pa-az-zi-rù*⸣ *ummi*[*ʾānū*] Finkel 2014, 362: 33 "apart from 120 kor (of dry bitumen) which the workmen stowed away".
3. OB lit. *ezub* 30 GUR *ú-pa*!?*-az-zi-rù* lú.meš*ummiʾā*[*nū*] ib. 58 "apart from 30 GUR (of lard) which the workmen stowed away". MPS (G, D), NR (G)

pazzurtu "contraband, smuggled merchandise, smuggling"; + OB

OB *ḫupšum ša pa-zu-ur-ta-ni u maṣṣarātum irtīqā* Shemshara 1, 36: 22 "the *ḫupšum*-troops of(!) our secret depot and the guards have absented themselves"; we expect, however, the genitive *pazzurtini*.

+ **ped-** "to help"; MB Qaṭna; Hurr. word

GN *ana* PN \ *be-tu-ni* "GN helped PN" QS 3, 5: 12, s. the disc. ib. p. 71.

pegû, *pegītu* s. *pagû*

peḫû I "sealed, closed; stupid"

1. Said of intellect (cf. CAD *p.* d): OB lit. *ana kâšim pe-ḫu-um* (// Sum. *pe-el*) *anāku* CUSAS 10, 14: 18, 20 "am I, (compared) to you, limited?"
2. Mayer 2008, 100: SB *bābu*(KÁ) *pe-ḫu-ú* OLA 40, 94 no. 6: 27 "locked gate". MPS (1), NR (2)

peḫû II "to close up, seal"

D NB *dūru nukkusu rab-kāṣir* [*ina libbi itt*]*ê u šamni ṭābi up-te-eḫ-ḫi* SAA 18, 157: 8' "the chief-tailor sealed the breached wall [with bitu]men and sweet-scented oil" (symbolic act).

pēḫû "caulker; encloser(?)"

OB *šu-ú pé-ḫu-ú i-ga-rum* ARM 28, 63: 36 "he, the encloser(?), the wall", s. comm. ARM 28 p. 93 n. c.

pelû I "red"

SB [*kul*]*bābū pe-lu-tum* KAL 1, 21: 60 "red ants".

pelû II "egg"

1. OB 6 *pe-lu-ú* Ì.DÙG.GA *umtallû* CUSAS 9, 65: 7 "6 eggshells, filled with perfumed oil" (an asyndetic relative clause, construction not understood in CUSAS 9 p. 66). Cf. CAD P 321 *pelû* d for the use of *pelû* as container for perfume in Mari.
2. OB 2 *pé-li lurmim* FM 2, 104 no. 62: 12 "two ostrich eggs".
3. OB 1 *gištappu tamlī pé-*⌜*li-i*⌝ ARM 32 p. 447 = ARM 24, 288+ i 38 "1 footstool with an eggshell inlay".
4. CAD P 320b *p.* a1': AbB 1, 113: 7 s. *paspasu*. MPS (1–3), NR (4)

pelû III "to be red"

G NB, Stol 2008, 352: *pe-li-ma* UET 7, 121 iii 6 "(stone) is red".
+ **D** Mayer 2017, 26: OB lit. *tûltum* … *ú-pé-el-li-a-am īnīšu* YOS 11, 5: 5 "the worm reddened his eyes". MPS (G), NR (D)

+ **pelulizzi** "a garment"; MB Qaṭna, Hurr. word

4 túg.me \ *be-lu-li-iz-zi* QS 3, 13: 5. According to ib. p. 89 perhaps from the Hurr. root *pil-* "to spin".

pēmtu "charcoal"

1. MA Bil. […] *u-me-ni-bir* // *pe-en-ti zurūma* Iraq 42, 32: 9 "scatter (plants) on the coals!"
2. NE BAM 1, 3 ii 8 (CAD P 325b *p.* c) // [gišE]R[E]N *ḫum-ṭám* BAM 5, 480 iv 5 "scorching cedar" (Worthington 2006, 21 and 28). Diff. Stol 2008, 352: [...] x *ṣil-lum-tú*GAR-*an-ma*. NR

pēmu "thigh"

1. OB lex. *ḫa-áš-úr-ĝu*10 = *kubur pe-mi-ia* CUSAS 12 p. 150: 30 (Ugumu) "the thick of my thighs". *úr-ĝu*10 = *pe-ma-a-a* ib. 32 "my thighs".
2. OB [*šumma izbum*] ... 4 *pe-e-mu-šu* CUSAS 18, 12: 70 "[If a miscarried foetus] ... 4 are his thighs".
3. SB Ugar. (Gilg.) I.ZI! GÍD!.DA *pe-na-*⌜*šu*!⌝ AulaOr. Suppl. 23, 42: 32 "his thighs are a long wall".

pe/indû "a red speckled stone"

(na4)ŠI.TIR = *pendû* also EA 22: 64 (Moran 1992, 58 n. 16). NR

peqqû "squirting cucumber(?)"

Stol 1987a, 84f.: in spite of Hebr. *paqqū ʿā*, prob. not "colocynth".

perʾazu s. *piʾʾazu*

perdu "an equid"

1. OA *pé-er-dam* AKT 1, 78: 10. S. Hecker, aATU (v. 0.3, 2012). Not **birtu* "a metal" (Bilgiç AKT 1 p. 96f. and 13). For *perdu* in OA s. Michel 2004, 190–200.

2. OB lit. *pe-er-di*!(text: GIŠ) *sisîm* CUSAS 10, 12: 27 "the mare(?) of a horse".

3. Stol 2008, 353:
a) OB 2 GAL SAG *līd pí-ir-di* 1/2 MA.NA^àm ARM 31, 26: 12 "(to make rhytons in form of) two big foal heads, each of 1/2 mina".
b) 4 GAL SAG *līd pí-ir*!-*di*! KÙ.BABBAR 1 5/6 MA.NA 3-*su* KI.LÁ.BI ARM 31, 37: 20 (s. also Durand 1998, 81).
c) For disc. s. Guichard, ARM 31 p. 282f. MPS (1, 2), NR (1, 3)

persu, *pirsu* "division; a piece of fabric (for repairing clothes?); weaned child or animal"

1. "a piece of fabric":
a) OB 4 *barkarrû pí-ir-su* ARM 30 p. 428 M.8599: 2 "4 *b.* textiles, piece (for repair?)".
b) 1 *uṭublu* SAG *pí-ir-su* ib. p. 397 M.11683: 2 "1 *u.*-fabric, piece".
c) S. also Durand, ib. p. 85 and 601.

2. Stol 2008, 353:
a) OB (silver for) *pisan pí-ir-si* ARM 25, 48: 17; r. 8; 134 r. 2 (s. also FM 7, 65) "box of the section(?)".
b) *alpī pí-ir-sà-*[*a*]*m azūz* ARM 6, 36: 5 "I distributed the oxen by section(s)(?)". Cf. CAD P 411b *p.* c.
c) *šītum pi-ir-su u karšu* YOS 11, 25: 6 (MesCiv. 6, 9 and 31f.) "salted meat, *p.*-entrails and stomach". Cf. CAD P 411b *p.* e.

3. Weaned animal: MA 2 ^gu4^ÁB^meš^ *pír-su* BATSH 9/3, 1: 2 "weaned cows" and passim with diff. animals, s. index ib. p. 196. MPS (3), NR (1–2)

perṣu "breach"

Stol 2008, 353: OB *gú*^pi-ir-ṣum^-*gìr* ASJ 20, 202 BM 54712 ii 7 (Izi). Cf. Izi Bo. A ii 147 (MSL 13, 137): *gú gìr* = *be-el-šú* (for *pilšu* "breach") = (Hitt.) *pát-te-eš-*[*šar*]. NR

\+ **peršaʾe** (an adverb); MB Qaṭna, Hurr. word

a-ḫi \ *be-er-ša*10*-e an-ziq* "my brother, I was ... annoyed" QS 3, 2: 43. S. the disc ib. p. 52.

pērtu "hair (of head)"

1. OB lex.:
a) *sík-àk-ĝu*10 = *itiq pe-er-ti-ia* CUSAS 12 p. 154 ii 2 (Ugumu) "lock of my hair".
b) ^giš^*tukul-sík-ĝu*10 = *kakki pe-er-ti-ia* ib. 4 "clump(?) of my hair.
c) *dal-sík-ĝu*10 = *talli pe-er-ti-ia* ib. 6 "part of my hair".

2. OB lit.:
a) *šākān qimmatim mēlul pé-re-te kûmma Ištar* CunMon. 8, 24 i 38 "making a hairdo, whirling of locks is yours, Ištar".

b) *sinnišātu pé*!*-re-te kadrā-ma* ib. 26 ii 4 "the women are untidy regarding (their) hair".

3. SB (Gilg.):

a) *appāt pe-er-ti-šu ḫannubā kīma Ni*[*ssaba*] AulaOr. Suppl. 23, 42: 31 "the tips of his hair grow like grain".

b) *apparī pērēta kī uqnâti* ib. 33 "with regard to his hair, he is tufted like blue wool".

4. Mayer 2017, 26: SB *ša per-ta arrakat* (// [*síg gíd-da*]) *gallābtaša* [*rabītu*? *anāku*] *ša per-ta kurrât* (// [*síg gud*$_8$*-d*]*a*) *ummu māšittašu* [*anāku*] FAOS 18, 145: 79f. "[I am] the [great(?)] hairdresser of the one whose hair is long. [I am] the mother who combs the one whose hair is short".

perʾu "bud, shoot, scion, descendant"

1. OB lex. *bēl pí-ir-ḫi-im* UET 6/3, 894 r. iv 11.

2. Mayer 2008, 101: OB *lumunšu pi-ri-iḫ-šu ul uwaššar* YOS 11, 15: 2 "his evil will not leave his descendants".

3. Stol 2008, 353: OB *mutēr pí-ri-iḫ* PN *ana išrētišu* MARI 4, 324 fig. 11: 4 "who restored the offspring of PN to his villages(?)".

4. Stol 2008, 353: MA 1 ^{udu}U$_8$ *pír-ḫi* GUKKAL AOAT 265, 187 Assur 3/1, no. 11: 1 "1 sheep of the fat-tailed breed". NR

peruzzu "a textile"; + MB Qaṭna

6 TÚG$^{me.meš}$ \ *be-ru-uz-zi-na* QS 3, 12: 16. S. ib. p. 86 for a Hurr. etym.

pessû, f. *pessūtu* "crippled, deformed"

OB as PNf:

1. *Pé-sú-tum* FM 4, 135 no. 3 iii 43 (after *Sukkuktum* "deaf") (also ib., 161 no. 9 iv 20').

2. *Pé-es-su*[*-tum*] FM 4, 179 no. 13 iv 23 (before *Sukkuktum*).

peṣû I "white"

1. Stol 2008, 352: OB of horses:

a) 1 *sisûm pé-ṣú-um* 1 *atānam pé-ṣi-tam* ARM 14, 40 r. 6' "1 white horse, 1 white she-ass".

b) *aššum sisîm* BABBAR *aqbīma umma šūma sisûm* BABBAR *ša narkabtim ul ibaššû lušpurma ašar ibaššû sisâm* BABBAR *lirdûnim* ARM 26/2 p. 526f. no. 533: 10–15 (Heimpel 2003, 406) "I spoke about a white horse, and he answered: 'There is no white chariot-horse available. I shall write, and where one is available, they will bring a white horse along'".

2. Stol 2008, 352: LB of oxen:

a) 1 *alpu pe-ṣu* JCS 35, 218: 2 "1 white bull".

b) 1*-et littu šībtu pe-ṣi-tu*$_4$ AOAT 330, 235 no. 32: 1 "one old white cow".

3. Stol 2008, 352: LB of grain:

a) *uṭṭetu pe-ṣi* OECT 10, 211: 1.

b) *ammātišu* ŠE *pe-ṣa-a-tú* BabA 1, 220 BM 55551: 14' "his forearms are white barley" (description of god's body). S. Reynolds, ib. p. 224. NR

petû I "open"

1. Mayer 2008, 100: OB *eqlam pa-at-a-*⌜*am*⌝ MHET 2/5, 772: 12 "field broken for cultivation".

2. Stol 2008, 352: MB Nuzi *ištū arḫi ša* MN *pa-ti-ú* AdŠ 4, 258: 33 "since the beginning of month MN".

3. Mayer 2008, 100: SB *kakkī pe-tu-ti* AfO 50, 21 BM 65454+: 16 (hymn to Ištar) "unsheathed weapons". NR

petû II "to open"

G 1. OA *šīmātim a-pá-ta-im* AKT 4, 45: 24 "to open the testament".

2. Mayer 2008, 100; Stol 2008, 352: with *panu* "to be friendly":
a) OB *iltum panū-ša pe-tu-ú-ma* AbB 9, 152: 18 "(if) the face of the goddess is friendly".
b) OB *pan* DN *pé-tu-ú* MARI 7, 273: 18 "the face of DN is friendly".
c) SB *pe-te-e pani* STT 123: 6 "to become friendly".
3. EA 137: 33 (CAD P 350b and AHw 860b) is emended by Moran 1992, 219 to *ep-*<*ša*>*-ti* "(for) I committed (sins against the gods)".
4. LB, used elliptically: *suluppē kī ip-tu-u ana danānu ina qātī*⸢*y*⸣ *ittašû* AUWE 5, 136 r. 6' "they have taken away the dates from me by force, after they had 'opened' (the storehouse)".
5. Mayer 2008, 100: SB KA/*pī-kunu ana* BAD-*e*/*pa-te-e* NUNDUN/*šapātīkunu ana katāmu lišānkunu ana dabābu/i ul anamdin* SpTU 2, 24: 11 // BM 45755: 6 "I will not permit (you) to open your mouth, to close your lips, to speak with your tongues".
6. On the name of the chief doorkeeper of the netherworld *Bí-*(*it*)*-ti* and *Bí-ṭu-ḫi-* s. Streck 2014–2016, 163 § 2.

Gtn Mayer 2008, 100: OB *kayyānu niṣrēt ilī ap-ta-na-at-ti-a-ak-kum* MARI 5, 258: 8 "I constantly reveal to you the secrets of the gods".

D EA *ù yu-pa-at-ti* : *ugāri šarri bēlika* EA 250: 47 (Moran 1992, 303 and 304 n. 8) "and he cultivated the fi[el]ds of the king, your lord".

+ Dtn Mayer 2017, 27: OB *pu-te-tu-um kabtam* Sumer 23 pl. 15 IM 49225: 23 "to constantly open is difficult for me(?)".

Dt OB lit. *šamû ellūtum up-*⸢*ta*⸣*-*[*t*]*u*?*-šum* ASJ 12, 8: 4' "the clear sky opens for him".

MPS (G, Dtn, Dt), NR (G, Gtn, D, Dt)

pīʾāqu "to become narrow, tight"

G Mayer 2008, 96: OB lit. *ip-te-eq-ma* Gilg. OB II 88 (// *ip-te-*GI Gilg. SB II 46) "he was embarrassed" (lit. "he became narrow"). George 2003, 185 derives the word from a hitherto unattested G of *puqqu*. MPS/NR

piʾātu "edge, border, bank (of a river)"

1. NA, with det. ÍD: *ina muḫḫi* ^{id}*pi-ia-a-ti ša* GN *ittalkū* ⸢*bīrtu*⸣ *ina libbi eppušū* SAA 15, 166: 9 "they went to the bank of the canal GN and are constructing a fort there".
2. The NA ref. in connection with rivers and canals in CAD *piātu* b are recorded in AHw 874 s. v. *pû* E 2 "Fluß-, Kanalmündung", understood as fem. pl. However, since a pl. is not required by any of the contexts, the interpret. of CAD is preferable.

piʾʾazu, + *perʾazu* "mouse"; + OB, + EA(?)

1. OB (foetus) *zumuršu kīma pì-a-zi-im pa-ra-am ša pì-a-zi ulab*[*biš*?] CUSAS 18, 19: 41 "its body is cl[ad(?)] like a mouse in a mouse's skin".
2. With Durand 1988, 120, Heimpel 2003, 185 n. 35 and Arkhipov 2012, 116f., the word listed in AHw 855 and CAD P 326f. as *perʾazu*, *peḫḫazu* "a precious metal" prob. belongs here. The word has to be normalized with double /ʾʾ/, which also explains why /i-a/ is never contracted.

pīdu I "pardon, indulgence, ransom"

Mayer 2008, 100: SB *ṭardu pi-du-*⸢*šu*⸣ (var. *pi-d*[*u-*, *pi-du-uš-šú*) *tanamdin* KAR 321 r. 2a // BM 61635+ iii 15' // BM 61649+ iii 21' "you give the ransom for the exile". NR

piglu s. *biqlu*

+ **pigmu** "section"; MB Emar; NWSem. lw.

eqlu mala ma-ṣú-ú ina pí-ig-mi GN Emar 6/3, 2: 2; 6: 2 "a field, as far as it extends, in the section of GN". Cf. Zadok 1991, 115; Pentiuc 2001, 140. NR

pīḫu "beer-jar"

1. OB 18 *pi-ḫu-um* CUSAS 9, 8: 7.

2. Stol 2008, 353:
a) PSBA 19 (CAD P 370a *p.* a1'b') read *pí-ḫu* 1 BÁN! KAŠ *si-bi*.
b) OB *pí-ḫu* 1 BÁN 5 SÌLA CT 45, 54: 7 "a beer-jug of 15 liter".
c) After UET 5, 607: 38, 4 *pīḫu* value 1 shekel silver.

3. For lit. s. Sallaberger 1996, 116.

MPS (1), NR (2–3)

pilaggu s. *balangu*

pilakku "spindle"

Mayer 2008, 100: OB lit. *ú-ki-al-lu pí-la-ak-ki* CunMon. 8, 26 ii 18 "(the men) hold spindles". NR

pilku II "work assignment, portion"; + OB, + MA

1. Stol 2008, 353: OB *ummānu ša* GN U4 7[kam] *pí-li-ik* U4 2[kam] *nadû-ma* AbB 14, 210: 7 "the troops of GN (assigned) for seven days have abandoned the work assignment of two days".
2. Stol 2008, 353: *pi-il-ku-um* UET 5, 726: 4 (CAD P 374a *pilku* A 1) belongs here.
3. MA *píl-ka-ni ṣi-il-a-šu-nu* "assign them portions!" Chuera 3: 5.

MPS (3), NR (1–2)

pillû "a plant, perhaps mandragora"

Stol 2008, 353: Read instead of NAM.DIL NÍTA GUL BAM 5, 494 iii 21 (CAD P 376b *p.* c1') rather *ḫu-bu-uš* SÚN (= *nar̮ṭabi*). NR

pilsu "view"

First ref. apart from PN: OB *ina pí-li-is īnīya* RATL p. 395 v 31 "under the view of my eyes".

pilšu "breach"

1. Note the spelling OB lit. *pí-in-ši-i-ka* (// Sum. *búr*) CUSAS 10, 14: 4.
2. Mayer 2008, 100f.: OB *ina liwīt dūr nītim šipik eperī pí-il-ši siḫpim u emūqiya rabîm ālam šuʾāti ... aṣbat* BagM 34, 144 viii 6 "I have taken this city by means of siege of the enclosure wall, embankment, breach, surprise attack and my great power".

MPS (1), NR (2)

pīlu, *pūlu* "limestone"

Pl. *pūlānū* also in NA 4! *pu-⌜la!-a!-ni!⌝* SAA 6, 288 r. 4.

+ **pimaḫunitinina?** "?"; MB Qaṭna, Hurr. word

ÉRIN[meš] *Su-ú-ti* \ *bi-ma-ḫu-ni(-)\ti-ni-na*? QS 3, 5: 52. S. disc ib. p. 74.

pinku "knob, boss "

1. OB (gold, the weight of) 1 *kisibirrim rabîm pí-in-ki* ARM 32 p. 274 A.3542: 3 "1 big coriander, a knob".
2. OB 1 *zēr šakirê pí-in-ku* ARM 25, 139 = ARM 32 p. 200 M.11193: 5 "1 seed of henbane(?), a knob".
3. OB [1] *zimizzi uqnîm rabûm [p]í-in-[ku]* ARM 32 p. 254 M.12682+ i 8 "1 big *z.* bead of lapis lazuli, a knob".
4. For disc. and further ref. from OB Mari s. Arkhipov, ARM 32 p. 88f.

+ pinnatu "part of the tail"; OB

Lex. KU-*kun-ĝu*10 = ⸢*pí-in-na-ti*⸣ CUSAS 12 p. 157 x 5.

pinnigu s. *pannigu*

pinnu, *pīnu* "button, stud"; + NA(?)

1. NA(?)⸢*pi-i-nu kis*⸣ [*su*] SAA 7, 62 iv 1 "button ..." (in list of precious items given to Mullissu).
2. Beaulieu 2003, 385: "an attachment or button to fasten the components of jewels". NR

pinzurru s. *bunzerru*

pipnu s. *bibnu*

pīqa "on (one) occasion"

1. Mayer 2017, 27: SB *pi-qam*? = *zamar* SpTU 3, 100: 15 "on one occasion = quickly".
2. Stol 2008, 353: For *pīqa lā pīqa* s. also disc. in Mayer 1989, 153f.

MPS (1), NR (2)

pīqat "perhaps"

For *pīqat* in OB cf. Wasserman 2012, 16–42.

piqdu "allocation, consignment"; + OB

1. OB 1 UDU.NÍTA *libbū pi-iq-di ana* É.GIR4.MAḪ CUSAS 9, 34: 2; cf. 37: 7 "1 ram from the consignment for the Egirmaḫ-temple".
2. OB (ewes and lambs) *ana nēpešti libbū pi-iq-di* ib. 365: 5 "for divination from the consigment".

piqqannu "dung pellet"

Mayer 2017, 27: Also metaphorically said of wool: SB A.GAR.GAR *šīpāti peṣâti ina maḫar* A.GAR.GAR *nabāsi* MC 13, 15: 9f. "pellets of white wool in front of pellets of red wool".

pirikānu, *parakānu* "a garment"

1. OA *pì-ri-kà-ni narbūtim wasmūtim* AKT 6c, 544: 21 "soft and fitting *p.*s".
2. OA *pá-ra-kà*-NIM *liqē*ʾ*ā* AKT 4, 61: 17 "take the *p.*!"
3. Disc. by Michel/Veenhof 2010, 238f., with new OA ref.

pirikku, + *piriggu* "a divine symbol or a cultic installation"

1. OB *aššum pí-ri-ik-ki-i*[*m ša ina i*]*šar-tim ṣeḫretim nadû ... pí-ri-ik-ku-um na-siḫ* FM 8, 57 no. 11: 33 "regarding the *p.*, [which] is situated [in] the small chapel ... the *p.* has been removed".

2. MB Emar 1-*en immeru ana kirî ša pí-ri-ki ša* DN Emar 6/3, 446: 49' "one sheep for the garden of the *p.* of DN".

3. MB Emar *ina pí-ri*!-*ki*!-*ma imtaḫrā* Emar 6/3, 28: 5. (s. Durand 1989a, 179) "they confronted each other by the *p.*".

4. In the fem. pl.:
a) MB Emar 2 *ḫissipū* DN *p*[*í*]-*ri-ka-ti* Emar 6/3, 274: 7 "2 vases-*ḫissipu* for DN of the *p.*s".
b) MB Emar DN *ša p*[*í*]-*ri-ga-ti inaqqû* Emar 6/3, 452: 15' "[...] they sacrifice [... to] DN of the *p.*"

5. CAD *pirikku* A "a divine symbol" and *pirikku* B "mng. unkn." are prob. a single lemma; s. Feliu 2003, 132–134 with previous lit. Either = *parakku* < Sum. *barag* "cult dais" (s. von Soden 1987, 103; Durand 1990a, 298; Streck 2003a, 36 n. 18; Mayer 2017, 27) or < Sum. *pirig* (CAD P 397). Cf. for the ref. under 4, above, the disc. in Pentiuc 2001, 40f. with diff. suggestions (*birrīku* "pool", *pilaqqu* "spindle", *brq* "to flash"). MPS (1, 4, 5), NR (2–5)

pirindu "slice"

Derives from *parāmu*, s. Watanabe 1987, 209 ad § 103. NR

piriṣtu, pl. *pirṣātu* "falsity, falsehood"

Lex. MSL 4, 119 OBGT XII 9, in CAD P 398 s. v. *pirištu* "secret". Cf., however, the following entry *tašg/qertu* "deceit" which makes clear that we are dealing with *piriṣtu*. NR

+ **pirišši** "a type of chair"; MB Qaṭna, Hurr. word

1. 1 gišGU.ZA \ *bi-ri-ši-na-še* QS 3, 12: 17 "one chair in *pirišši* style".
2. [x] gišGU.ZA \ *bi*! (copy: GA)-*ri-ši*!-*n*[*a-še*] ib. 18: 31.
3. For a Hurr. etym. s. ib. p. 86.

pirištu "secret"

1. Unique form with affricate /s/: OB *pi-ri-IZ-ti* RATL 143: 9.
2. Mayer 2008, 101: SB *pi-riš-tú kankat* StPohl SM 10/2 T 158: 159 (s. George 1986, 140) "the secret is sealed".
MPS (1), NR (2)

pirizzaru "a month; a festival"

Disc. by Jacquet 2011, 56f. with further ref.

pirku I "transversal"

1. Stol 2008, 353: OB "region, area":
a) Ref. in CAD P 407 *p.* d1' belong to sec. 3 "region, area".
b) (Field) *pí-ri-ik* DN OECT 15, 39: 2.
c) MU.DU KISLAḪ *pí-ir-ki* A.DAM. MA MDOG 125, 55: 44 (s. also comm. on p. 59); KTT 120: 19 "income of the threshing floor in the region of the steppe".

2. Stol 2008, 353: OB *inūma pi-ir-kam ša* PN *uterrūnim* BagM 24, 152 n. 202 ii 25 "after they have returned the *p.* of PN".

3. Stol 2008, 353: MA measure *pirik ritte* "handsbreadth", s. Freydank 1991, 71:
a) *ina sūte ša pi-rík ritte* MARV 8, 46: 29; 6, 24: 12.
b) *ina sūte ša* PAD *ile pi-rík*/*ri-ik ritte* MARV 3, 42: 3; 8, 60: 4

4. Stol 2008, 353: NA *pi-ir-ki ina irtišu* SAA 10, 310: 2' "[has] lines in his chest" (med.).

5. Stol 2008, 353: NA *pi-ri-ik bīte* CTN 4, 248: 10 "transversal of a house".

6. Mayer 2008, 101: SB *pi-rik mātāti usappiḫšunūti* BagM 21, 384 no. 18 i 18 "(the Assyrian) scattered them (the deportees) across the country". NR

pirmaḫ "design. of horses"

Stol 2008, 353: instead of *pirzumuḫ* (AHw 867a; CAD P 408f.) read *pirmamuḫ* (van Soldt 1980, 78 and 170). NR

+ **pirqūtu** "redemption"; LB
PN *u mārūšu ina tuppi pi-ir-qú-ti-šú-nu ušzīzū* OIP 122, 38: 45 "they reaffirmed (the status of) PN and his children (as recorded) in their tablet of redemption". Weisberg, ib. p. 255 connects *pirqūtu* with Aram. *prq* "to isolate, segregate".
MPS, NR

+ **pirsātānītu** "woman sharing the secret knowledge, female initiate"; LB

tuppu lúKU4.Émeš munus*pir-sa-*⌜*ta*⌝*-na-a-tú* BabA 1, 107f. BM 80711: 1 "a letter from the temple-enterers (and) the female initiates". Cf. Jursa, ib. p. 108.
NR

pirsu s. *persu*

+ pirṭu "disposal(?)" OB

Stol 2008, 353: OB 908 NUN.SÌLA[ku6] *ana pi-ir-ṭí-im* ŠU.TI.A PN [lú]⌈SU.SI.IG⌉ BagM 20, 247 n. 44: 6 "PN, an official (responsible for the disposal of animal carcasses) has taken 908 (spoiled?) fishes to clear (them) away". Sanati-Müller, ib. p. 237: perhaps *pi-ir*-TI-*im* derives from *parāṭu* "to clear away". NR

pīru "elephant"

1. OB lit. *arrak ša pi-ri-im iṣṣeḫrakka*! CUSAS 10, 12: 9 "it (the penis) is very long. An elephant's seems smaller than yours (lit. has become small with respect to you)".
2. SB *ḫutpalû ša idīšu šinni* AM.SI Gilg. SB VIII 123 "the mace in in his hand was made of ivory"; cf. also l. 119.

pisannu s. *pišannu* I

pisnuqiš "powerlessly"

SB *pi-is-nu-*⌈*qiš*⌉ JCS 66, 76: 35 (Gilg.).

pisnuqu "powerless"

Instead of *pa-ás-na-qì* Gilg. Y iv 21 (CAD P 425b) read *-qi*4 (George 2003, 214 ad l. 254).

pīsu "shovel"

OB, Mayer 2008, 101: *pi-i-sà-am* … *šūbilīm* AbB 14, 110: 50 "send me a shovel". NR

piṣṣu (qualifying beads, mng. uncertain)

Plene spelling: OB *uqnûm pí-iṣ-ṣu-ú* ARM 25, 209 = ARM 31, 194: 1 "lapis lazuli *p.*". Cf. disc. Arkhipov 2012, 41 with n. 130.

pišannu, *pisannu* I "box, chest; drainpipe"

1. OB *pišan ērištim* (= [gi]*pisan šu-kam-ma*) CT 45, 75 r. 16; TCL 1, 199: 13 etc. "basket of an expecting (mother)"; s. Stol 2000, 172 n. 9).
2. For OB Mari s. Durand 2009, 180 with numerous ref.
3. SB *išātu kīma mê pí-šá-an-ni ay is-saḫir* Tsukimoto 1999, 193: 34 "may the fever not turn back, like water of a drainpipe". MPS (2–3), NR (1)

pišertu, *pašertu* "release";

1. For OB *aban/abnē* (*ša*) *pašertim* "pierres pour la délivrance" s. disc. in Durand 1983, 236.
2. MA (n barley) *in*[*a bī*]*t*? *pa-še-er-te* BATSH 9/3, 85: 3 "in the [hou]se(?) of disposal(?)". But s. *pi-šèr-ti* ib. 8. Many ref. for *pišerti karūʾe* "release of the barley-heap" (cf. CAD P 428 *p.* 1b) s. ib. p. 196 (index). MPS (2), NR (1)

+ pišri "a wooden implement used in textile manufacturing"; MB Qaṭna, Hurr. word

1. 11 [giš] \ *pí-iš-ri ša* [lú.meš]UŠ.BAR[me] QS 3, 14: 1 "11 *p.*-implements for the weavers".
2. 6 [giš] \ *pí-iš-ri ša* [gada]TÚG[me], 3 [giš] \ *pí-iš-ri ša* [gada]BAR.DUL ib. 10f. "6 *p.*-implements for linen garments, 3 *p.* for linen cloths".
3. S. also ib. 3, 4, 15, 18f. and the disc. in QS 3 p. 91 according to which *p.* is not the loom.

pišru I "release; interpretation"

1. a) OB lit. *ṣeḫram išaqqīʾam mê pi-iš-ri-im* CUSAS 32, 31 iii 11 "it gives the child water of dispelling (of evil) to drink".

b) Also OB lit. *pí-iš-ri* YOS 11, 20: 12; OA *pí-iš-ri-im* Or. 66, 60: 16. Cf. George, comm. CUSAS 32 p. 97.

2. Stol 2008, 354: OB *Ištar-pi-iš₇-ra-*AN ARM 7, 263 i 2 (CAD P 430a *p.* d) = "Ištar of (mountain) Bišri" (ARM 21, 18 n. 4; MARI 4, 527 n. 3).

3. OB, qualifying textiles: *ḫawu/uṣû ša pi-iš-ri* ARM 30 p. 85f. and p. 127f.? Or read *bišri* "from Bišrī"?

4. *iṣ pišri* "magic staff": GIŠ.BÚR = *iṣ-ṣi piš-ri* CTMMA 2, 69: 1 "solving wood". MPS (1, 3), NR (2–4)

piššatu, + *piššetu* "anointing-oil"

1. Lex. *ì-ba* = *pí-iš*!*-še-tum* Emar 6/4, 541: 31 (Ḫḫ I).

2. a) OB *pi-iš-ša-ti ammīni īṣat* CUSAS 9, 10: 17 "why is anointing-oil for me scarce?".
b) *ul pi-iš-ša-ta ul lubāra iddin* ib. 22 "he gave me neither anointing-oil nor a garment".
c) S. also *pi-iš-ša-ta* ib. 13. (sesame oil and cedar resin) *a-na pi-iš-ša-at dalātim* "as lubricant for doors" ib. 143: 3 (cf. CAD P 432 *p.* 2b).

pīštu, *pīltu* "abuse, scandal"; + OA, + NA

1. OA *ša bâš pānī pí-ša-tí-ka tumannā* AKT 6b, 408: 33 "to the shame of (my) face you recount your insults".

2. OB lit. *pi-iš-tum* (// Sum. *in*) *šārum meḫûm* CUSAS 10, 14: 8 "the insult is wind and storm".

3. Mayer 2008, 101:
a) NA lit. *pi-šá-te-*⌜*e-šu ma'dāte*⌝ SAA 3, 29 r. 7 "his many obscenities".
b) NA lit. *ana tēlte u pil-te ina pī nišī ittaškin* ib. 9 "he became a proverbial expression and obscenity in the mouth of mankind".
c) NA lit. PN *ša pi-šá-tu-šú ma'dū* ib. 30: 5 "PN, whose abuses are many".

4. Mayer 2008, 98: SB *ikkib rubê parūti pi-šat lā qabê īpussu* SpTU 3, 58 iii 32 "what he did to him is a taboo for the prince, an offence, an unutterable insult". MPS (1–2), NR (3–4)

pitḫu "perforation"; + MB Emar

1. MB Emar *pí-it-ḫa dalāti* Emar 6/3, 463: 1 "opening of the doors".
2. According to Pentiuc 2001, 141 NWSem. lw., but can well be derived from Akk. *pitḫu*. Streck 2000, 109f.: no Amor. etym.

pitiltu "rope (made of palm fibres)"

1. OB lit. *liptilkum iṣ arti pí-*[*t*]*i-il-tam* "let (someone) twist ribs of palm leaves into ropes for you" Finkel 2014, 359: 11 (construction with two acc.).
2. SB *šībūti i*[*zabb*]*ilū pi-*⌜*til*!?*-ta*⌝ Gilg. SB XI 54 "the old men brought rope of palm-fibre". Cf. George 2003, 881.

pitnu I "strong, sturdy" s. *patnu* II

pitnu II "box; a stringed musical instrument"; + OB

1. OB *pi-it-nu* ... *liblūnim mummu*[*m lā*] *rē*[*q*] FM 9, 126 no. 23: 7 "may they bring a *p.* The conservatory shall [not] be unemployed". For further ref. s. ib. p. 323. Cf. the disc. of Ziegler, ib. p. 76f.
2. *pi-it-nu-um* ARM 28, 86: 22 in broken context (cf. a female singer in l. 26).
3. OB lit. *kīma pi-it-ni-im ḫu-ú-du* ZA 75, 198: 24 "rejoice like a harp!"

pitqu "smelted metal, ingot; pen"

1. OB *pí-it-qú* ARM 24, 123: 8; ARM 25, 196: 1; 215: 2; 362: 1, 2, 5, 9 "(silver), smelted metal".

2. OB (silver) *billatum ša* 1 *patrim pí-it-qí-im* ARM 25, 320 = ARM 32 p. 380 M.10655: 7 "alloy for 1 dagger, smelted metal".

3. OB (bronze, the weight of axes etc.) *pí-it-qí* ARM 25, 204 = ARM 32 p. 346 M.11195: 11 "smelted metal".

4. Counted, mng. "ingot":
a) OB (bronze, the weight of) 2 *pí-[it]-qí* ARM 32 p. 264 A.3146: 8.
b) OB (5 talents of bronze, the weight of) 2 *pí-it-qí ša alê* ARM 21, 258: 39 "2 ingots for drums".
c) OB (silver, the weight of) 1 *pí-it-qí ša ištū* GN PN *ublam* ARM 25, 179 = ARM 32 p. 383 A.4535: 2 "1 ingot, which PN brought from GN".

5. Stol 2008, 354: OB *pi-ti-iq* PN BiMes 17, 75 Ki 660: 3, r. 3, 9 "(sheep) of the pen of PN".

6. For UET 5, 481: 31 (CAD P 441b *p.* 4) s. *bitqu*.

7. For disc. and further ref. from OB Mari s. Arkhipov, ARM 32 p. 27f.

MPS (1–4, 7), NR (5–6)

pitru "half"

1. Lex. 30 *ma-na* = NA4 *pí-ti-ir* Emar 6/4, 553: 213 (Ḫḫ XVI) "30 mina = stone of one-half (of a talent)".
2. The same word as CAD *pitru* B "one-half of a sar" (AHw *pitru* 1 "ein unbebautes Gelände od Grundstück") and CAD *pitru* D "a stone vessel" (AHw *piṭru* 7 "ein Stein?"). Reading *pitru* instead of *piṭru* is favored by the spelling *pi-ti-ir* (never *pi*-DI-*ir*). S. also *bitru* in Emar.

pitrustu "ambiguous omen"

OB dual (s. CAD P 442 *p.* a) also in *pi-it-ru-iš-ta-an* CUSAS 18, 22: 22, r. 26.

pittu I "area, vicinity"

For the passage UET 6/2, 414: 12 (CAD P 443 s. v. *pittu* A) s. *bittu* II.

pītu I "opening, aperture"

1. OB prob. "clasp" (lit. "opening device"), attached to hides used as containers:
a) 2 *mašak alpim* 2 *pí-tá-an* ARM 19, 164: 2 "2 oxhides, 2 clasps".
b) 6 *maša[k ...]* 6 *p[í-t]um* ib. 157: 2.
c) For further ref. s. ib. p. 164 (index). S. the disc. by Limet, ib. p. 33; Limet 1985, 517 n. 18 and 520 ad 3.5. For *pītu* in the mng. "clasp (of a necklace)" s. CAD P 447 *p.* A 3. S. also Arkhipov, ARM 32 p. 89f. with further ref. from OB Mari.

2. Stol 2008, 354: OB ^{iti}KA-*ti erṣetim* VS 9, 132: 7 "month of breaking up the soil", cf. *pí-ti erṣetim* CAD P 447a *p.* 2e.

3. Bo. said of a woman: *ikkūm*? *bākitiya pí-ta-a-ki* KBo. 36, 27: 18 "instead of(?) my wailing woman, your two openings". Or *bi-ta-a-ki* "your houses" (cf. Schwemer 2004, 67)?

4. Mayer 2008, 101:
a) SB *ūm* BAD *bābi bēli rabû* DN *u qarrādi* DN2 SpTU 4, 167 obv. B a1 (hemerology; s. also b3, c2 and r. B b1, c3) "the day of the opening of the gate of the great lord DN and the warrior DN2".
b) SB *ina pi-it bābi rummî sikkūri* [*ina*? *né-gél-te*?]-*e āli u bēlišu* BM 64518: 9 (unpubl.) "during the gate opening, the bolt loosening, [the wakening up(?)] of the city and his lord".

MPS (1, 3), NR (2, 4)

pitūtu "headband, diadem"

Pl. in NA [*p*]*i-tu-a-te* in broken context SAA 5, 282 r. 3. NR

+ **piṭirtu?** "loosening"; OB

KA-*inim-ma pi-ṭi-ir-tum* ZA 75, 200: 61 "incantation 'loosening'". Prob. not a PNf WE-*ṭi-ir-tum* as supposed by Wilcke, ib. p. 201, 207, s. Scurlock 1989–1990.

piṭru I "release"

1. OB "loose silver" vs. "sealed silver" (CAD P 448 s. v. *piṭru* adj.), s. Stol 1982, 151 and Stol 2004b, 903.
2. For AN.KUD BI-IT-*ru ša šá-*[*me-e*] Emar 6/4, 567: 5' (CAD P 449 *p.* lex. sect.) s. *bitru*.
3. Borger 2008, 446: DUḪ ^{giš}BANŠUR RAcc. 133: 211 and 143: 410 (CAD P 450b disc. sect.; AHw 1366b s. v. *tuḫḫu*) = *piṭir paššūri*, cf. *pi-ṭir paššūri* K.9876: 18 (CAD P 450b *p.* 6).
4. Mayer 2008, 101: a part of the body (CAD P 450 *p.* 2): SB [*si-ḫi-i*]*l-ti šīrī ilʾibannima* [*u*]*nnišu pi-ṭi-ri-ia* Rm. 499: 3' (UFBG 536, coll. Geller) "pain of my flesh afflicted me and weakend my *p.*"
5. Stol 2008, 354: LB *ina utūni u pi-iṭ-ru* LÁ Sack 1994, 7: 9 "(gold) being lost in the furnace and *p.*" (unclear; or *pitru*?). NR

pizallūru, + *pišḫallūrtu* "gecko"; + OB

1 *unuq ubān*[*im*] KÙ.GI ŠÀ.BA 1 *pí-iš-ḫa-al-lu-ur-ti uqnîm* ARM 23, 535 iv 33; ARM 25, 118 = ARM 32 p. 368 A.1259: 53 "finger ring of gold, on it a lapis lazuli gecko". Further similar ref. ARM 32 p. 103.

+ **PI-zi-rí-um** "an item of jewelry"; Ur III

Civil 2006, 60: "a small item (nine of them weigh one shekel) of gold jewelry. The word remains obscure in form and mng., and a connection with *be$_5$-en-zé-er* is most unlikely". Ref.:

1. 9 PI-*zi-ri-um* KÙ.SIG$_{17}$ ḪUŠ.A KI.LÁ.BI 1 GÍN UET 3, 676: 1 (AHw 871b s. v. *pizzer*(*ium*) "eine Pflanze"; CAD P 453a *pizzir* disc. sect.) "9 *p.* of red gold weighing 1 shekel".
2. PI-*zi-ir tu-di-da* UET 3, 477: 3 "*p.* of a dress-pin".
3. ŠU.NÍĜIN 1 *ki-lí-lum* PI-*zi-rí-um* KÙ.SIG$_{17}$ ḪUŠ.A UTI 6, 3800 r. ii 13 "together: 1 head ornament (and) *p.* of red gold".
4. ŠU.NÍĜIN 2 *ki-lí-lum* PI-*zi-rí-um* KÙ.SIG$_{17}$ UTI 6, 3800 r. iii 10.

MPS, NR

+ **pū?** "here(?)" EA; NWSem. lw.

ù p[*u*]*-ú en-ni-ip-ša-*<*at*> LÚ^{meš} GAZ^{meš} EA 104: 53. CAD E 216 interprets *p*[*u*]*-ú* here as *pû* "mouth; agreement": "they have come to an agreement with the *Ḫāpiru*-people". Moran 1992, 177: "and an agreement has been made with the ʿApiru". Sivan 1984, 130 and 259 compares the word with Hebr. *pō* "here". Moran, ib. p. 178 n. 5: "perhaps yielding better sense … 'and (t)here (too) (the city) has gone over to the ʿApiru'". NR

pû I "mouth"

1. New idiom: OA *ana pá-e lā tuṣṣiʾ* AKT 6a, 236: 35 "don't make excuses(?) (lit. don't go out to the mouth/word)".

2. Mayer 2008, 102: OA lit. *arhiš illukū māʾū i-pí-ša* PIHANS 100, 396: 5 "the (amniotic) fluid quickly runs from her (cow's) (uterus's) mouth".

3. OB *mār šipri ša* PN *ana ṣēr bēliya it-talkam bēlī pí-šu lā uwaššaršum* ARM 28, 98: 39 "a messenger of PN has come to my lord. My lord should not let him speak!".

4. OB *sikkata ana pî maḫāṣu* (CAD *p.* 1a1'a'): *a-n*[*a pî*]- ⌜*i*⌝ *bēl awātiya sikkatam lā amaḫḫaṣu* ARM 28, 105: 12' "(because) I cannot drive a peg into the mouth of my adversary".

5. Stol 2008, 354: KA-*šu ukīn* UCP 10, 91: 18 "(before the judges) he made firm his declaration".

6. Stol 2008, 354, in PN:
a) *Pu-um*-DINGIR OECT 15, 132: 17 "The word is god".
b) *Puzur-*^{d}*Pu-ú* Sefarad 66, 10 iii 6 "(Under the) protection of The Word".

7. OB *Pí-i-ka-si-i* ZABR 9, 165: 12 (s. also p. 167 for other ref.) "Mouth of the (river) Kasû".

8. Mayer 2008, 102: DN *ašakkan ana pi-i qutrēnim ša* ⌜*qutturika*⌝ *erēnam ellam* YOS 11, 22: 14 "DN, I place pure cedar on the opening of the censer to fumigate(?) you".

9. Mayer 2008, 102; Stol 2008, 354: "speech, language":
a) SB *kīma kaspi ina* KA *nišī balāṭu libši* BBR 26 iii 9 // SpTU 2, 12 ii 14 "may (my) life be like silver in people's talk".
b) SB *kīma ina qabê* DN *kīma* DN_2 *ina* KA *nišī balāṭu lū dār* BBR 26 iii 11 // CT 51, 195: 3' // SpTU 2, 12 ii 16 "according to the command of DN may (my) life last for ever in people's talk like the beer-goddess".
c) SB *šūt/ša pa-a šaknū tapaqqidī kīma* DN Ištar 1: 10 (Zgoll 2003, 193) "you (Ištar) care for those equipped with a mouth (= ref. to the people) like DN".

10. LB *ki-i pi-i ša-ṭir* BM 77429: 30 "written after dictation". Cf. Jursa 2009, 151.

11. Mayer 2008, 102: SB *a-na pi-i patri aškun* BagM 21, 344 no. 2 ii 7 "(men) I have placed for the mouth of the sword (= killed)".

12. Mayer 2008, 101f.: For Iraq 18, 62: 28 (CAD P 455a *p.* 1a1'a') s. the improved text in *Mīs pî* 134: 36: *pi-i-šú* (var. KA-*šú*) *ana mākālê uzun-šu ana na/ešmê liššakin* "may his (of a deity's image) mouth be enabled to eat, his ear (be enabled) to hear".

13. Stol 2008, 354: *ina* KA *Sippar* CT 4, 39b: 11 (CAD P 469b *p.* c) does not belong here; KA is an unusual spelling for KÁ "gate".

MPS (1, 3, 4, 7, 8), NR (2, 5–7, 9–13)

pû II, *pāʾu* "chaff"

1. OA *šummamin wašbāti awāssu ana pá-e iddīʾūnim* AKT 6a, 75: 50, cf. 76: 52 "if you had been present, would they have treated (lit. thrown) his word like chaff?"
2. OB *zēram pé-e-em tu*[*ḫḫī*] ARM 27, 156: 10 "seed, chaff, br[an]".
3. Genitive *pīʾi*: MB *kīma pitilti pi-ʾ lā tippattil* Lamaštu p. 264: 8 "like a fiber of chaff, you will not become twisted".

NR

+ **pû III** "a bird"; OB

OB *pu-um*^{mušen} Edubba 7, 100: 29 (in list of birds). Variant of *paʾû* "a bird" (Al-Rawi/Dalley, ib. p. 106)? Cf. also *baʾu* ib. 65.

pūʾāgu "to take away forcibly"

For OA ref. s. *būʾāʾu*.

pudru "dung cake"

OB lit. *pu-ud-ru-um* CUSAS 32, 30 r. iii 20' (in recipe).

pudû s. *būdu* III

puggu s. *buggu*

+ pugl- "to assemble"; MB Qaṭna, Hurr. word

$^{\text{lú.meš}}$*mar-ia-ni-na ša* ^{uru}*Qàṭ-na* \ *pu-uk-lu-uš-te* QS 3, 4: 5 "assemble the *maryannū* of Qaṭna!"

pugudātu "bridle, rein(s)"

Stol 2008, 354: LB [*ištēn imēru*] *ilḫi ukāpi pu-ug-da-tum … ultu bīt puṭṭurišu ni-te-eb-lu … imēru šâšu pu-ug-da-ti ilḫi ukāpu … īmurūma* AfO 50, 260 BM 29378: 16, 20 "we have taken from his lodging [a donkey], an *ilḫu*-cloth, a pack-saddle, a bridle ... they inspected that donkey, the bridle, the *ilḫu*-cloth, the pack-saddle". NR

puḫādu "lamb"

1. Stol 2008, 354: OB *pu-ḫa-da-am barmam* YOS 11, 23: 2 (Starr 1983, 30) "speckled lamb" in an extispicy prayer.

2. Mayer 2008, 102: SB ^{udu}SILA$_4$ *sāmu* SpTU 2, 17 iv 15' "brown lamb".

3. Mayer 2008, 102:
a) *ukkuš* ^{udu}SILA$_4$-*ma* BBR 100: 20 "the male lamb was kept away".
b) *ukkuš* ^{udu}SILA$_4$-*ma akarrabkunūši* KIR$_{11}$ ib. 38 "the male lamb was kept away, I dedicate to you a female lamb". NR

puḫāttu "female lamb"

1. Syllabic spelling: OB $^{\text{sila4}}$*pu-ḫa-tum* FM 8, 125 no. 37: 6'.

2. Mayer 2008, 103:
a) SB KIR$_{11}$ (^{f}SILA$_4$) *taḫannaqma* SpTU 3, 84: 4 "you strangle a female lamb".
b) Without det.: SB SILA$_4$ *birīt tulêšu tanaddi* ib. 9 "you put the (female) lamb between her(!) breasts". MPS (1), NR (2)

puḫdinu s. *b/puḫdinnu*

puḫḫu D "to exchange"

Dt OB *ša … up-te-ḫu* MHET 1, 4: 4 (AOAT 303, 113 n. 309) "(field), which was exchanged". MPS, NR

puḫru "assembly"

1. Stol 2008, 354: OB *ištū awīlum* GAL.UKKEN.NA *īrubam awīlum ana* GAL.UKKEN.NA *kī'am iqbī umma šūma aššumika nuḫassis* MHEO 1, 104 Di 628: 4'f. "after the gentleman, the head of the assembly, had entered, the (other) gentleman said to the head of the assembly: 'We thought about you'". Cf. CAD P 493b *puḫru* A in *rabi puḫri*; Janssen MHEO 1 p. 92f.

2. Stol 2008, 354 *ina puḫri* "publicly, openly":
a) OB *u ina pu-úḫ-ri šillati idbuba* AbB 6, 124: 16 "he slandered me in public".
b) *in pu-uḫ-ri-im mimmu tušaddinu birrā* AbB 9, 111: 16 "establish publicly whatever you have collected".
c) S. also Fs Garelli 65 A.3976: 8.

3. *puḫram nadānu* "to hold an assembly":
a) OB *aššum pu-uḫ-ri-im nadānim* PN *taṭrudam ta'tamam ša* GN [*u*]*p-ta-ḫi-ir-ma* QuadSem 16, 35 A.3243 // A.3651: 4 "you have sent PN concerning holding an assembly. I have gathered the assembly of GN".
b) *lā tallakā ana* GN *bârum ibârkunūti u pu-ḫu-ur-ku$_8$-nu lā tanaddanā* ARM 26/2 p. 62f. no. 306: 42 "do not go to GN: you will be certainly caught. And do not gather your assembly!"

4. SB, Mayer 2008, 103: *puḫra* (UKKIN) *pu-uḫ-ḫu-ra-a-tú* (var. *pa-ḫa-ra-tu$_4$*) *kīma kurgarrî* SpTU 2, 24: 3 // BM 45755: 2b "(why do you keep) the assembly assembled like a cultic performer?". NR

pūḫu "exchange; substitute"

1. OB *a-na-ku lu pu-ḫu ša ba-la-ṭí-ka* "may I be a substitute for your life" CUSAS 9, 4: 5, 19.

2. Mayer 2008, 103: in rit. context:
a) *pu-ḫu-ú-a ša ukinnū … dinānū'a ša ibbanû …* K.5022+ r. 3f. (Šamaš 78 B, Mayer 1976, 419) "the replacement figure of me that they have set up … the substitute figure of me that was made".
b) *ṭiṭṭa akriṣ ṣalam iṣi u qanî ana pu-ḫi-ia [ēpu]š ēpuš pu-u-ḫi šá* NU.SAĜ.Í[L.M]U K.2387+ r. 4f. (Šamaš 78 A // ib B r. 10f. "I pinched off clay, I made a figure of wood and cane as a substitute for me; I have made a substitute for me, which is a replacement for me".
c) *[pu-ḫ]u-ú-a maḫrātunu dinānū'a maḫrātunu* ib. A r. 17 // B r. 22 "you have received the replacement for me, you have received the substitute for me".
d) [NU.SA]Ĝ.ÍL-*ia ša* DN *īpušu ana pu-ḫi-ia (u) dinānīya šū illak* ib. A r. 21f. // B r. 26 "the substitute figure for me, which DN has made, it will go for my replacement and for my substitution".
e) [DN] *annû* NU.NÍG.SAĜ.ÍL.MU DN *annû pu-ḫ[u-ú-a* DN *annû] dinānū'[a]* K.6034+ (Šamaš 92, Mayer 1976, 421) "DN, this is my substitute figure; DN, this is my replacement figure; DN, this is my substitution".

MPS (1), NR (2)

puḫurtu, *puḫuštu* "throng, crowd"

Stol 2008, 354: SB *pu-ḫu-uš-ti Esaĝil* CLBT pl. 4 D 4 vi 15 "assembly of Esaĝil". NR

puk(k)u s. *buk(k)u* I

pūku "a garment"

OA:
1. TÚG *pu-ki-im* RA 60, 119: 24.
2. 1 TÚG *pu-ku-um* Fs. Garelli 231 no. 4: 6.
3. *šitrum ša pūkim* Kt 91/k 466: 1; Kt 93/k 542: 9; Kt 91/k 501.
4. Disc. by Michel/Veenhof 2010, 239.

MPS, NR

pulḫītu "distress, consternation, fear"

SB *[aššu] … pu-ul-ḫi-te ša niš[ī]* Gilg. Assyrian Ms y_2: 15 "[for the purpose of] … fear of people", var. of ⌜*pul-ḫa-a*⌝*-ti* Gilg. SB II 219a, 228, 299, which shows that the mng. of *pulḫītu* and *puluḫtu* are similar. Diff. George 2003, 360: casus obliquus *pulḫête* < *pulḫī'āte*.

pulițē "citizenry"

Mayer 2008, 103:
1. The form *pulițū* does not exist. The most common form *pulīṭē* renders either sg. πολιτης or pl. πολιται.
2. New spelling [lú]*pu-li-ṭe₄-e* Astronomical diaries no. -134 B obv. 17, no. -124 B r. 17', no. -90 obv. 30', no. -77 B r. 16' etc. NR

pulițū s. *pulițē*

puluḫtu, + *paluḫtu* "fear(someness)"

1. OB *pa-lu-uḫ-ti* DN "fear of DN" AbB 12, 64: 4.

2. Mayer 2008, 103:
a) *ulawwa pu-lu-*⌜*uḫ*⌝*-ta-*⌜*šu*⌝ *birkī-ka* OB Gilg. OB Schøyen₂ 20 (George 2003, 234) "terror of him (= Huwawa) will encircle your legs".
b) SB *ša melammē tullât kīma ūme pul-ḫa-tú (// pul-ḫa-a-ti) kiṣṣurat* CT 25, 10

ii 5 // ib. 15 ii 5 // AfO 50, 21 BM 65454+: 4 "(goddess), who is bedecked with fearsome radiance, is clad in fear like a storm". MPS (1), NR (2)

pulukku "drill, stake, boundary marker"

1. OB *pu-ul-lu-uk-ka-tum*, quoted CAD P 510 1c, s. now RATL 28: 19.

2. Stol 2008, 354: read ARM 21, 258: 813 *pu-lu-ka-*[*tim*] (cf. CAD P 511a *p.* 3).
3. OB 2 *pu-lu-ku* ZABAR ARM 32 p. 246 M.12668 iii 49 "2 needles/drills of bronze".

4. Mayer 2008, 103:
a) SB *ša... saparša pu-lu-uk dadmē saḫru* AfO 50, 21 BM 65454+: 8 "(goddess), whose net surrounds the borders of the settlements".
b) *šarrat pu-lu-uk dadmī* BM 75974 r. 36 "queen of the boundaries of the inhabited world". MPS (1, 3), NR (2, 4)

punnigu s. *pannigu*

pupuri "a vessel"; + SB

pu-pu-ri Emar 6/4, 778: 80 = AOAT 251, 196 Ef 80; note the parallel *pu-pu-ri* ib. manuscript Br. Pace Pentiuc 2001, 43 not *pu-uṣ-ri.*

puqqu "to pay attention to"

G Cf. *pīʾāqu* for Gilg. OB II 88 (uncertain).

D 1. OB lex. *lal-da-bu-u* = *pu-uq-qu* MARI 5, 412 BM 38590: 21.
2. Mayer 2008, 104: *ina qereb šamāmī kalîš pu-uq-qu-ši* BM 75974 r. 18 "in the midst of the sky they are attentive to her".
3. Mayer 2008, 104: *puqqu* + *ana*: *ana namraṣīt nūrika ú-pi*!*-iq bēlī*! BAM 3, 231 i 23 // BAM 4, 332 i 8' "I was attentive to the radiance of your light, my lord".

Dt Mayer 2008, 104: First ref. for present tense (elsewhere only stative attested, interpreted as Dt in AHw 879f. but as Dtn in CAD P 512–514): *ana nakās napištiya up-ta-qu* KAR 224 r. 15 // K.3581+7946: 7 (s. Farber 1977, 254 ad 23'f.) "is greately attentive to cut my life". MPS (G, D), NR (D, Dt)

puquddû "(formal) delivery, legal consignment"

OB 1 *ḫaṣṣinnu* 3 [urudu]ŠU.KIN.NÍG. GAL *ša pu-qù-de-e labīri* 1 [urudu]ŠU.KIN.NÍG.GAL *pu-qù-de-e* PN 1 *ḫaṣṣinnu* 4 [urudu]ŠU.KIN. ⸢NÍG.GAL⸣ *ša unūt ekallim pu-qù-de-e* PN BabA 1, 163 BM 78557 "1 copper axe, 3 copper sickles, part of the old allocation; 1 copper sickle allocated to PN, (in total) 1 copper axe and 4 copper sickles, part of the utensils of the palace allocated to PN". Cf. van Koppen 2002a, 163f. and n. 24. NR

puquttu "thorn"

Stol 2008, 354: SB Ú.GÍR.LAGAB *šadî* BAM 4, 409: 31 "thorn from the mountain". NR

purīdu "leg"

1. OB lex.: *du-un-ĝu*₁₀ = *pu-ri-di* CUSAS 12 p. 150: 34 (Ugumu) "my leg".
2. SB (Gilg.) *qanā pu-ri-id-šu* AulaOr. Suppl. 23, 42: 36 "his leg is a reed long".

purkullu s. *parkullu*

purkullūtu s. *parkullūtu*

+ purnussu "a vessel"; OB, Hurr. lw.

1. 4 ^{gal}*pu-ur-nu-sú* KÙ.BABBAR ARM 25, 501 = ARM 31, 34: 4 "4 *p.* of silver".
2. 1 *pu-ur-nu-sú* KÙ.BABBAR 11 GÍN *šuqultašu qadu guḫaššu* ARM 31, 37: 35' "1. *p.* vessel of silver, 11 shekel is its weight, together with a wire".
3. 1 *pu-ur/úr-nu-us-sú* ZABAR *guḫaššu* KÙ.BABBAR ARM 24, 85 = ARM 31, 109: 11; ARM 25, 504 = ARM 31, 172 r. 3 "1 *p.* vessel of bronze (with) a wire of silver".
4. 1 *pu-ur-nu-sú ṣeḫrum* KÙ.BABBAR ARM 25, 501 = ARM 31, 34 r. 13 "1 small *p.* vessel of silver".
5. 1 *pu-ur-nu-sú* (*ṣeḫrum*) ZA[BAR] ARM 24, 101 = ARM 31, 264: 11; ARM 25, 521 = ARM 31, 134: 8 "1 (small) *p.* vessel of bronze".
6. Disc. with further ref. Guichard, ARM 31 p. 259–261. MPS, NR

purruru "scattered"

OA *meḫrat taḫsistim pá-ru-ur-tí* AKT 7a, 61: 21 "copy of the broken memorandum".

purrusētu "separated"

Stol 1995, 179: 2 ÁB *pu-ru-se-e-tum* CT 8, 28c: 12 (CAD P 522b "mng. unkn."), refers to mother-cows separated from their calves. Cf. *pirsu* as a design. of a weaned animal. NR

pursāsu "wig"

OB lit. *naḫlapāti pu-ur-sa!-si tušešmî zikrī* CunMon. 8, 26 ii 3 "you made men obey (the rules of) garments (and) wigs". NR

pursītu, + *puršītu* "(offering) bowl"

1. OB *pursīt uḫūli* "soap bowl":

a) 1 ^{gal}*pu-ur-si-it ú-ḫu-li* 11 GÍN *šuqultaša* ARM 25, 501 = ARM 31, 34: 13 "1 *p.* bowl with soap, its weight is 11 shekel".
b) 1 *pu-ur-sí-it ú-ḫu-li* KÙ.BABBAR ARM 25, 517 = ARM 31, 235: 7.
c) 1 BUR.ZI *ú-*[*ḫu-li*] ARM 31, 37: 11'.

2. OB 1 ^{gal}BUR.ZI-*tum* KÙ.BABBAR ARM 24, 96: 6 "1 *p.* of silver".

3. OB [...B]UR.ZI-*tum ṣeḫertum* KÙ.BABBAR ARM 24, 103 tr. lat. 1 "small *p.* of silver".

4. 3 BUR.ZI *Kaptarāyu* ARM 25, 393 = ARM 31, 85: 12 "3 Cretan *p.* bowls".

5. 1 GAL PAP BUR.ZI *ša ḫarḫarr*[*im*] ARM 31, 154 r. 3 "1 *p.* bowl ... withring".

6. SB *pur-ši-it damī ina*[*šši*] Emar 6/4, 737: 3 "it carr[ies] a bowl of blood".

7. Cf. Guichard, ARM 31 p. 261–264 for disc. and further ref.

MPS (1–7), NR (1)

pūršašillu s. *būršašillu*

puršumu "old man"

OB lit. *pu-ur-šu-mu-um ša tāmuru ilka werru* Gilg. OB Nippur 7 "the old man you saw is your strong god".

pūru I "(stone) bowl"

Stol 1987b, 64; 2008, 354: OB 30 BUR *narṭabi*(SÚN) *ša ana* GN PBS 8/2, 185: 6 "30 bowls of beerwort, which are for GN". Diff. CAD P 519b *p.* a2' *purkullu*: 30 BUR.GUL "30 (string of onions) for the stone cutter". NR

pūru II "lot, plot"

1. Stol 2008, 354: MA *ana batiq ša puri* MARV 3, 37:10 (AoF 19, 286) "due to the interruption of the lot".

2. NA 1-*en pur* SAA 14, 205 r. 3 "1 plot". MPS (2), NR (1)

purussû "decision"

1. Mayer 2008, 104: *dīn* NN *purussâ šuršû* "to obtain a decision on the matter of NN":
a) MB *dīnšu pu-ru-us-sa-a ay ušaršī* Sumer 38, 125 iv 27 "may he (Šamaš) not obtain a decision on his matter".
b) SB *aššum dīni* ⌜*pur*!*-si*!⌝*-i šuršî* KAR 58 r. 5 (coll., s. already Or. 72, 236) "in order to obtain a decision on the case".
c) SB *adi dīnī* EŠ.BAR *tušaršû* K.2132: 14' (ŠRT pl. XII; dupl. of BAM 4, 323: 32b, quoted in CAD P 532b *p.* b) "until you obtain the decision for my case".
d) *ultu*/*ištu dīnī* EŠ.BAR *tušteršû* K.2132: 15'a // BAM 4, 323: 33b "as soon as you have obtained the decision of my case".

2. Mayer 2008, 104: *purussâ parāsu*: SB EŠ.BAR*-a-a ana damiqti lipparis* SpTU 2, 22 iii 19 "may the decision about me be favorable".

3. Mayer 2008, 104: *purussû* + *akāšu* Dt: SB *ša* EŠ.BAR*-šá lā uttakkaš* AfO 50, 21 BM 65454+: 3 "(Ištar,) whose decision can not be driven off".

4. Mayer 2008, 104f.: *purussû* + *ešēru* Št "to obtain the omen's meaning":
a) *šumma amēlu... itti bārî u šā'ili dīnšu* (*u purussû-šu*) NU SI.SÁ (*uštešser*) BAM 3, 315 ii 15, iii 7 f.; 316 ii 12'; 468: 2; SpTU 22+85 i 27 f., ii 19 f.; STT 95+295 iii 136 (symptom) "if a man – his case (and his decision) is not given correctly by the haruspex and dream interpreter".
b) *ana purussê-šu parāsi*(*mma*) *dīn-šu ana* SI.SÁ BAM 3, 316 ii 14' or *ana šu-te-šu-ru* SpTU 22+85 i 30; STT 95+295 (iii) 137 "in order to make the decision for him, to give correctly his case". *itti bārî u šāʾili dīn-šu* (*u purussû-šu*) *uš-te-šer* BAM 3, 315 iii 15; SpTU 22+85 i 50 (result) "his case (and his decision) are given correctly by the haruspex and dream interpreter". NR

\+ **purustu** "division"; OB

Stol 2008, 35: *pu-úr-sà-at Ḫana* A.3572: 4 (Durand 1992, 114 and 116) "the divisions of the Ḫaneans". NR

purūʾu "harassment, denunciation"

OA *mimma pu-ru-i lā tašakkan* AKT 6b, 408: 39 "do not slander me!"

\+ **p/bussulum** "a food product(?)"; Ur III

1. 5 *sìla ì-šaḫ* 1/2 *ma-na pù-sú-lum pù-sú-lum-šè* CUSAS 3, 972: 37f. (CUSAS 4 p. 142) "5 liters lard, 1/2 mina *p.* for *p.*
2. [*pù*]*-sú-*LUM *pù-*⌜*sú*⌝*-lum-šè* CUSAS 3, 975: 39f.
3. *pù-su-lum* CUSAS 3, 1272: 4.

pusummu "veil"

For Gilg. O. I. r. 20 and TIM 9, 46: 17 (CAD P 537f.) s. *puzzuru.* NR

pūṣu "whiteness, white spot"

Stol 2008, 354 (s. also Stol 1993b, 348b): Lex. *še ḫád-e-dè* = ŠE*-im pu-ṣu* = *duḫ-nu* SpTU 3, 116 iv 22 (Ḫg) "dried grain = grain with white spots = millet" (interpr. after DCCLT). NR

puṣuddu "mongoose"

Borger, 1987, 145f.: delete Iraq 16, 186 vi 49 (CAD P 541b). Cf. *buqlu.* NR

puṣūtu s. *buṣūtu*

\+ **pušḫu II** "soothing"; SB

SB *tuqtarrib ṣindu pu-uš-ḫu ana pagrišu ša kulbābi lā i-ṭir-šú* ORA 7,

246: 8' "you brought bandage (and) soothing to the body of the one whom an ant did not carry away". T. Oshima, ib. p. 247 with comm. on p. 264, connects the word with *pušḫu* I "rat", which is less convincing cf. also Mayer 2017, 27).

pušikku "combed wool"

For OB Mari s. Durand 2009, 146 with ref.

+ **pušlu** "a creeping creature(?)"; SB ⸢*maš*⸣*-ka pu-uš-li* Emar 6/4, 548 p. 97: 2 (Ḫḫ XI) "hide of a *p.* creature", s. DCCLT MB Ura 07 for the broken Sum. and a possible connection with *pašālu* "to crawl" and *pašultu* "a crawling creature".

pušqu "narrowness; straits"

1. Fem. pl.: SB *ḫarrān rubê púš-qá-tum itt*[*iq*] Emar 6/4, 698: 36 "the caravan of a prince will p[ass] in difficulties".

2. Mayer 2008, 105 ad CAD P 544b *p.* 1d: *pušqu* beside *ud-de-e* only in KAR 321. Duplicates BM 61635+ iii 16' and BM 61649+ iii 22' have *im-ṭe-e* "loss(es)" (pace Oshima 2011, 234: 27').

MPS (1), NR (2)

putinnu s. *butinnu*

putrintu "a profession"

Durand 2009, 230f. reads in ARM 22, 144: 3 *pu-ut-ri-ni-tum* (sg.).

****putru**

Del. *putru* (CAD P 546a) and read the only ref. with AHw 1583b and Borger 2008, 447 *pu-ut-*[*tu*?] S. *puttu* I below.

NR

puttu I "a kind of beer"

1. Stol 2008, 354: Lex. *kaš* x x *ba* = *pu-ut-ti* SpTU 3, 115 ii 4 (Hh) "beer ... = *p.*".

2. Borger 2008, 447: Lex. *šita*$_4$$^{ši-ta}$*-munu*$_4$ = *pu-ut-*[*tu*?] MSL 11, 73: 16 (quoted in CAD P 546a s. v. *putru*). Cf. AHw 1583b.

NR

puttu II "an ornament or decorative object"

Stol 2008, 355: Cf. OB KÙ.SIG$_{17}$ *pu-ut-tu* A.11844: 9 "golden *p.*(?)", quoted in CAD P 355a under *petû m.* Cf. *pītu* "clasp" (s. above and CAD P 447a *pītu* A 6).

NR

pūtu I "forehead, brow"

1. OA, in the mng. "person, self" (CAD *p.* 7): *ana pu-tí-a-ma šālannima u lāpulkama u a-pu-tí-a-ma lallik* AKT 6a, 263: 25, 27 "ask me personally and I will answer you and I will leave by myself". Larsen, ib. p. 416 translates "right here, right now", but presents in his comm. the alternative "in person".

2. Cf. prob. also: OA *aḫīma a-pu-*<*tí-a*> *ašâl* ib. 268: 14' "I will question my brother perso<nally>(?)".

3. Mayer 2008, 105: For Gurney, AnSt. 5, 98: 30 (Cuthean Legend, CAD P 553a *p.* 7) s. Westenholz 1997, 306: 29f. (cf. comm. ib. 306ff.): *ina narê ul išṭur ul ēzibamma pagrī u pu-u-ti šuma*(MU) *ul ušēṣīma ul aktarrabšu* "on a stela he did not write (and) did not leave (it) to me, myself, he did not make a name for himself so that I coud not pray for him" (cf. CAD P 553a: *pu-u-ti-ia*$_5$).

MPS (1, 2), NR (3)

\+ **puṭṭuru** "guestfriend(?)"; LB

Jursa, AfO 50, 261b: *bīt puṭṭuri* LB equivalent of OB *bīt napṭarim* "guesthouse":

1. *ilḫi ukāpi pugdātu ... ultu bīt pu-ṭu-ri-šú ni-te-eb-lu* AfO 50, 260 BM 29378: 16 "we took from his lodgings an *ilḫu*-cloth, a pack-saddle, a bridle".

2. *ultu bīt pu-ṭu-ru ša* PN YOS 7, 192: 6, 10 "(I brought a donkey, belonging to the lady of Uruk,) from the lodgings of PN"; diff. CAD P 555a *p.* 2: "separated(?) building". NR

puwatu "dyer's madder, red dye"

For disc. s. van Soldt 1990, 347f.

NR

puzru "concealment"

1. OAkk. Beydar in PN: *Puzur*$_4$-BE Subartu 2, 23 v 8 "(In the) protection of the lord".

2. OB (the acquaintance) *īḫuz pu-*[*iz-ra-*]*am* Ištar Bagdad 68 "went into hiding".

3. OB *kalīʾāku ina rādim lā* ⸢*ēʾir*⸣ *ana pu-<uz->ri-im* Ištar Bagdad 32 "I am held back in the rainstrom; I did not go to the shelter".

4. *puzru* as a synonym of *pirištu* in Mari s. Villard 2001, 51f.; Durand 1997, 94 n. g (Stol 2008, 355): secret counsil of the king.

5. MB Ekalte (if a tablet) *ina pu-uz-ri šaṭru* WVDOG 102, 91: 11 "is written secretly"

6. Borger 2008, 447: Streck Asb. 52 vi 31 (CAD P 556b *p.* 1a2') read *pu-uz-ra-šin* instead of *pu-uz-ra-<ti>-šin*.

7. NA "private parts": *eṭlu ša ardati ardatu ša eṭli ina rebīt āli inaṭṭalū puzur*[*šun*] BIWA p. 151, C VIII 127 "a young man of a girl, a girl of a young man, they are looking at the private parts of each other in the main street of the city". MPS (1, 5), NR (2–4, 6–7).

puzzuru "concealed"

Streck 2007, 152; Mayer 2008, 105: OB *irtaḫiṣ qīštam mūšab Enūnakī pu-zu-*⸢*ra*⸣*-mi-ip-te-e* (= *puzzuram iptē*) Gilg. OB Ishchali 38' = OB IM 18 "he trampled through the forest; he discovered the secret abode of the Anunnaki". S. George 2003, 266. Pace CAD P 559b *p.* disc. sect. not *pusummu*. NR